MUTTS

SUNDAY MORNINGS

By Patrick McDonnell

Andrews McMeel
Publishing

Kansas City

"HEY, PEOPLES, READ ALL ABOUT IT!"

MUTTS   CATS AND DOGS   MORE SHTUFF   YESH!

OUR MUTTS   A LITTLE LOOK-SEE   MUTTS SUNDAYS   THE MUTTS LITTLE BIG BOOK   **YESH!**

Mutts is distributed by King Features Syndicate, Inc. For information write King Features Syndicate, Inc., 888 Seventh Avenue, New York, New York 10019.
Sunday Mornings copyright © 2001 by Patrick McDonnell. All rights reserved. Printed in the United States of America. No part of this book may be used or reproduced in any manner whatsoever without written permission except in the case of reprints in the context of reviews.
For information, write Andrews McMeel Publishing, an Andrews McMeel Universal company, 4520 Main Street, Kansas City, Missouri 64111.

03 04 05 QUD 10 9 8 7 6 5 4 3 2

ISBN: 0-7407-1853-3

Library of Congress Catalog Card Number: 2001088685

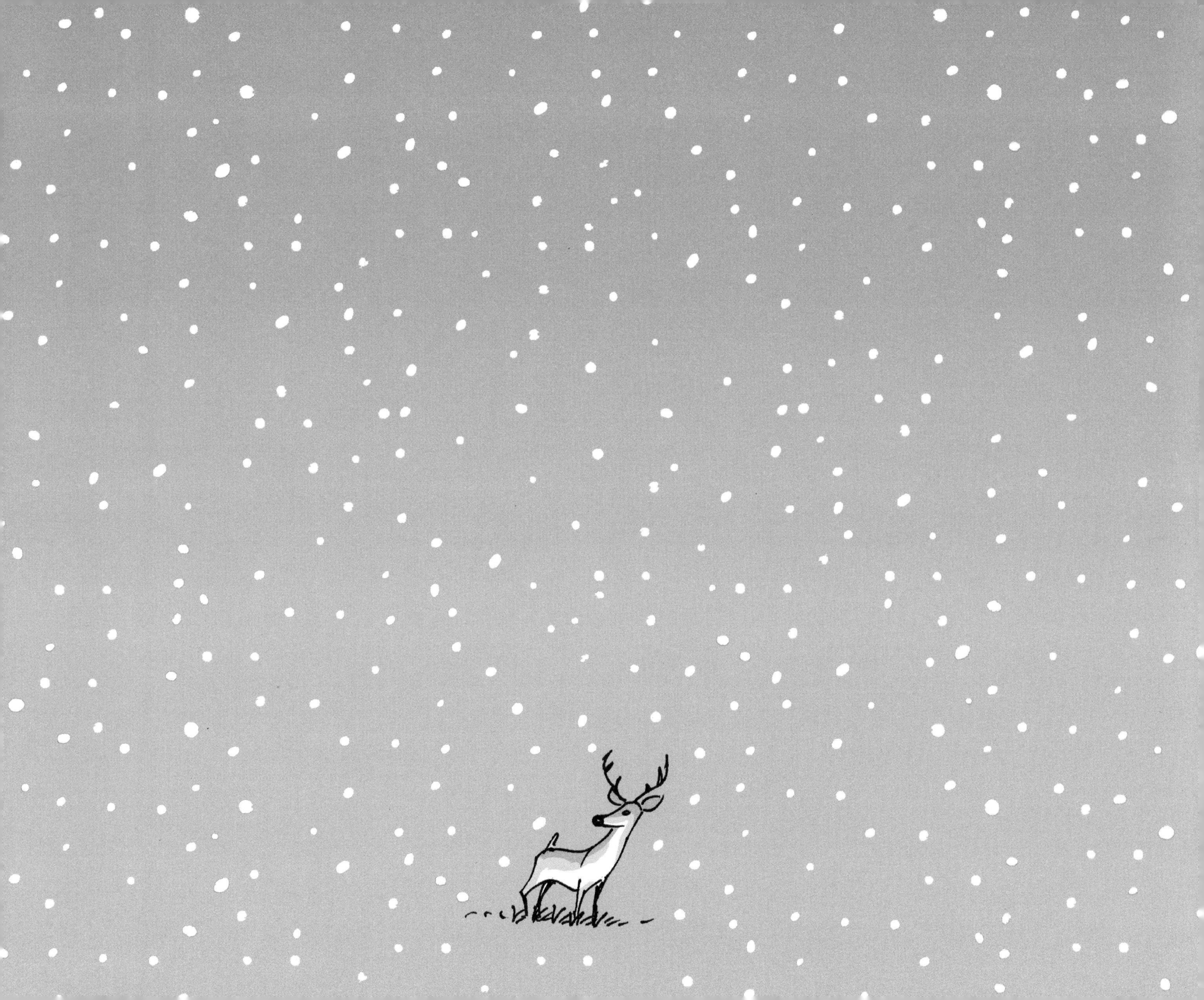

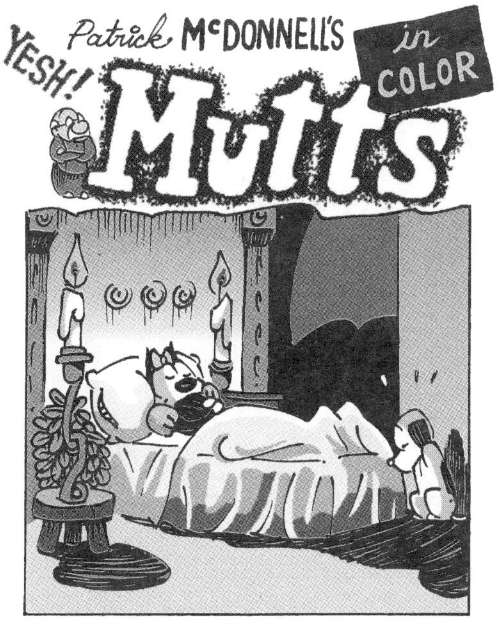
Patrick McDONNELL'S
YESH!
in COLOR
Mutts

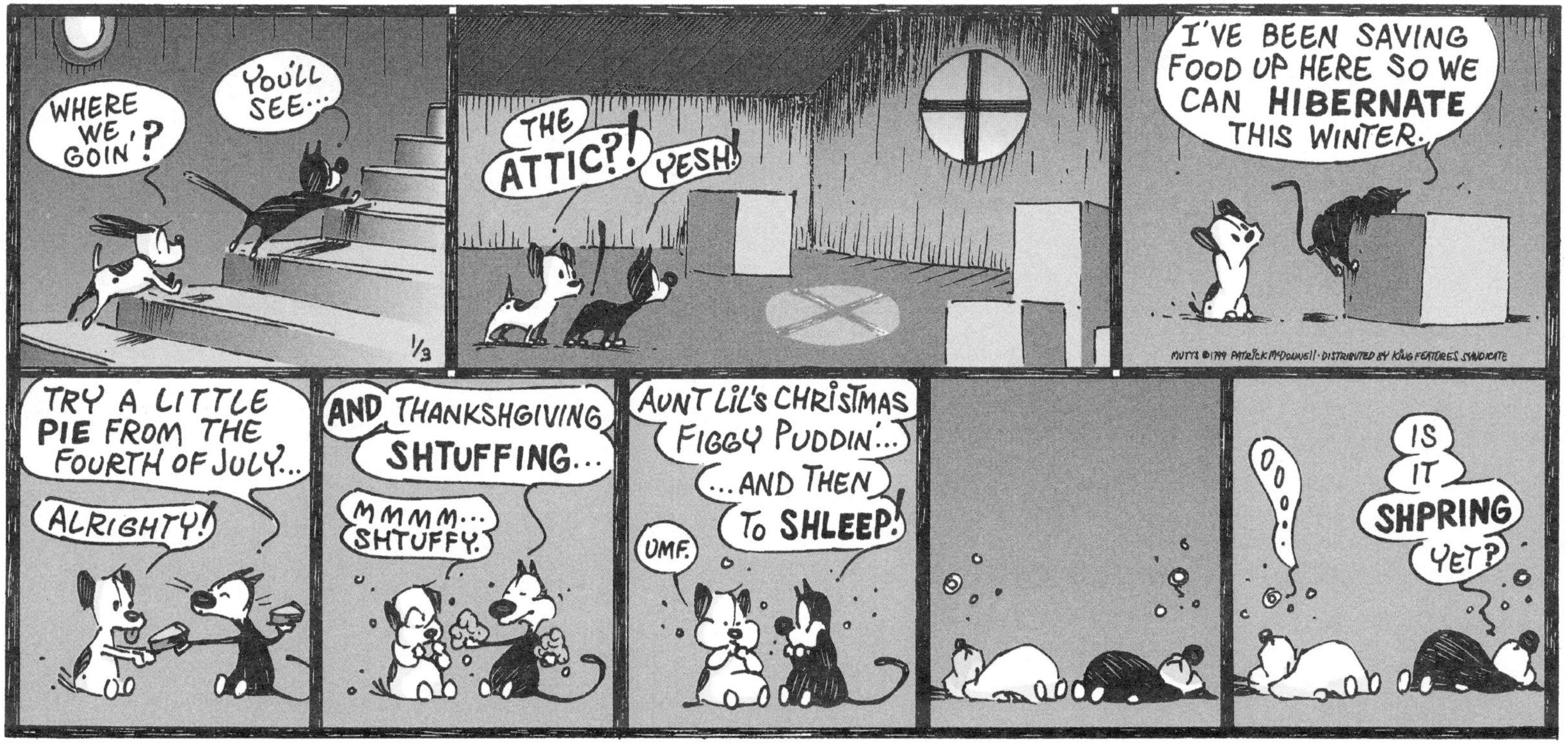
WHERE WE GOIN'?
YOU'LL SEE...
1/3
THE ATTIC?!
YESH!
I'VE BEEN SAVING FOOD UP HERE SO WE CAN HIBERNATE THIS WINTER.
MUTTS ©1999 PATRICK McDONNELL · DISTRIBUTED BY KING FEATURES SYNDICATE
TRY A LITTLE PIE FROM THE FOURTH OF JULY...
ALRIGHTY!
AND THANKSHGIVING SHTUFFING...
MMMM... SHTUFFY.
AUNT LIL'S CHRISTMAS FIGGY PUDDIN'...
...AND THEN TO SHLEEP!
UMF.
IS IT SHPRING YET?

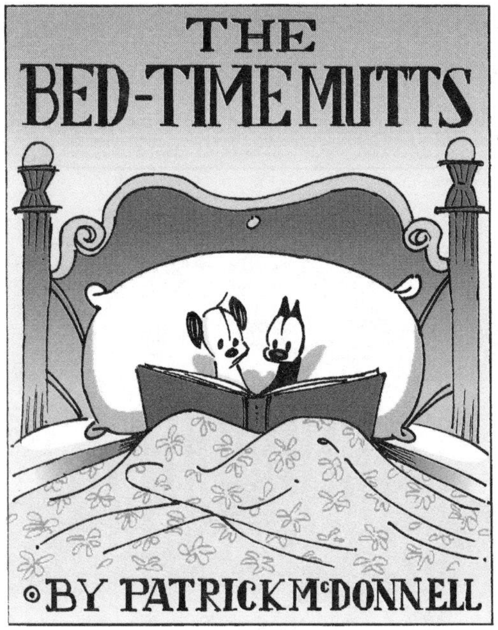
THE
BED-TIME MUTTS
© BY PATRICK McDONNELL

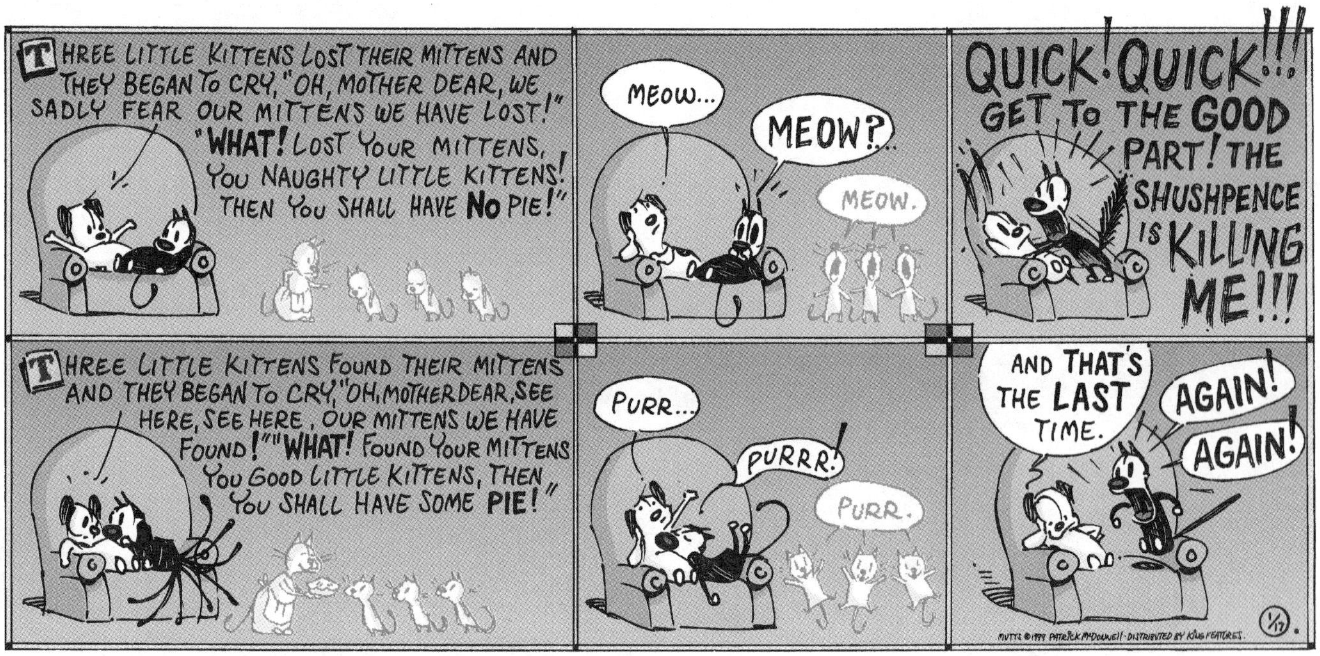
THREE LITTLE KITTENS LOST THEIR MITTENS AND THEY BEGAN TO CRY, "OH, MOTHER DEAR, WE SADLY FEAR OUR MITTENS WE HAVE LOST!"
"WHAT! LOST YOUR MITTENS, YOU NAUGHTY LITTLE KITTENS! THEN YOU SHALL HAVE NO PIE!"
MEOW...
MEOW?
MEOW.
QUICK! QUICK!!! GET TO THE GOOD PART! THE SHUSHPENCE IS KILLING ME!!!
THREE LITTLE KITTENS FOUND THEIR MITTENS AND THEY BEGAN TO CRY, "OH, MOTHER DEAR, SEE HERE, SEE HERE, OUR MITTENS WE HAVE FOUND!" "WHAT! FOUND YOUR MITTENS YOU GOOD LITTLE KITTENS, THEN YOU SHALL HAVE SOME PIE!"
PURR...
PURRR!
PURR.
AND THAT'S THE LAST TIME.
AGAIN!
AGAIN!
MUTTS ©1999 PATRICK McDONNELL · DISTRIBUTED BY KING FEATURES.
1/17

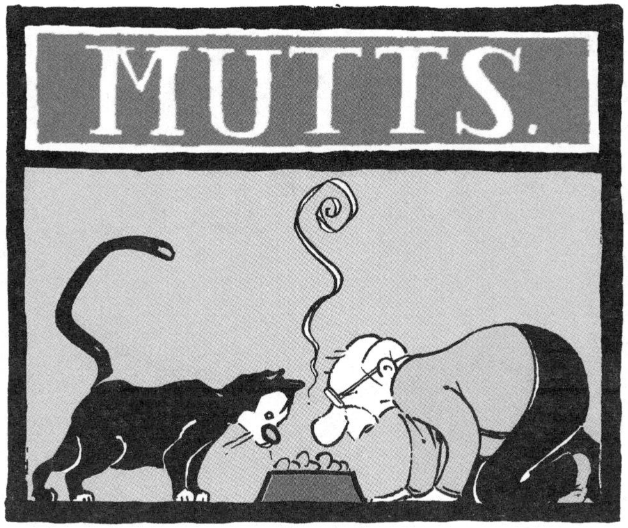
MUTTS.

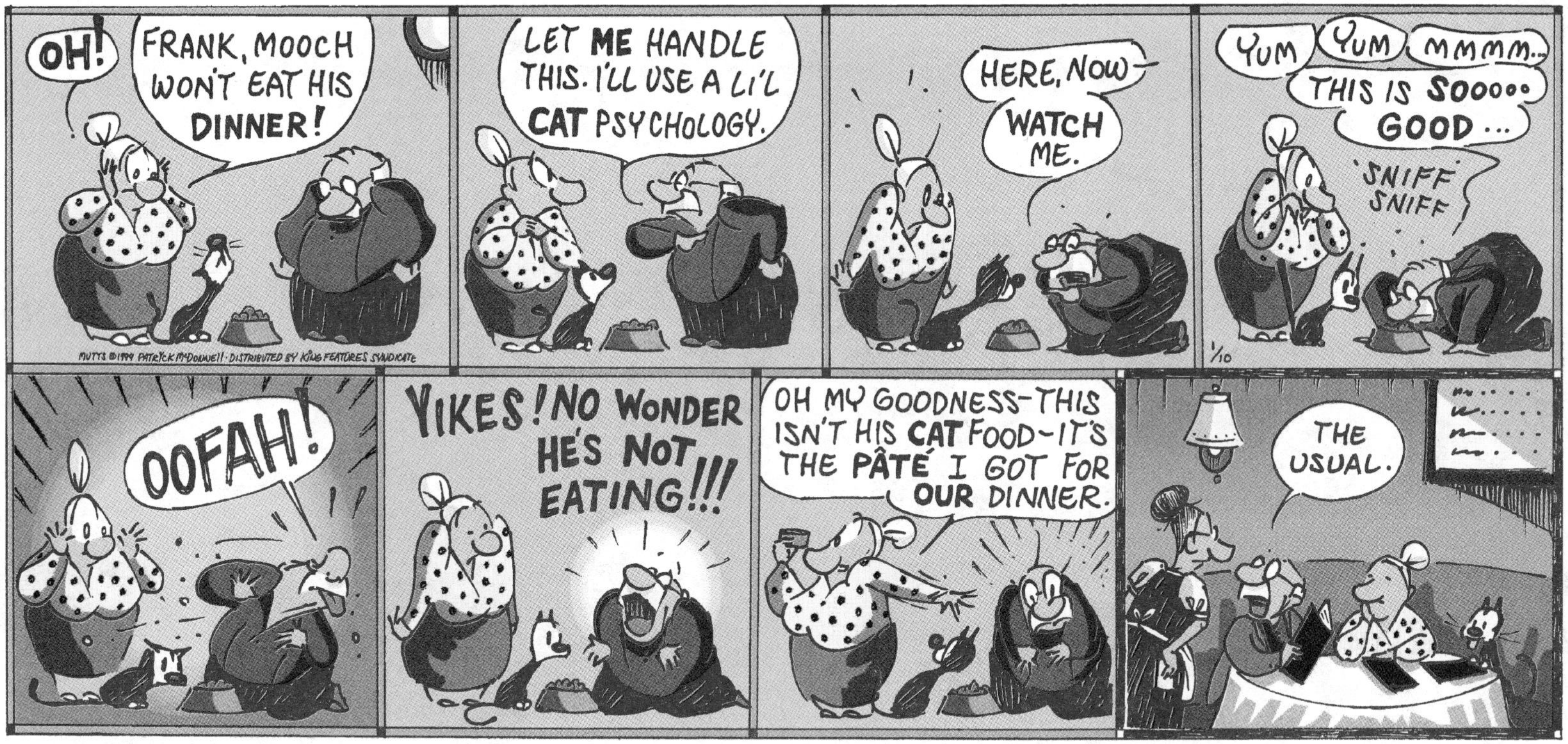
OH!
FRANK, MOOCH WON'T EAT HIS DINNER!
MUTTS ©1999 PATRICK McDONNELL · DISTRIBUTED BY KING FEATURES SYNDICATE
LET ME HANDLE THIS. I'LL USE A LI'L CAT PSYCHOLOGY.
HERE, NOW–
WATCH ME.
YUM
YUM
MMMM...
THIS IS SOOOOO GOOD...
SNIFF SNIFF
1/10
OOFAH!
YIKES! NO WONDER HE'S NOT EATING!!!
OH MY GOODNESS–THIS ISN'T HIS CAT FOOD–IT'S THE PÂTÉ I GOT FOR OUR DINNER.
THE USUAL.

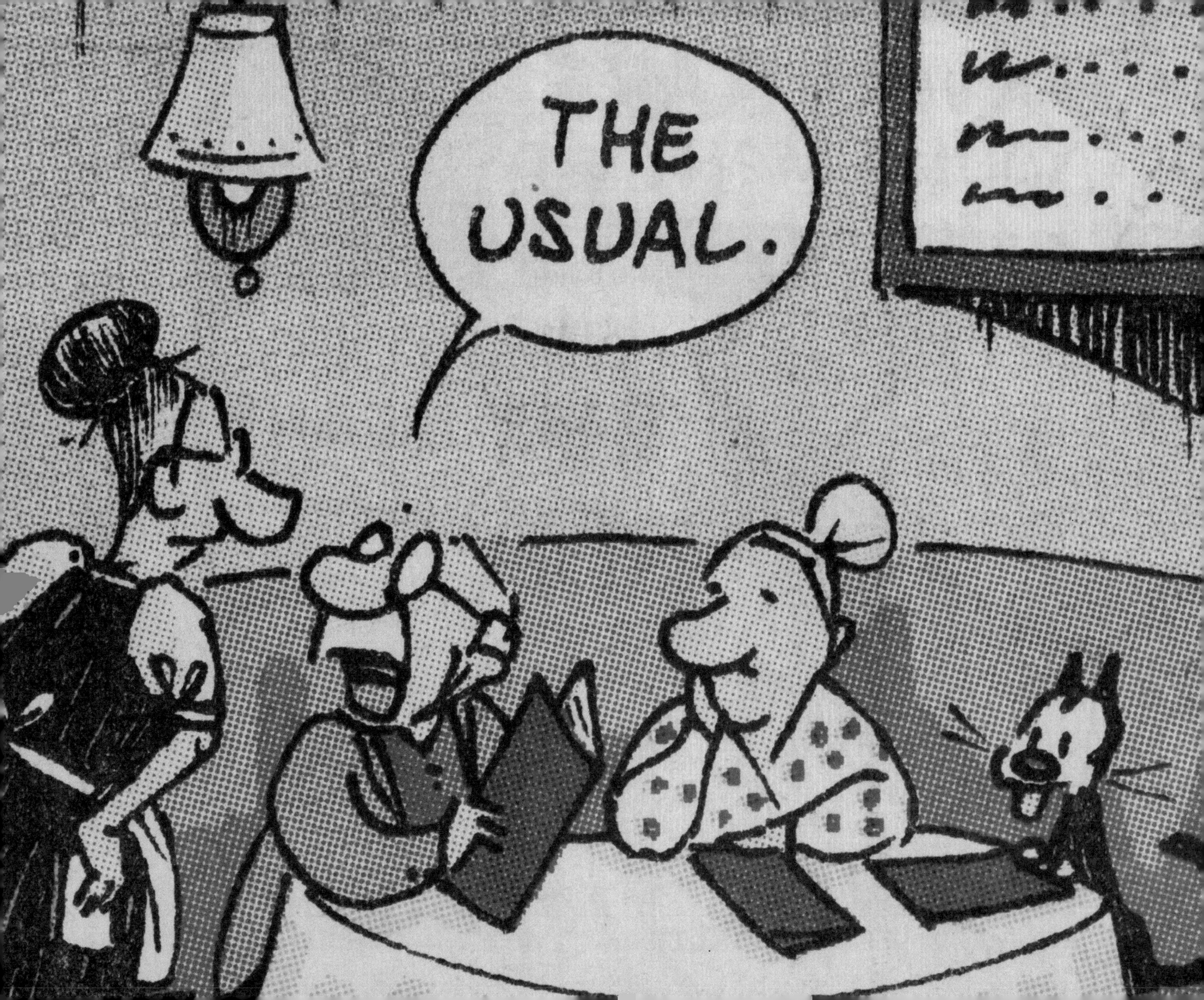
THE USUAL.

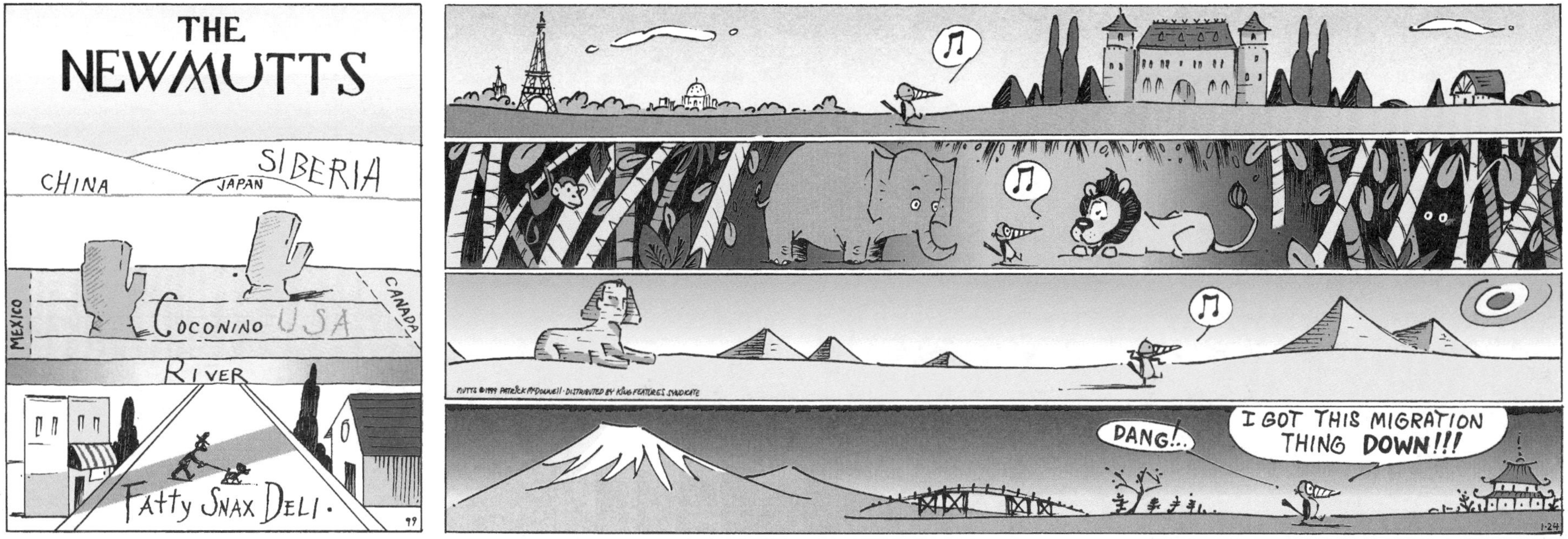
THE NEWMUTTS
CHINA
JAPAN
SIBERIA
MEXICO
COCONINO USA
CANADA
RIVER
Fatty Snax Deli
DANG!..
I GOT THIS MIGRATION THING DOWN!!!

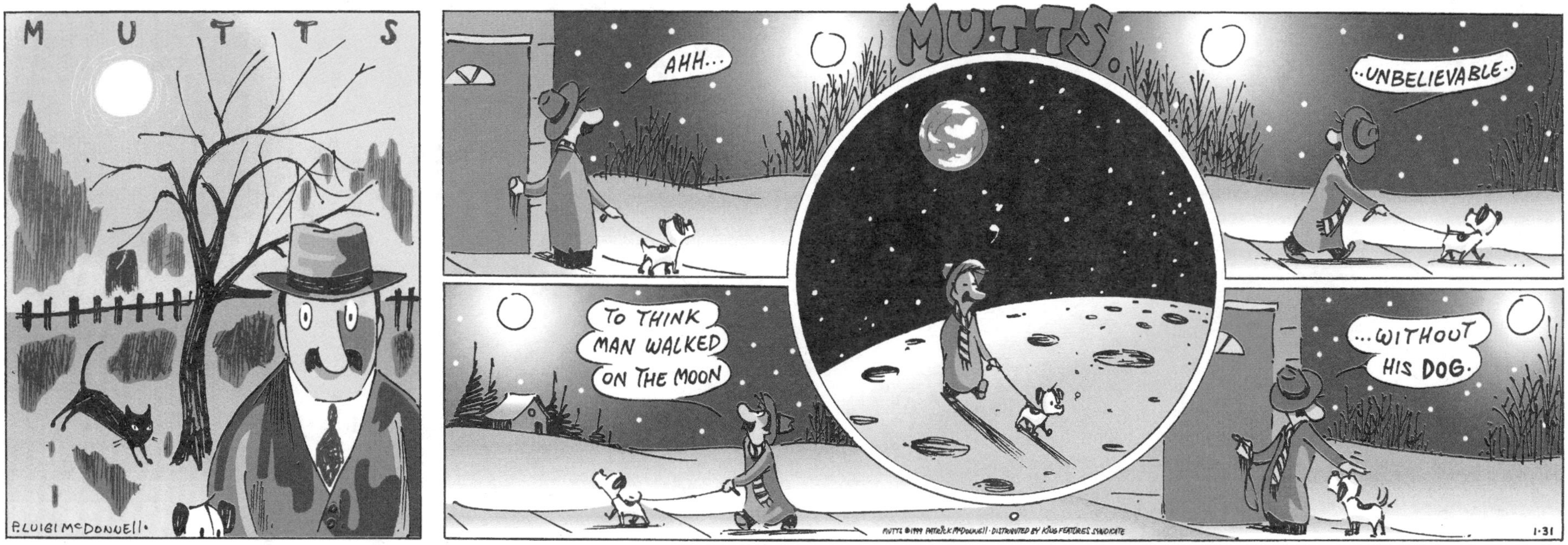
MUTTS
P. LUIGI McDONNELL
MUTTS
AHH...
..UNBELIEVABLE..
TO THINK MAN WALKED ON THE MOON
...WITHOUT HIS DOG.

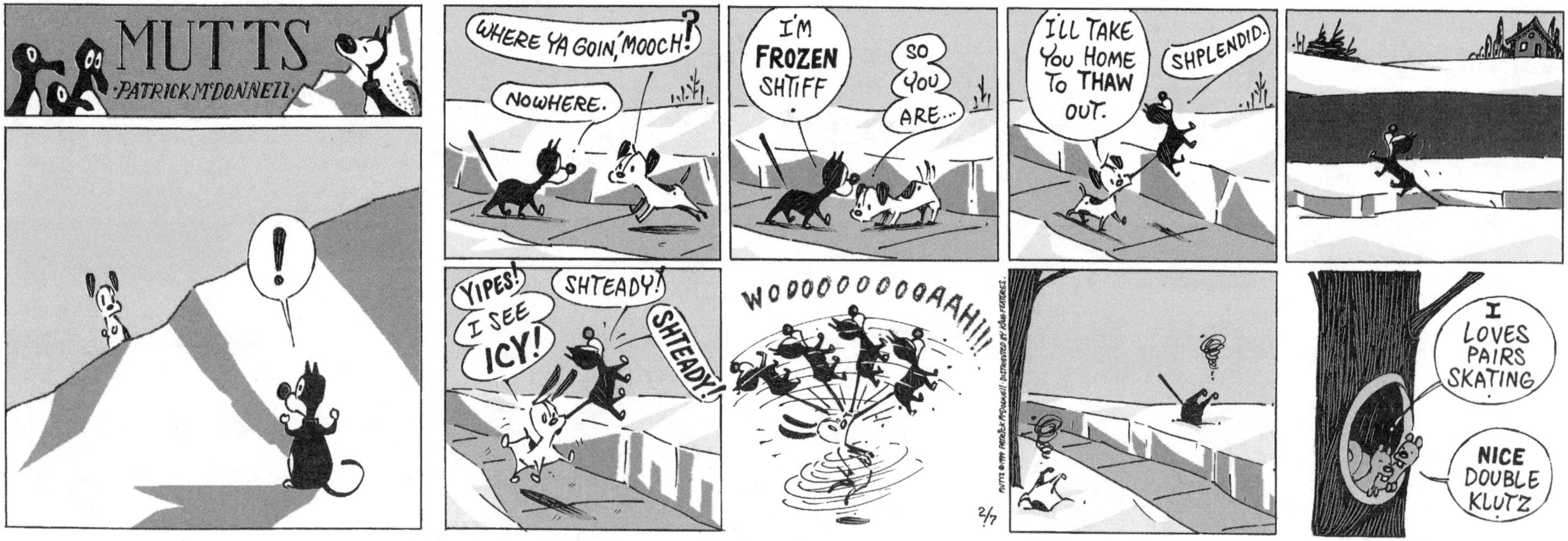
MUTTS
·PATRICK McDONNELL·
!
WHERE YA GOIN', MOOCH?
NOWHERE.
I'M FROZEN SHTIFF.
SO YOU ARE...
I'LL TAKE YOU HOME TO THAW OUT.
SHPLENDID.
YIPES! I SEE ICY!
SHTEADY!
SHTEADY!
WOOOOOOOOOOAAH!!!
MUTTS ©1999 PATRICK McDONNELL · DISTRIBUTED BY KING FEATURES.
2/7
I LOVES PAIRS SKATING.
NICE DOUBLE KLUTZ.

MUTTS

MOOCH AND NOODLES ARE HAVING A POETRY CONTEST TO WOO SHNELLY.
HOW ROMANTIC!
ROSES ARE RED..
VIOLETS ARE BLUE..
SUGAR IS SWEET!
AND SO ARE YOU!
YA @☆#!!
OOPS!
WOOPS!
BRAVO! BRAVO!
SPLUNK
MUTTS ©1999 PATRICK McDONNELL · DISTRIBUTED BY KING FEATURES SYNDICATE
POETRY IN MOTION!
CLAP CLAP CLAP
2·14

E 1

F P 2

T O Z 3

L P E D 4

M U T T S 5

GO ON, MUTT! YOU CAN FLASH THOSE OL' PUPPY EYES ALL DAY- YOU'LL GET NO SNACKS FROM ME! I NEVER LOSE A STARING CONTEST!!!
2·21
FATTY SNAX DELI
OKAY, I'M FULL.
LET'S GO!
MUTTS ©1999 PATRICK McDONNELL · DISTRIBUTED BY KING FEATURES

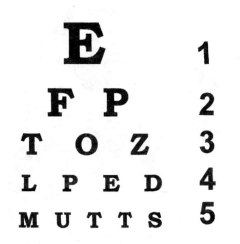

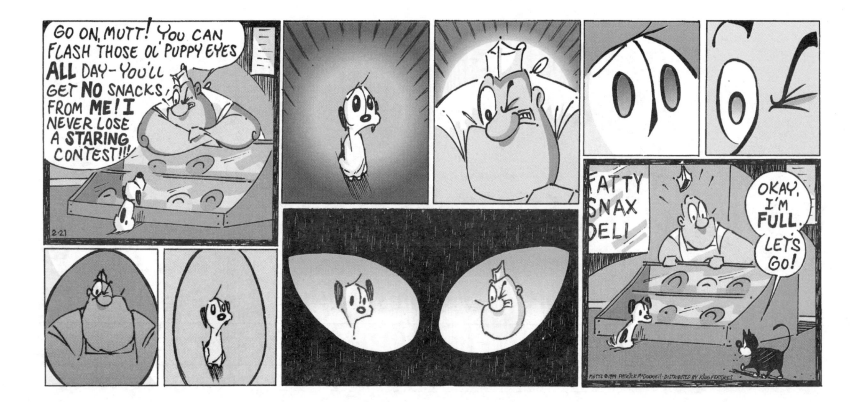

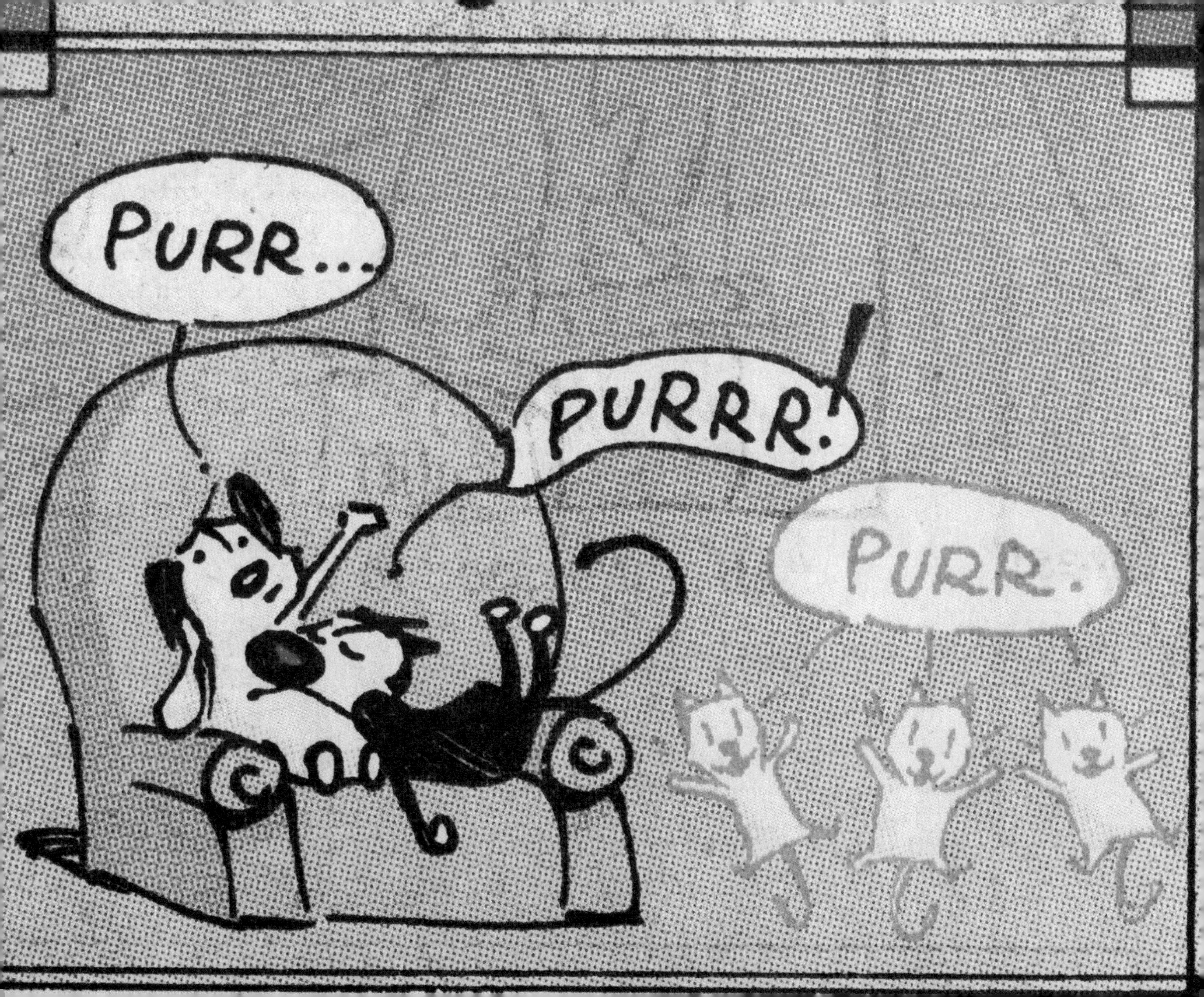
PURR...
PURRR!
PURR.

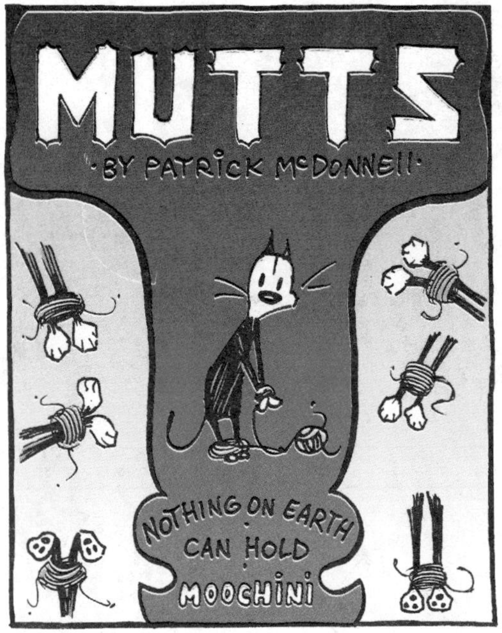
MUTTS
BY PATRICK McDONNELL
NOTHING ON EARTH CAN HOLD MOOCHINI

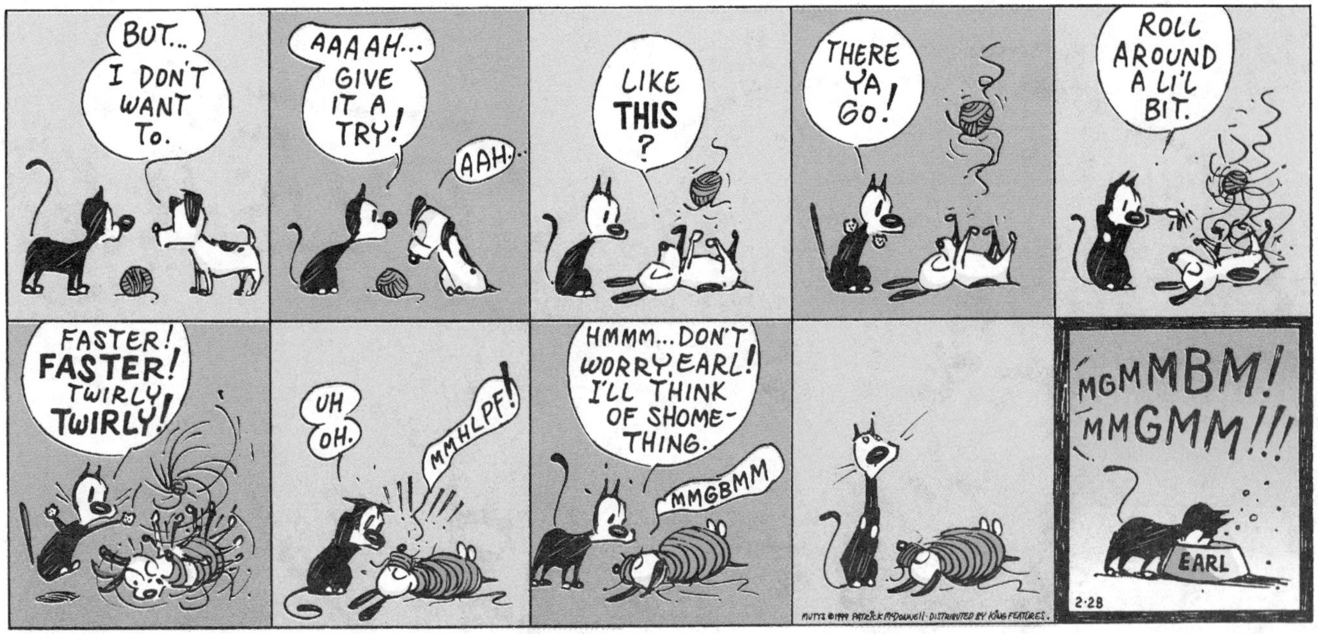
BUT... I DON'T WANT TO.
AAAAH... GIVE IT A TRY!
AAH...
LIKE THIS?
THERE YA GO!
ROLL AROUND A LI'L BIT.
FASTER! FASTER! TWIRLY TWIRLY!
UH OH.
MMHLPF!
HMMM... DON'T WORRY, EARL! I'LL THINK OF SHOME-THING.
MMGBMM
MUTTS ©1999 PATRICK McDONNELL · DISTRIBUTED BY KING FEATURES.
MGMMBM! MMGMM!!!
EARL
2·28

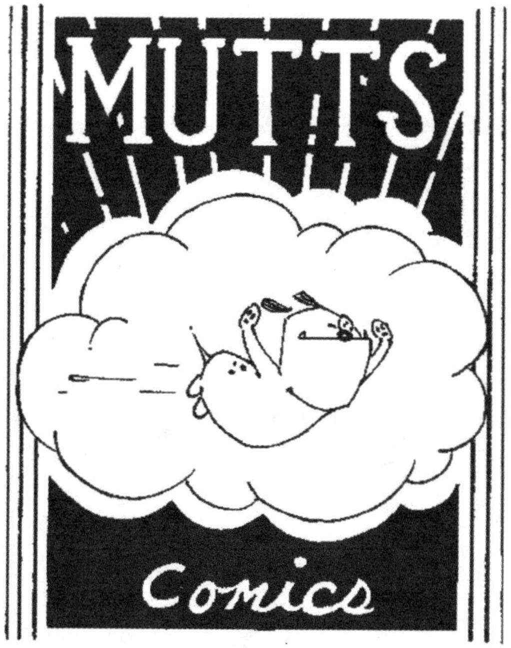
MUTTS
Comics

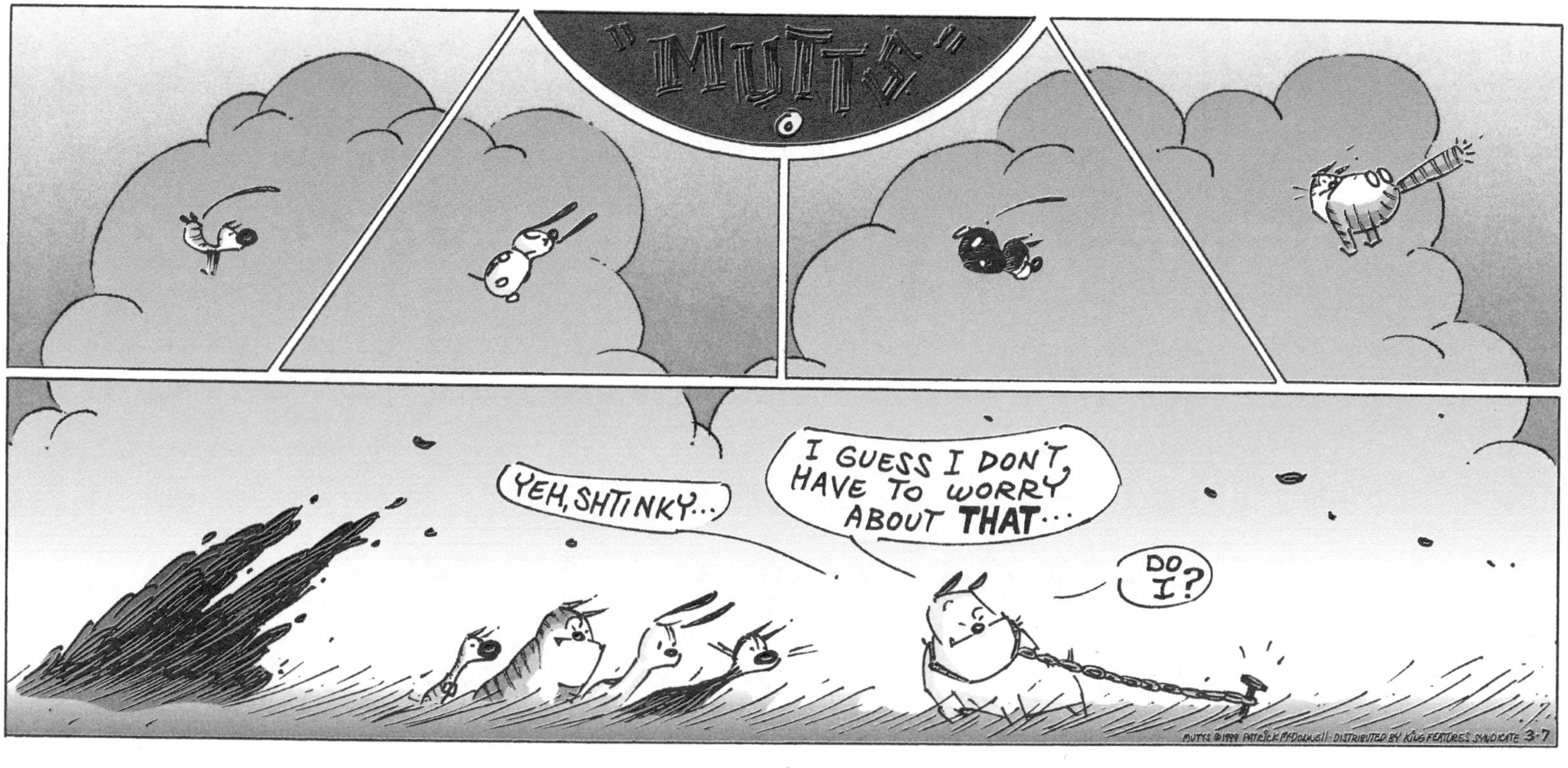
"MUTTS"
YEH, SHTINKY...
I GUESS I DON'T HAVE TO WORRY ABOUT **THAT**...
DO I?
MUTTS ©1999 PATRICK McDONNELL · DISTRIBUTED BY KING FEATURES SYNDICATE 3-7

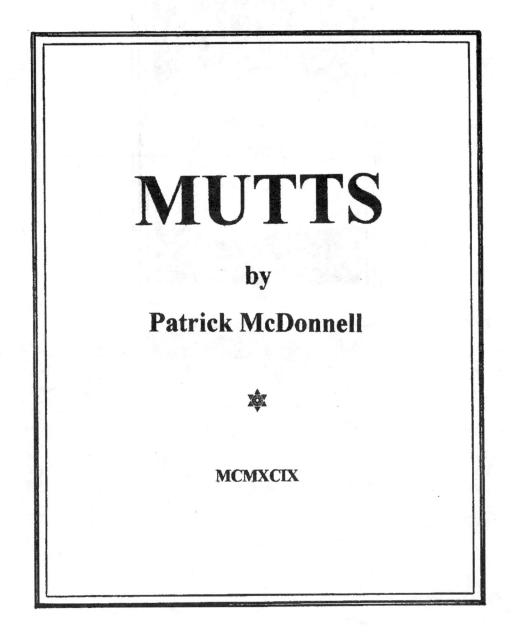

MUTTS

by

Patrick McDonnell

✶

MCMXCIX

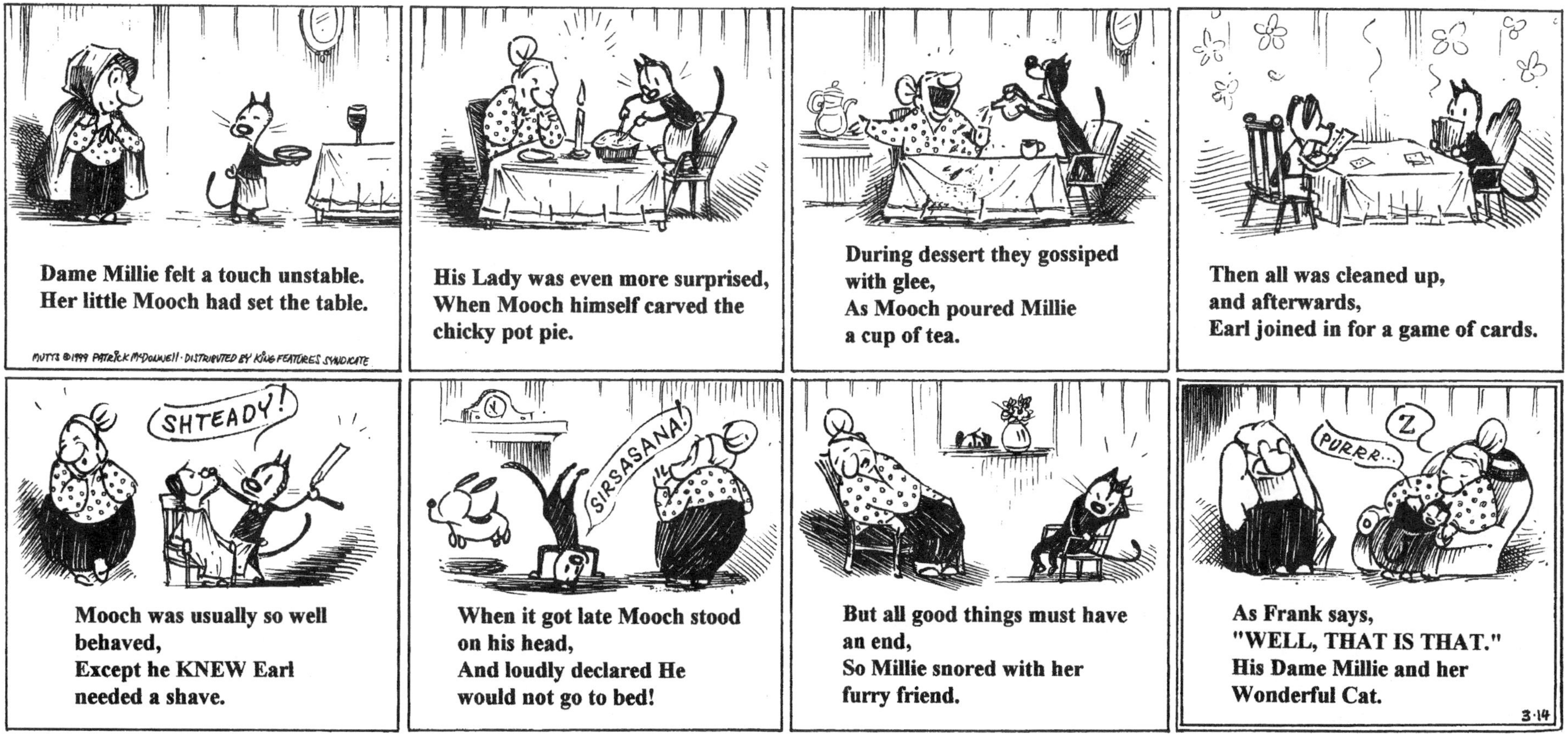
Dame Millie felt a touch unstable.
Her little Mooch had set the table.
MUTTS ©1999 PATRICK McDONNELL · DISTRIBUTED BY KING FEATURES SYNDICATE
His Lady was even more surprised,
When Mooch himself carved the
chicky pot pie.
During dessert they gossiped
with glee,
As Mooch poured Millie
a cup of tea.
Then all was cleaned up,
and afterwards,
Earl joined in for a game of cards.
SHTEADY!
Mooch was usually so well
behaved,
Except he KNEW Earl
needed a shave.
SIRSASANA!
When it got late Mooch stood
on his head,
And loudly declared He
would not go to bed!
But all good things must have
an end,
So Millie snored with her
furry friend.
PURRR...
Z
As Frank says,
"WELL, THAT IS THAT."
His Dame Millie and her
Wonderful Cat.
3·14

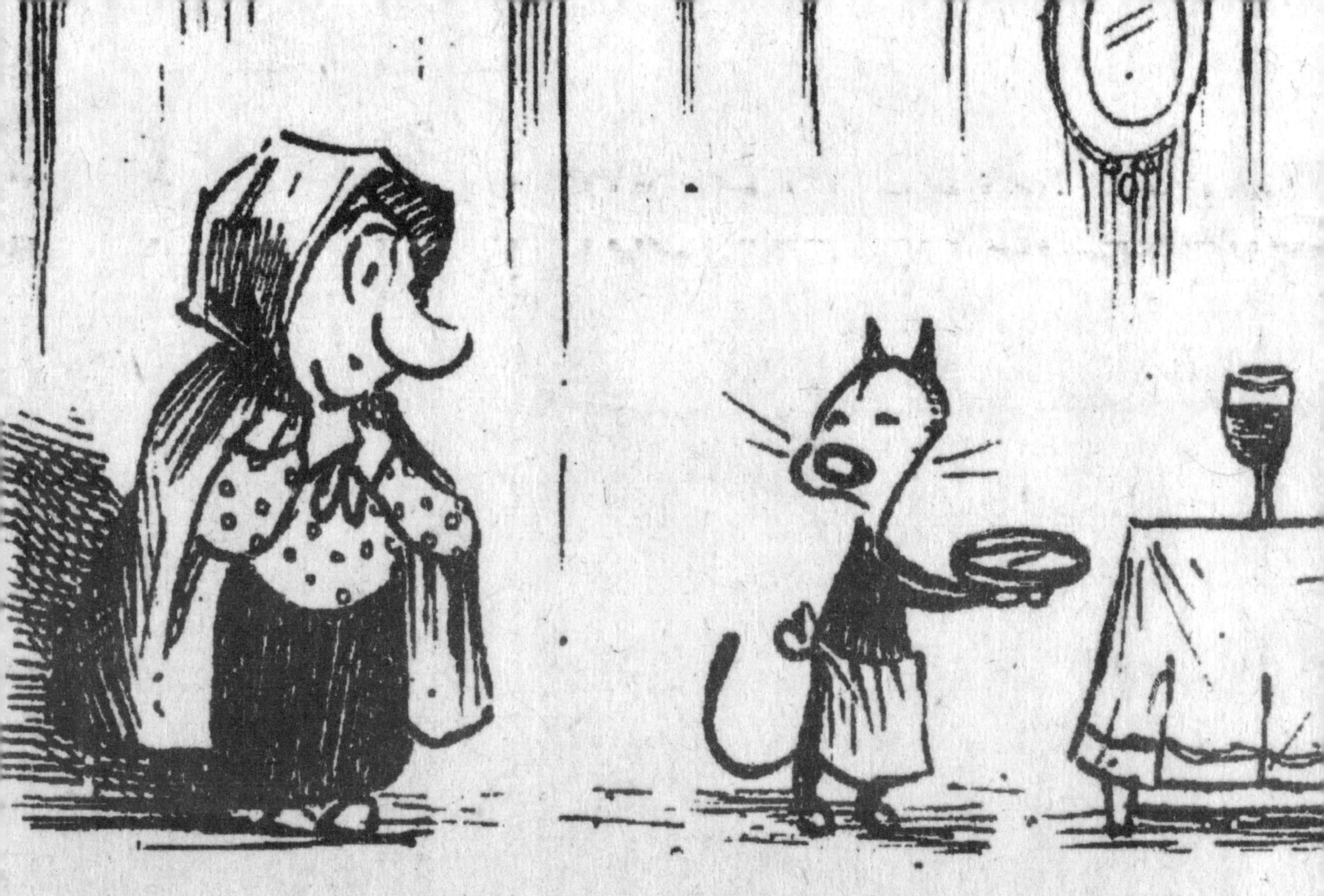

Dame Millie felt a touch unstable.

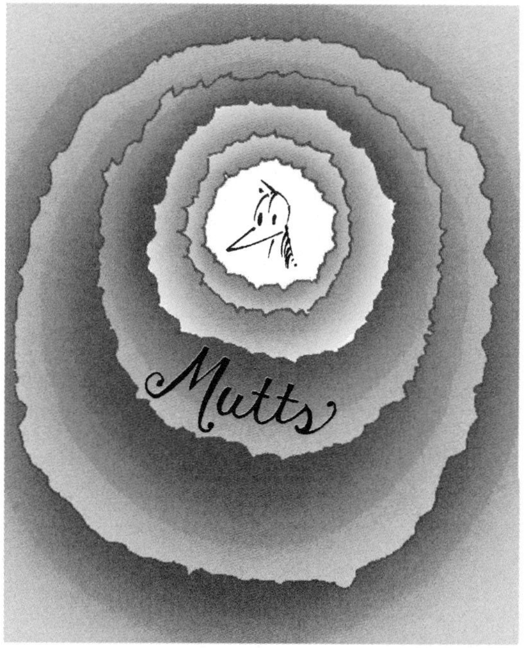
Mutts

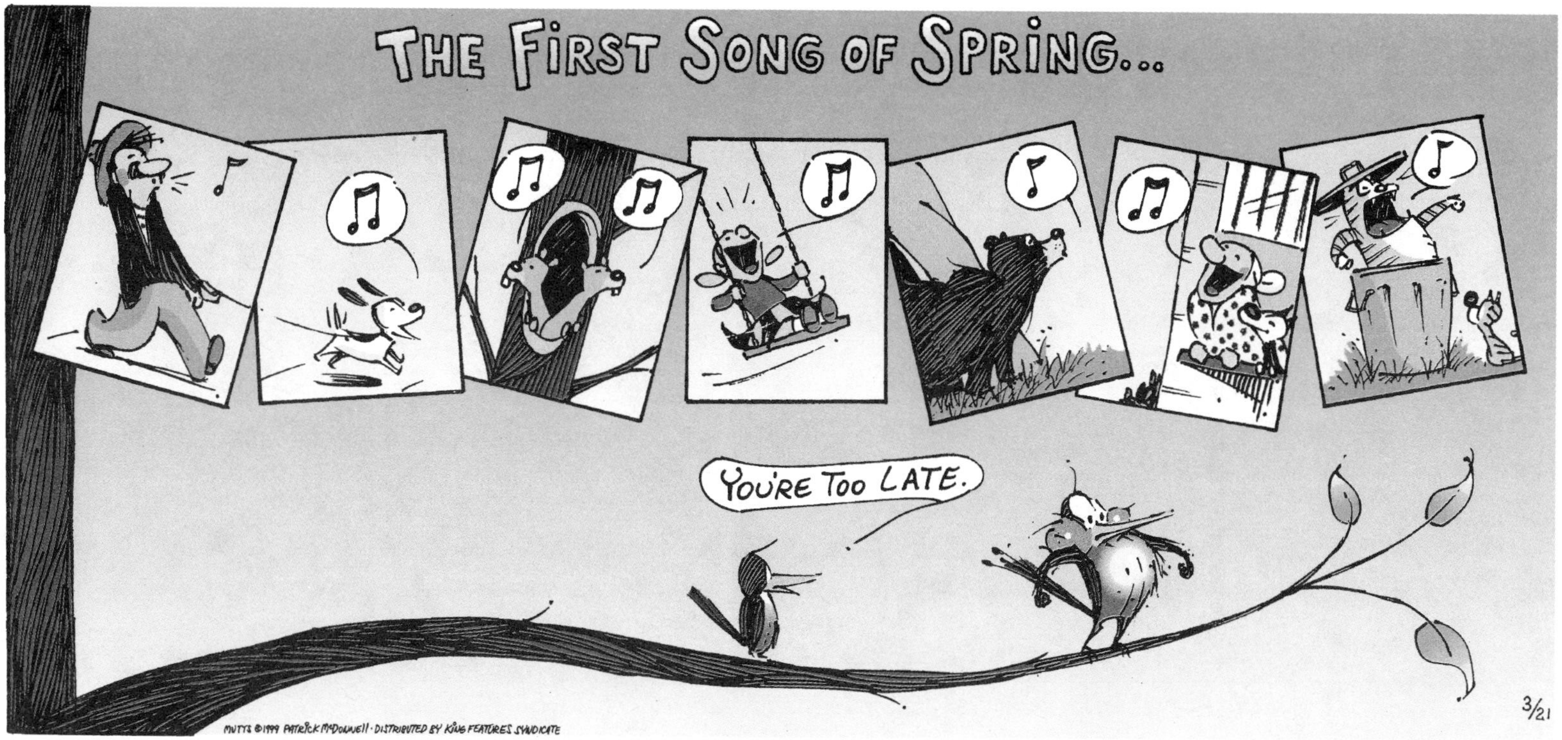
THE FIRST SONG OF SPRING...
YOU'RE TOO LATE.
MUTTS ©1999 PATRICK McDONNELL · DISTRIBUTED BY KING FEATURES SYNDICATE
3/21

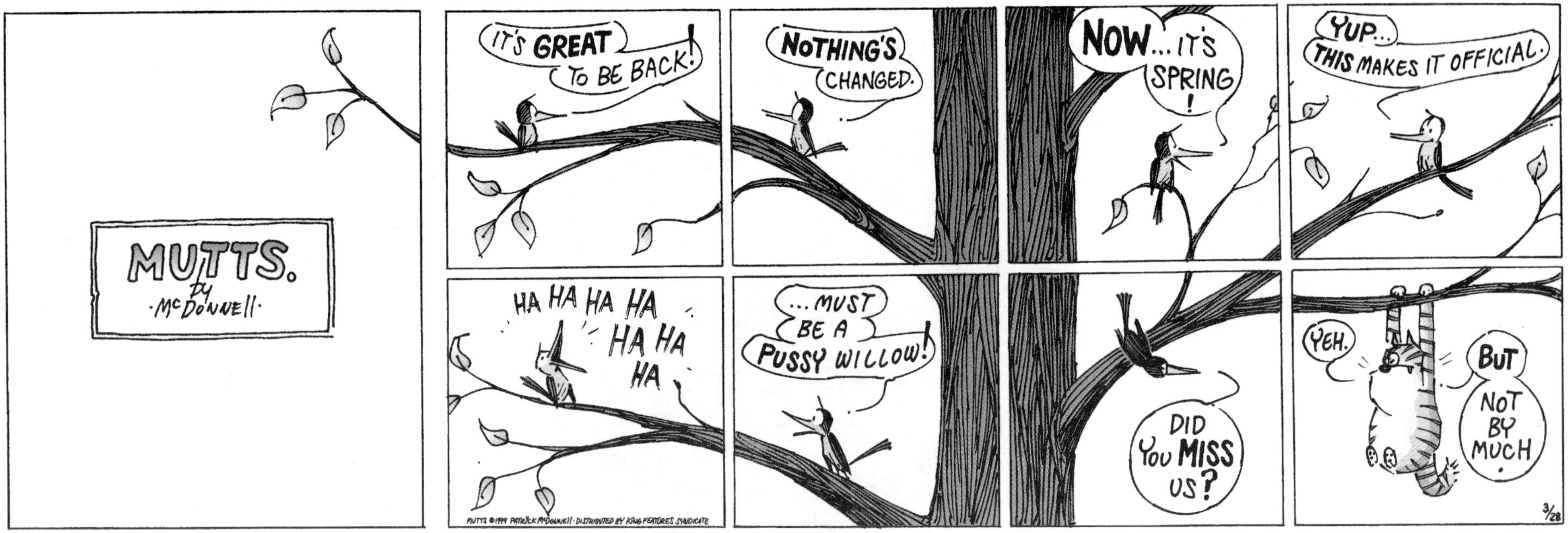
MUTTS.
by McDonnell
IT'S GREAT TO BE BACK!
NOTHING'S CHANGED.
NOW... IT'S SPRING!
YUP... THIS MAKES IT OFFICIAL.
HA HA HA HA HA HA HA
...MUST BE A PUSSY WILLOW!
DID YOU MISS US?
YEH.
BUT NOT BY MUCH.
MUTTS ©1999 PATRICK McDONNELL · DISTRIBUTED BY KING FEATURES SYNDICATE
3/28

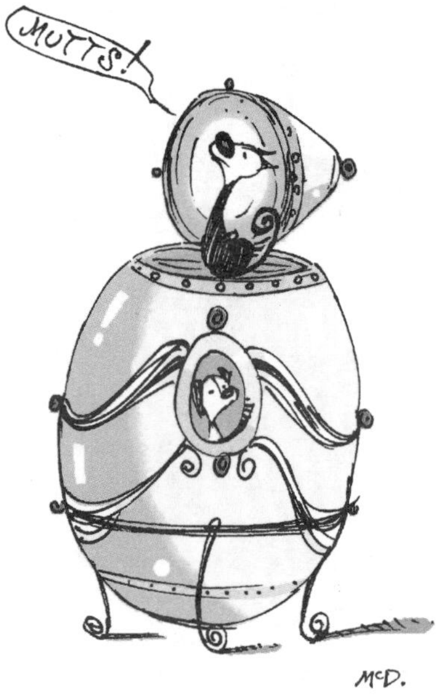
MUTTS!
McD.

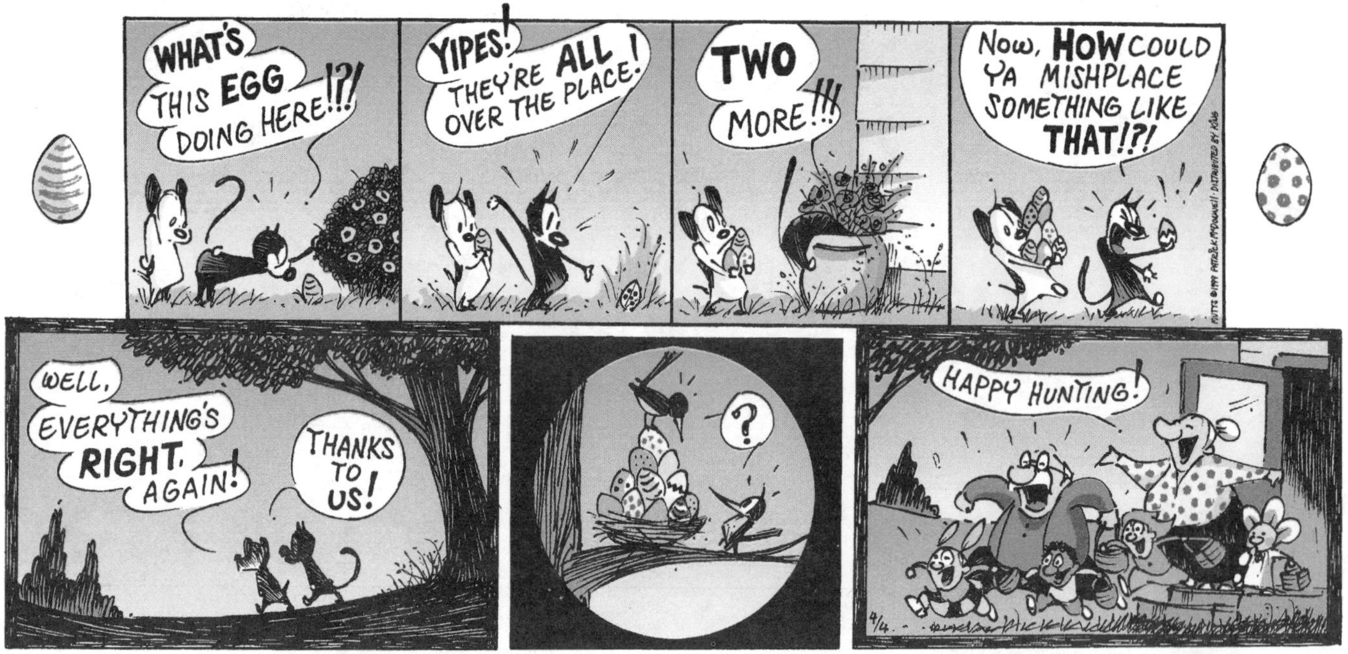
WHAT'S THIS EGG DOING HERE!?!
YIPES! THEY'RE ALL OVER THE PLACE!
TWO MORE!!!
NOW, HOW COULD YA MISHPLACE SOMETHING LIKE THAT!?!
WELL, EVERYTHING'S RIGHT, AGAIN!
THANKS TO US!
?
HAPPY HUNTING!
4/4

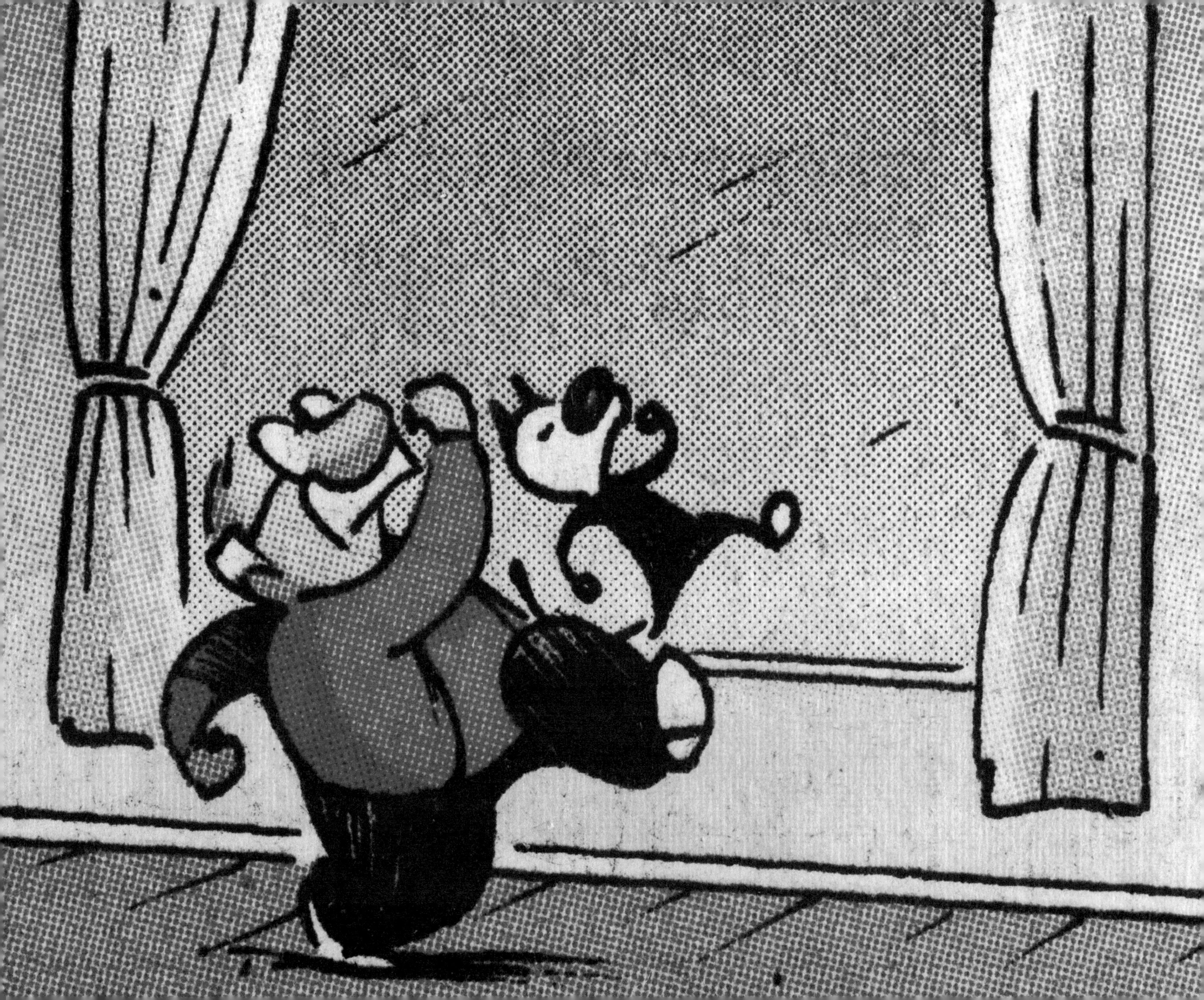

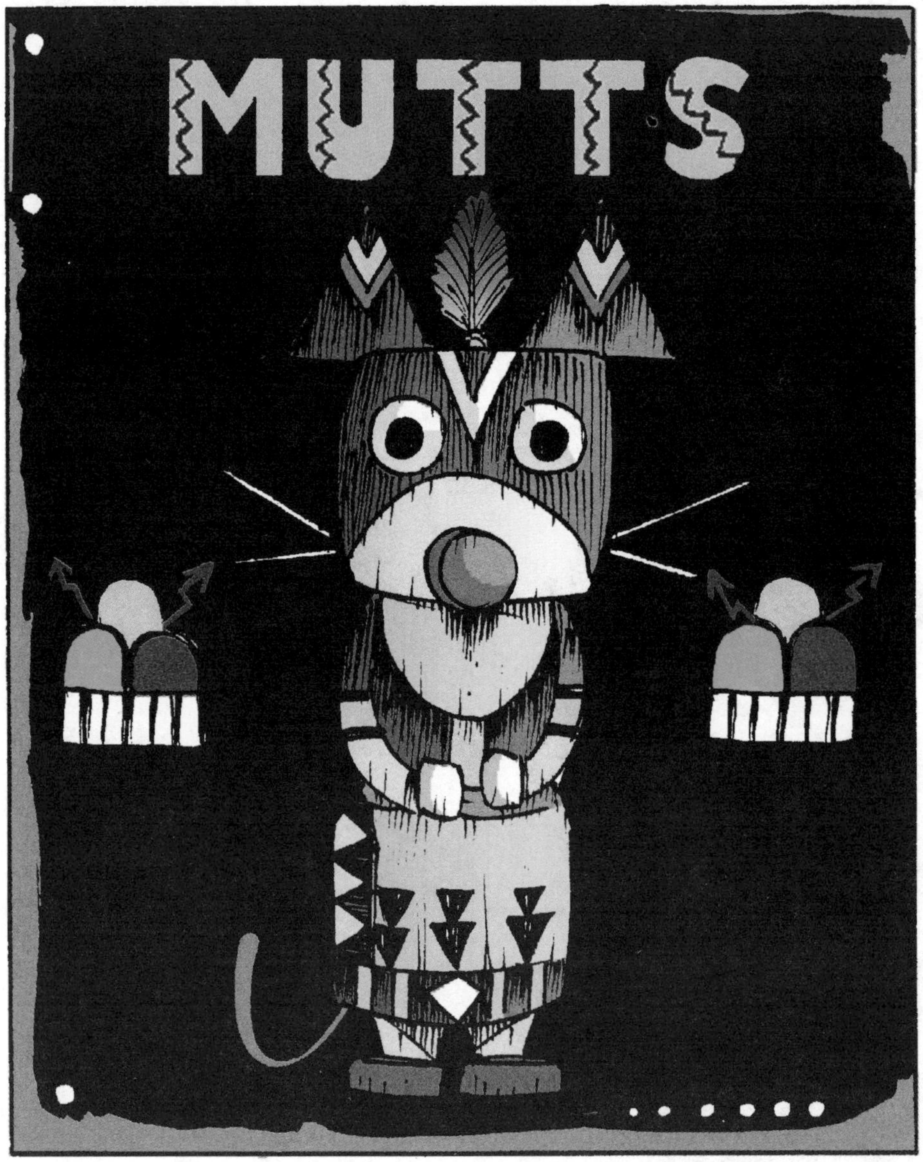
MUTTS

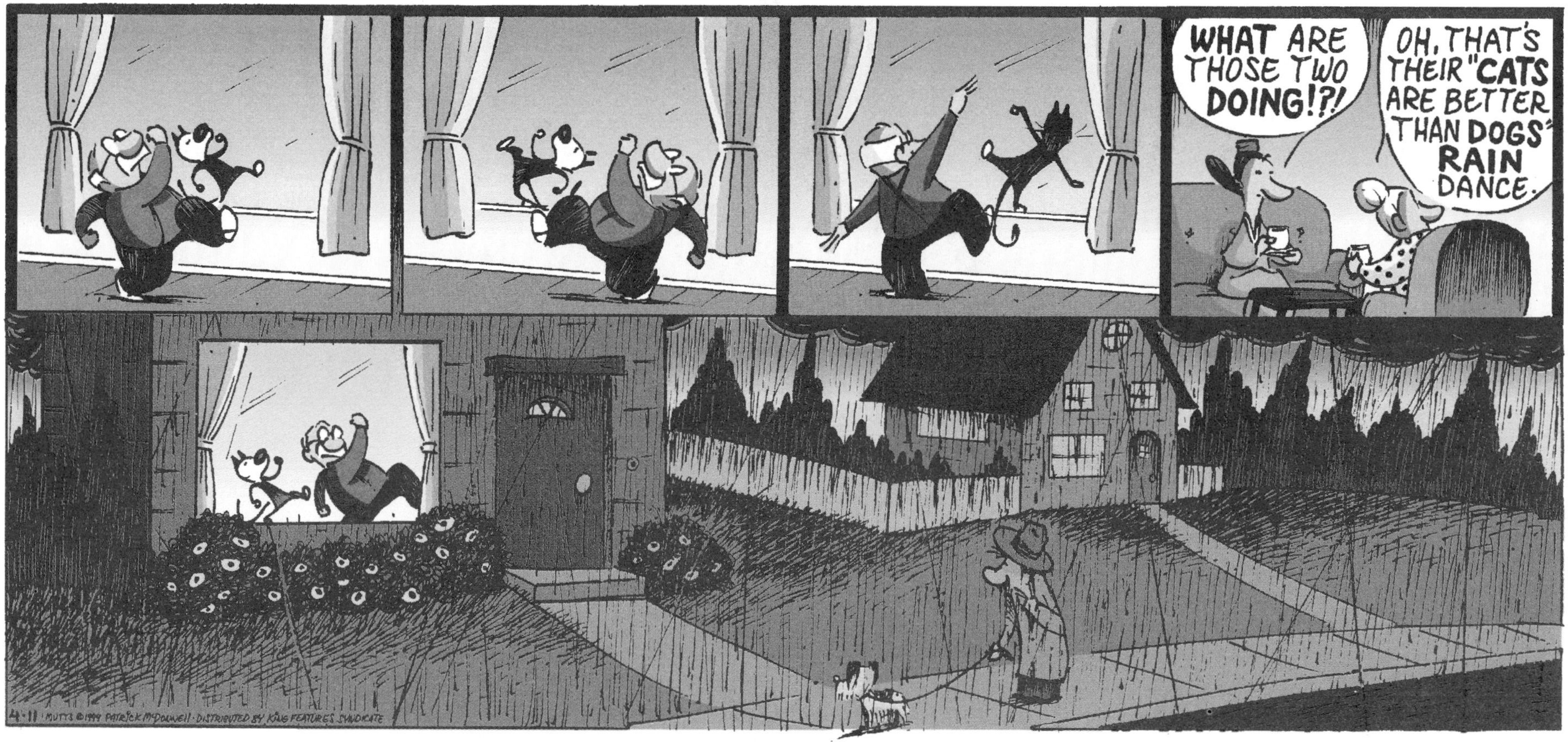
WHAT ARE THOSE TWO DOING!?!
OH, THAT'S THEIR "CATS ARE BETTER THAN DOGS" RAIN DANCE.
4·11 · MUTTS ©1999 PATRICK McDONNELL · DISTRIBUTED BY KING FEATURES SYNDICATE

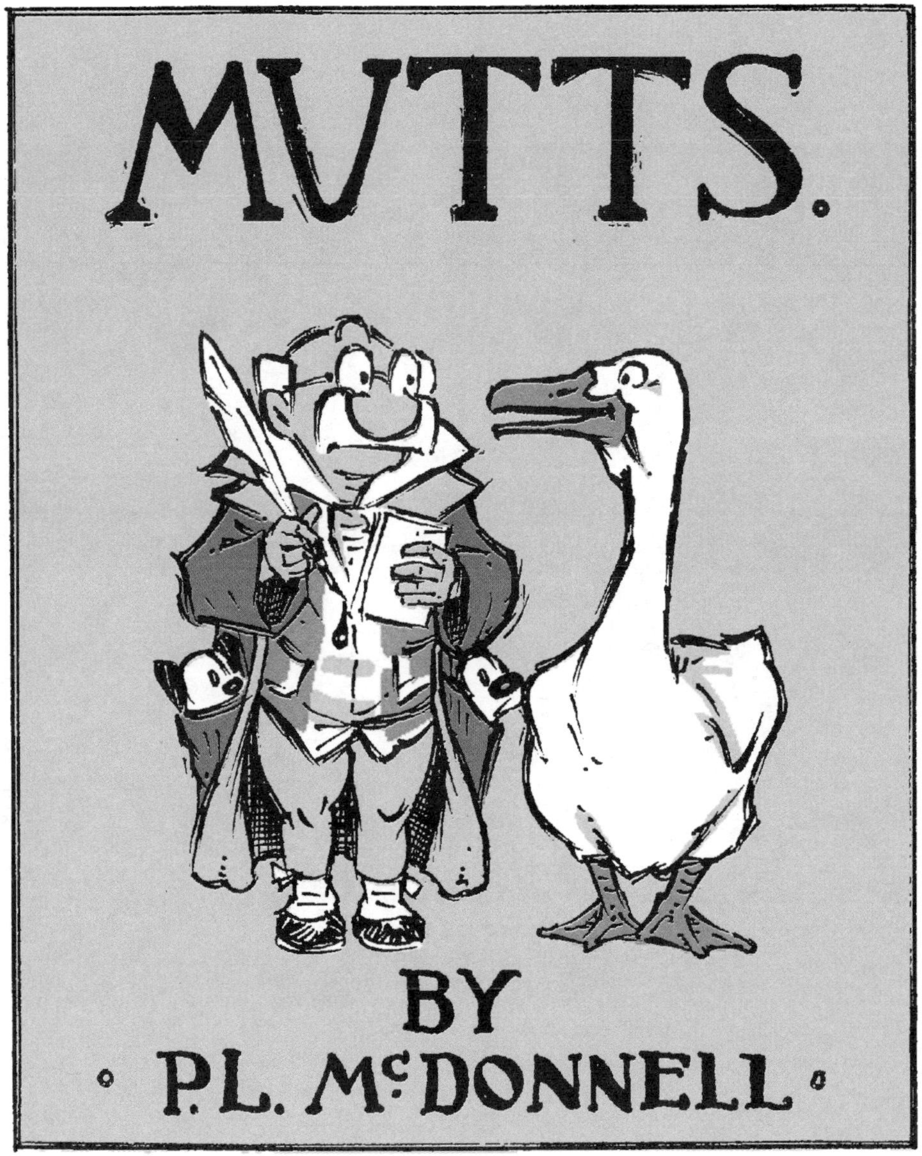
MUTTS.
BY
P.L. McDONNELL

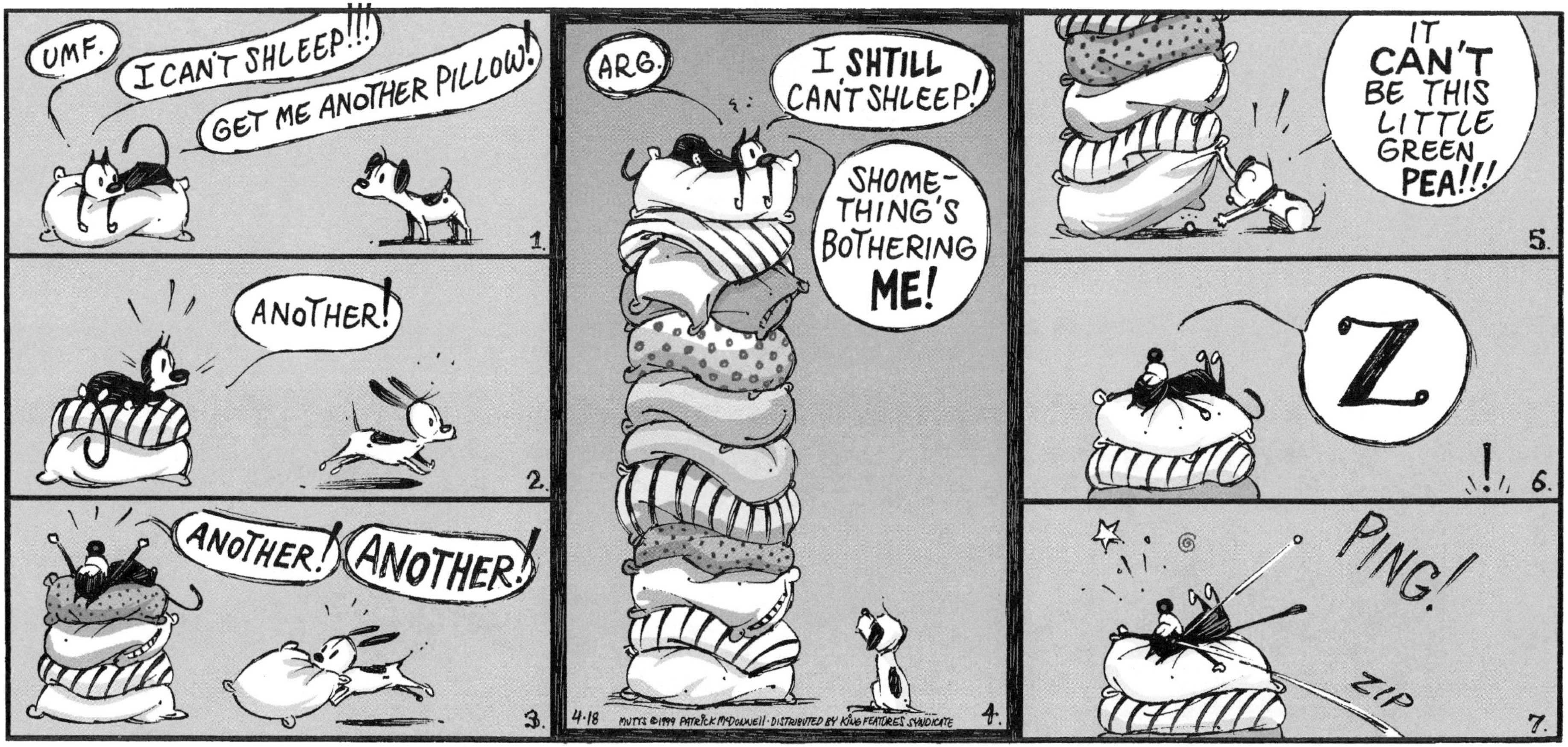
UMF.
I CAN'T SHLEEP!!!
GET ME ANOTHER PILLOW!
ANOTHER!
ANOTHER!
ANOTHER!
ARG.
I SHTILL CAN'T SHLEEP!
SHOME-THING'S BOTHERING ME!
4·18 MUTTS ©1999 PATRICK McDONNELL · DISTRIBUTED BY KING FEATURES SYNDICATE
IT CAN'T BE THIS LITTLE GREEN PEA!!!
Z
PING!
ZIP

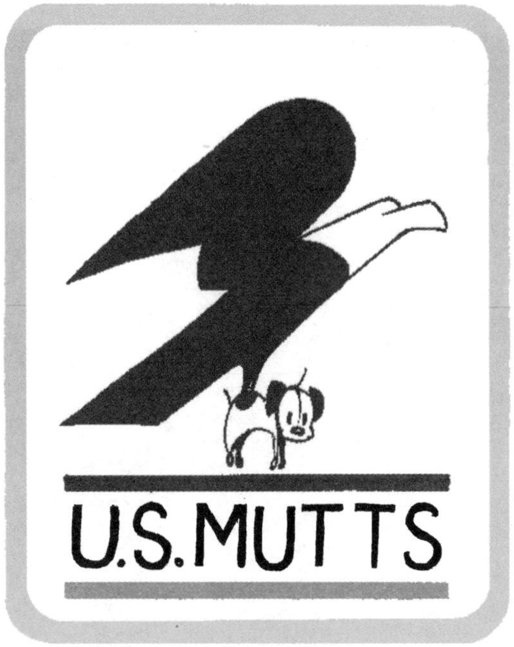
U.S. MUTTS

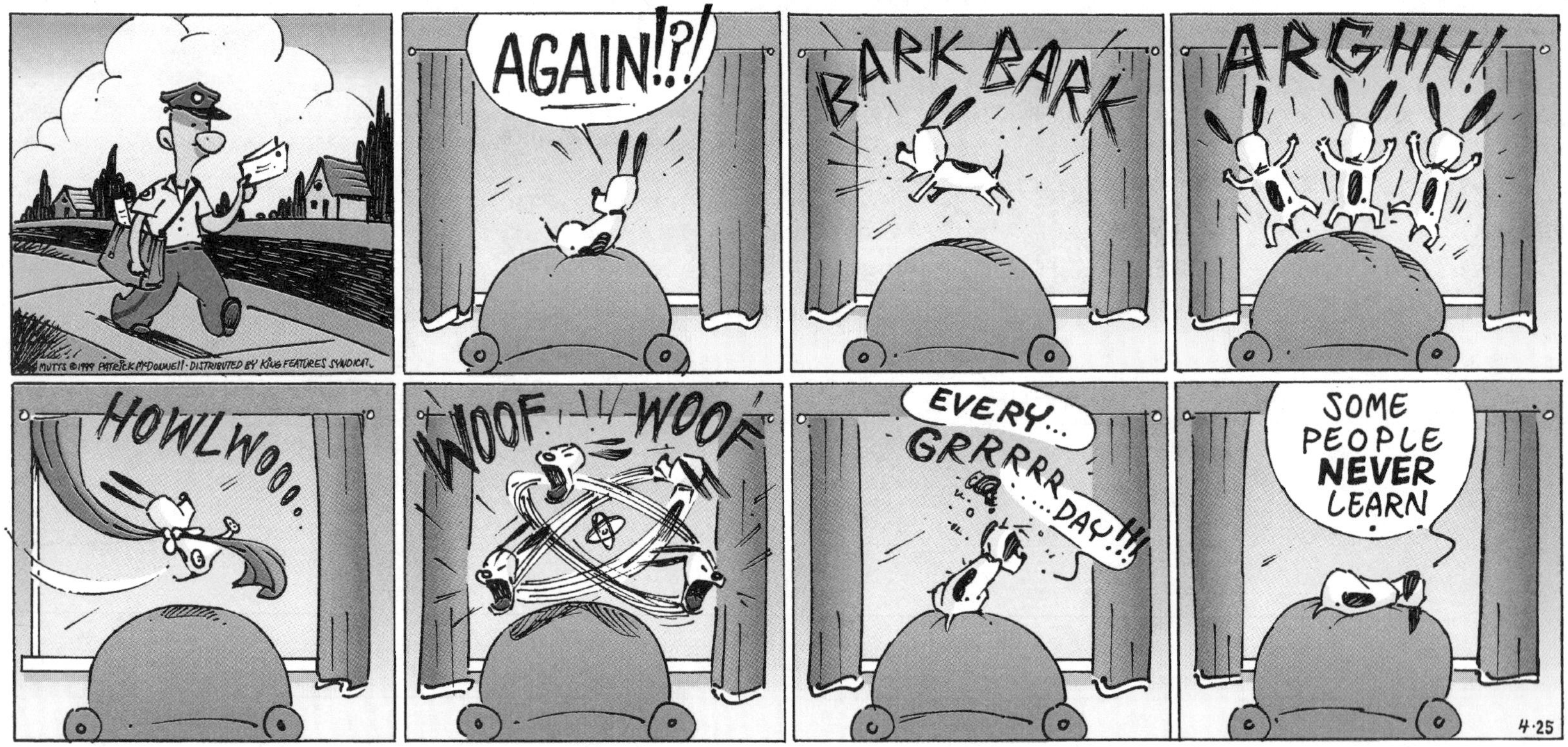
MUTTS ©1999 PATRICK McDONNELL · DISTRIBUTED BY KING FEATURES SYNDICATE.
AGAIN!?!
BARK BARK
ARGHH!
HOWLWOOO..
WOOF WOOF
EVERY...
GRRRRR
...DAY!!!
SOME PEOPLE **NEVER** LEARN.
4·25

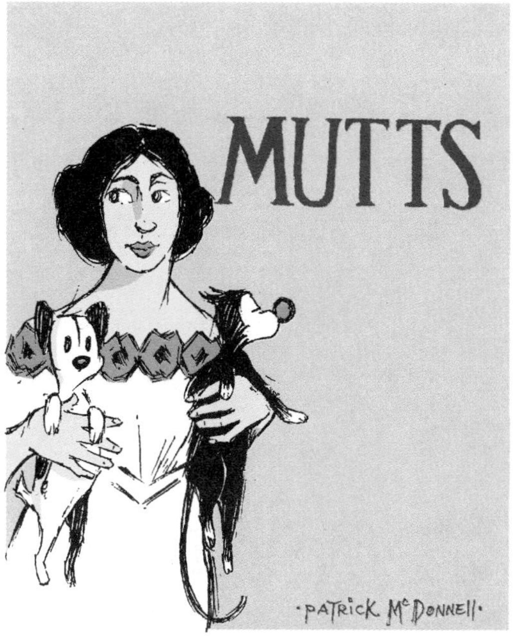
MUTTS
·PATRICK McDONNELL·

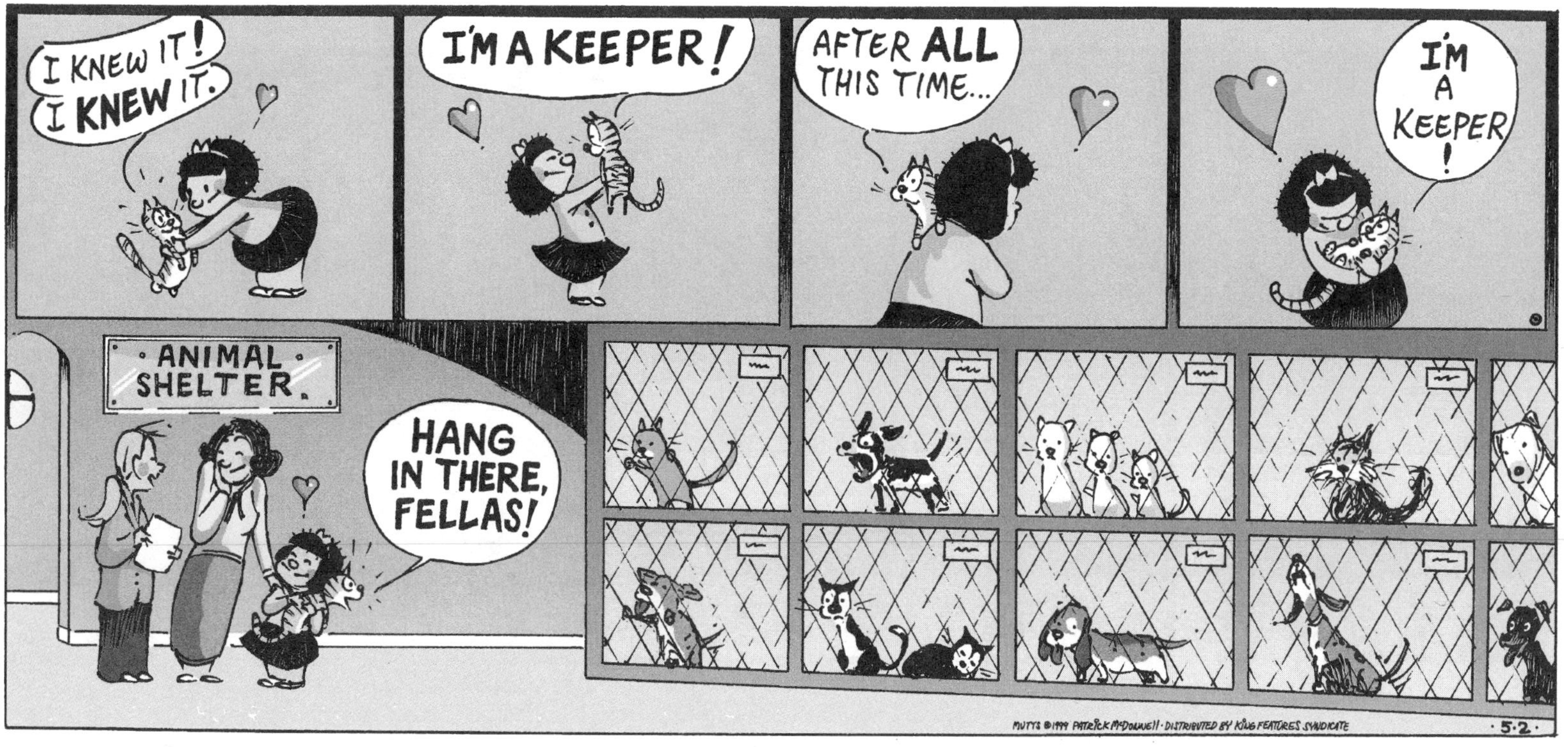
I KNEW IT! I KNEW IT.
I'M A KEEPER!
AFTER ALL THIS TIME...
I'M A KEEPER!
ANIMAL SHELTER
HANG IN THERE, FELLAS!
MUTTS ©1999 PATRICK McDONNELL · DISTRIBUTED BY KING FEATURES SYNDICATE
·5·2·

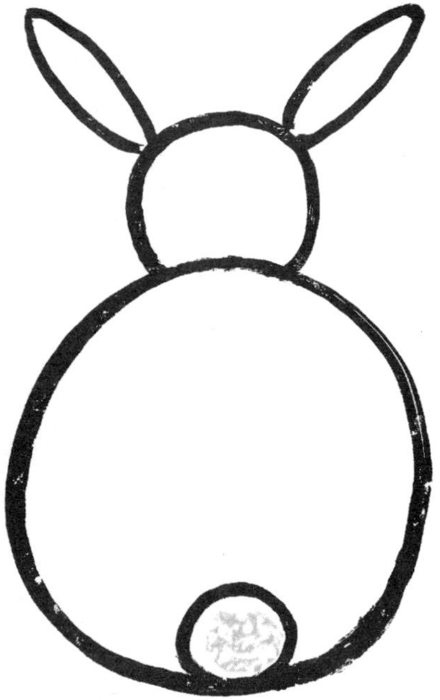

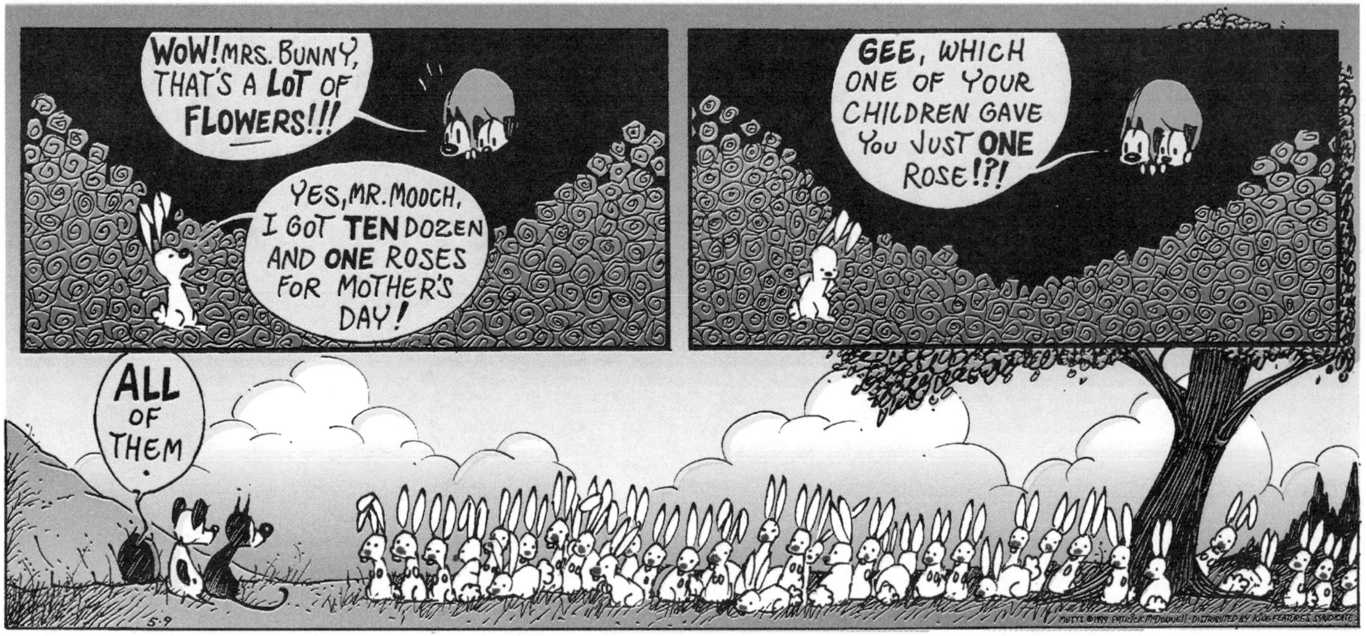
WOW! MRS. BUNNY, THAT'S A LOT OF FLOWERS!!!
YES, MR. MOOCH, I GOT TEN DOZEN AND ONE ROSES FOR MOTHER'S DAY!
GEE, WHICH ONE OF YOUR CHILDREN GAVE YOU JUST ONE ROSE!?!
ALL OF THEM.
5-9
MUTTS ©1999 PATRICK McDONNELL · DISTRIBUTED BY KING FEATURES SYNDICATE

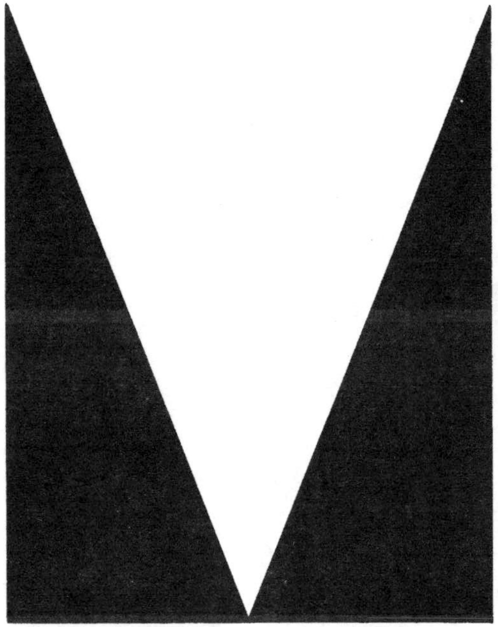

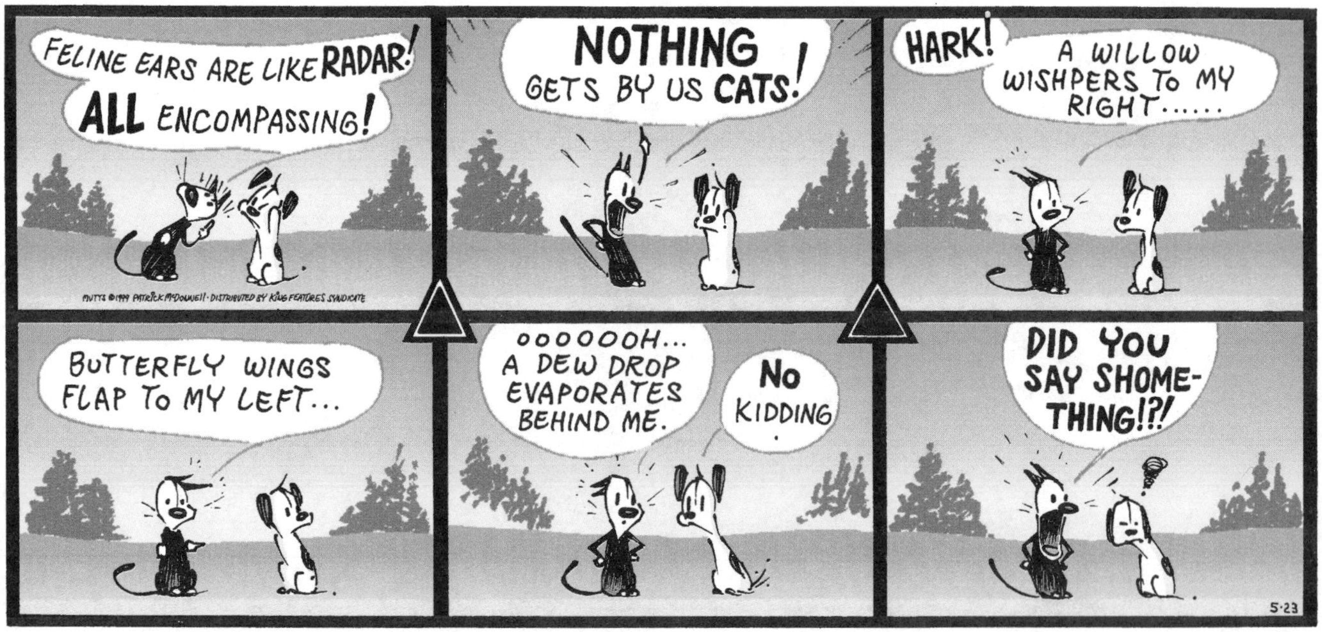
FELINE EARS ARE LIKE RADAR!
ALL ENCOMPASSING!
MUTTS ©1999 PATRICK McDONNELL · DISTRIBUTED BY KING FEATURES SYNDICATE
NOTHING GETS BY US CATS!
HARK!
A WILLOW WISHPERS TO MY RIGHT......
BUTTERFLY WINGS FLAP TO MY LEFT...
OOOOOOH... A DEW DROP EVAPORATES BEHIND ME.
NO KIDDING.
DID YOU SAY SHOME-THING!?!
5-23

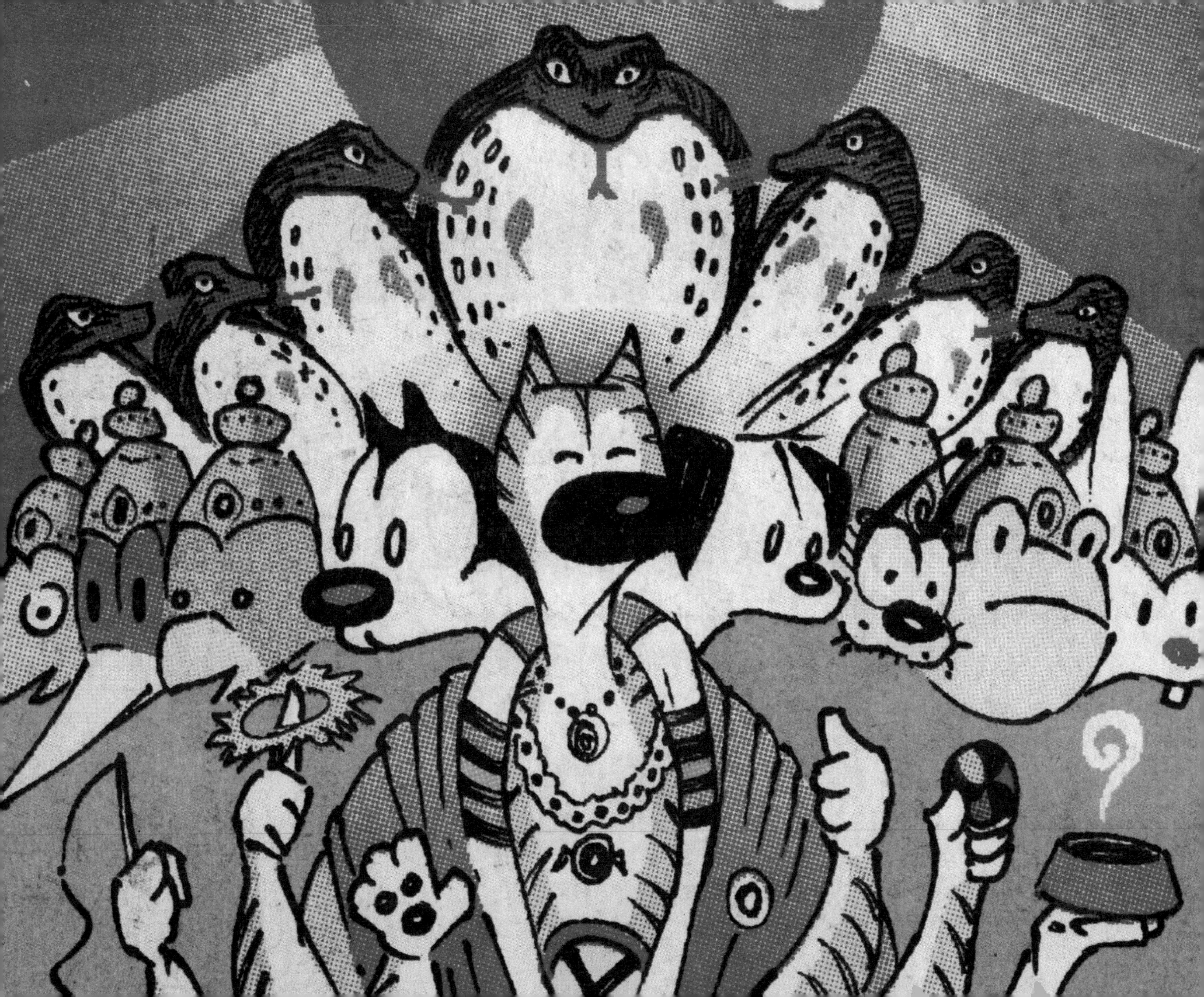

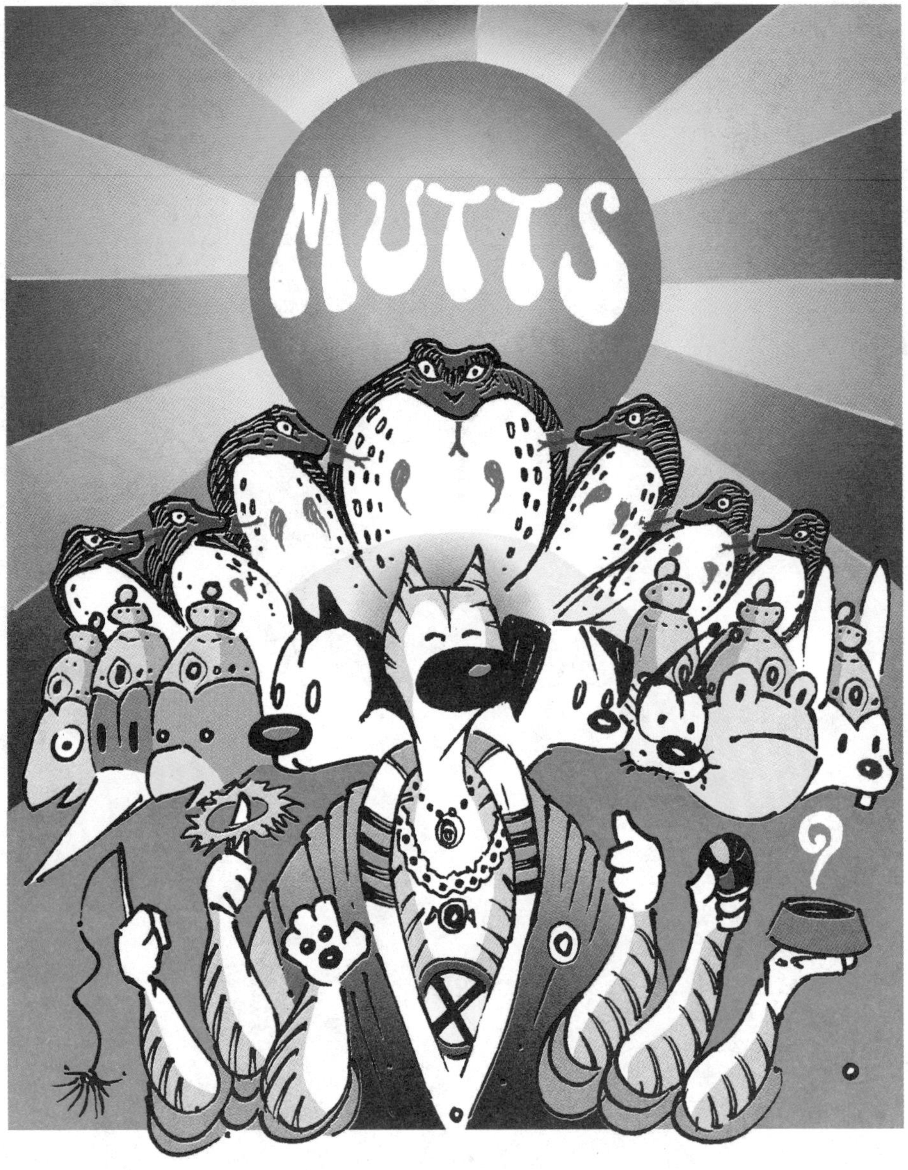
MUTTS
?

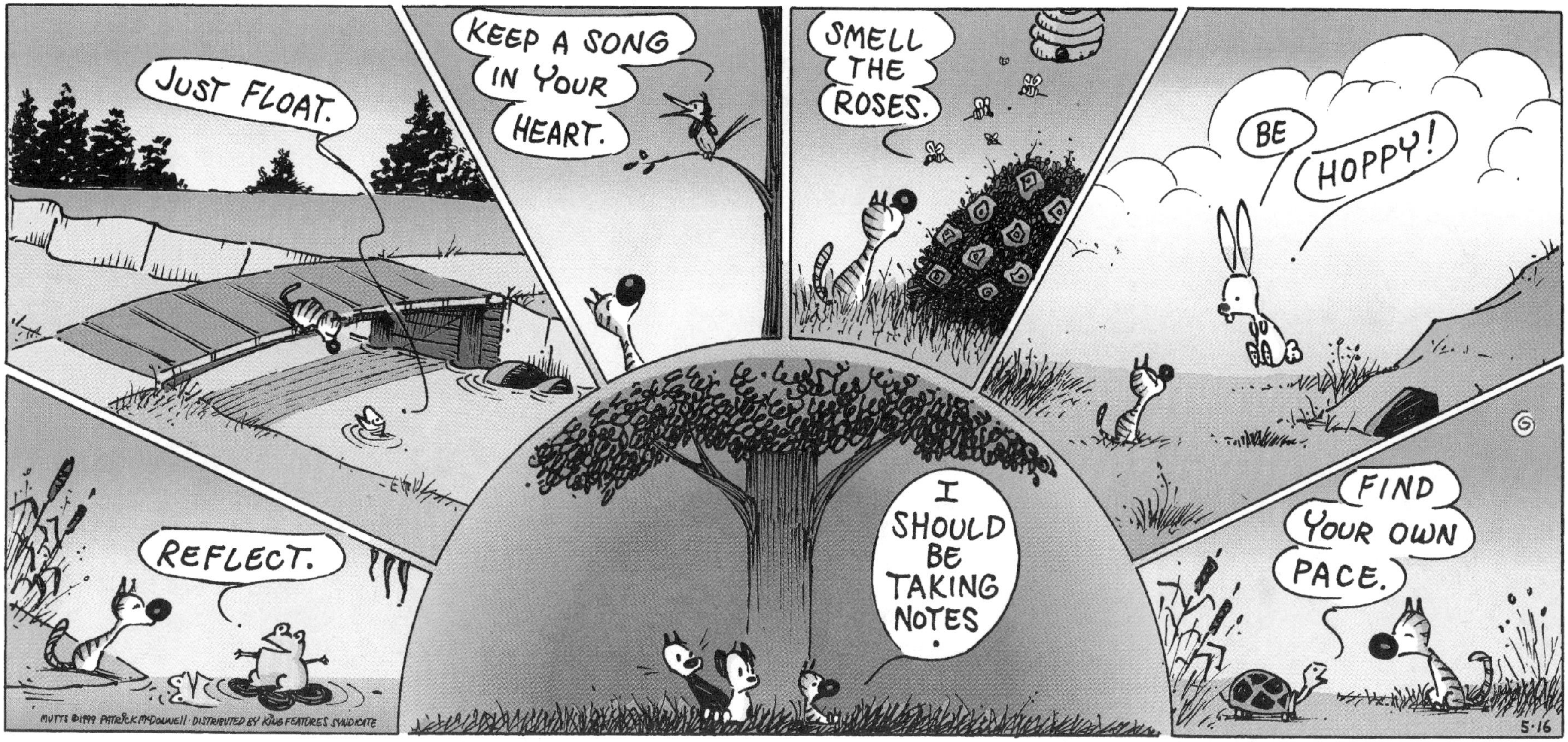
JUST FLOAT.
KEEP A SONG IN YOUR HEART.
SMELL THE ROSES.
BE HOPPY!
REFLECT.
I SHOULD BE TAKING NOTES.
FIND YOUR OWN PACE.
MUTTS ©1999 PATRICK McDONNELL · DISTRIBUTED BY KING FEATURES SYNDICATE
5·16

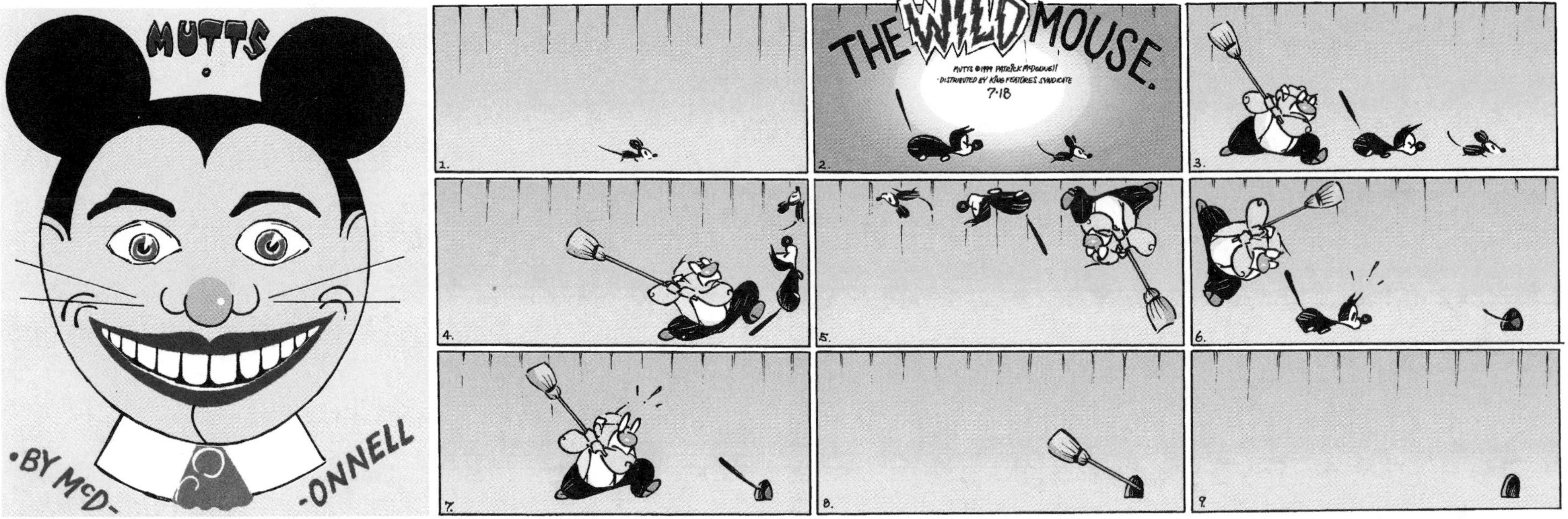
MUTTS
•BY McD- -ONNELL
THE WILD MOUSE.
7·18

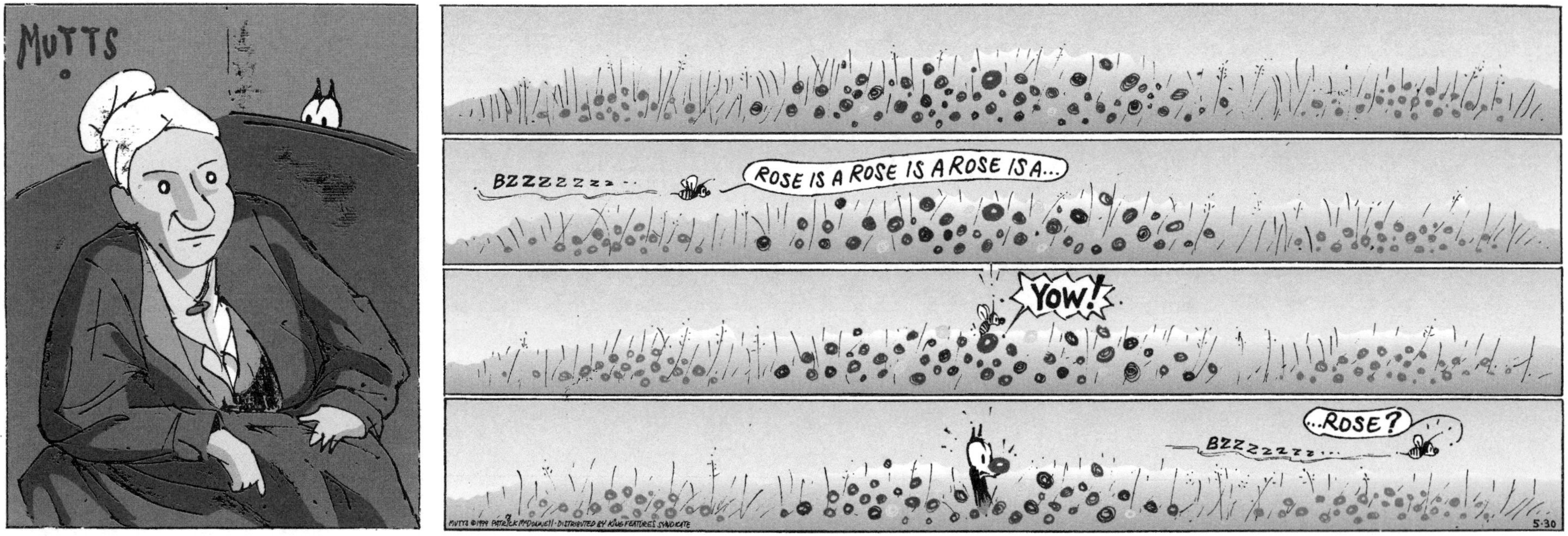
MUTTS
BZZZZZZZ...
ROSE IS A ROSE IS A ROSE IS A...
YOW!
...ROSE?
BZZZZZZZ...
5·30

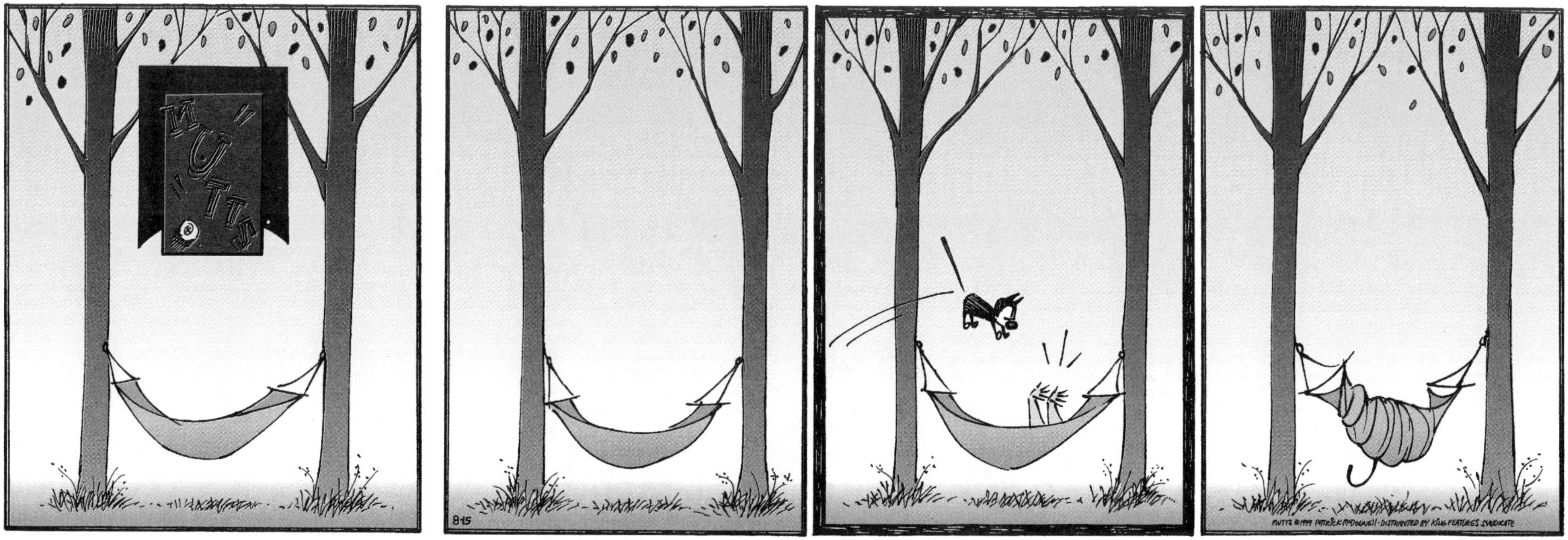
MUTTS
8-15
MUTTS ©1999 PATRICK McDONNELL · DISTRIBUTED BY KING FEATURES SYNDICATE

MUTTS
BY McDONNEll

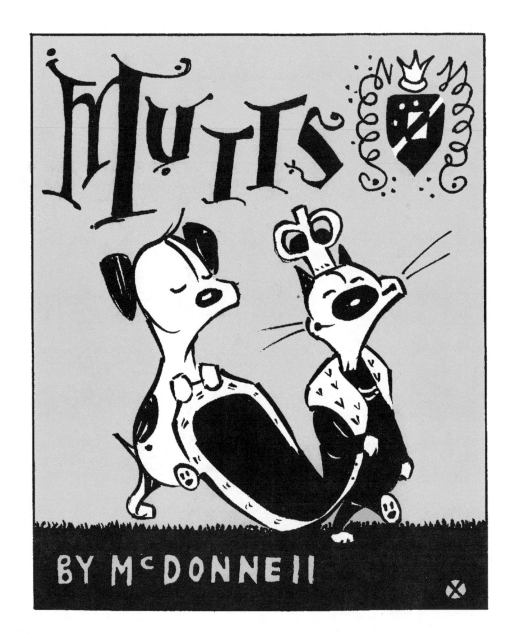

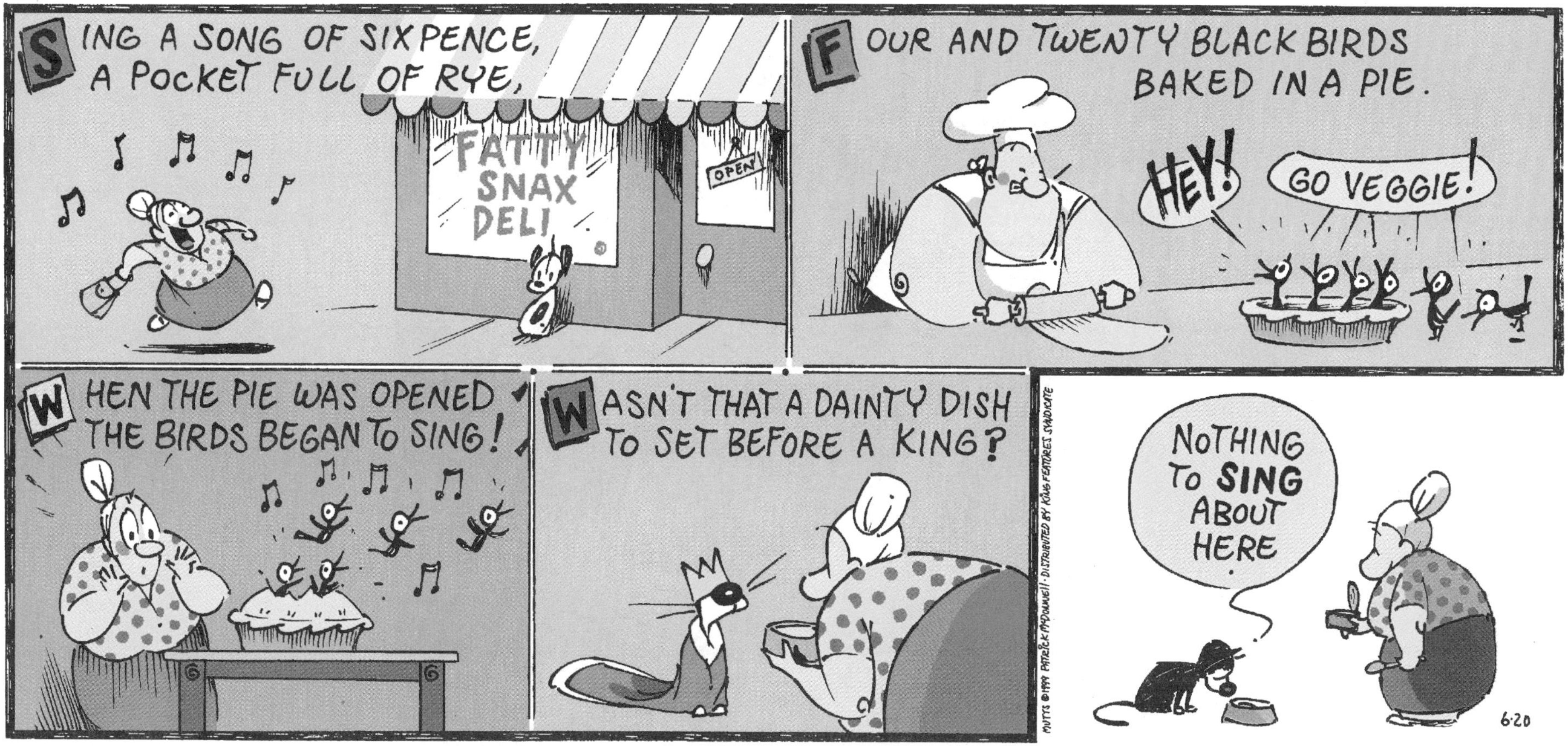
SING A SONG OF SIXPENCE,
A POCKET FULL OF RYE,
FATTY SNAX DELI
OPEN
FOUR AND TWENTY BLACK BIRDS
BAKED IN A PIE.
HEY!
GO VEGGIE!
WHEN THE PIE WAS OPENED
THE BIRDS BEGAN TO SING!
WASN'T THAT A DAINTY DISH
TO SET BEFORE A KING?
MUTTS © 1999 PATRICK McDONNELL · DISTRIBUTED BY KING FEATURES SYNDICATE
NOTHING TO SING ABOUT HERE
6·20

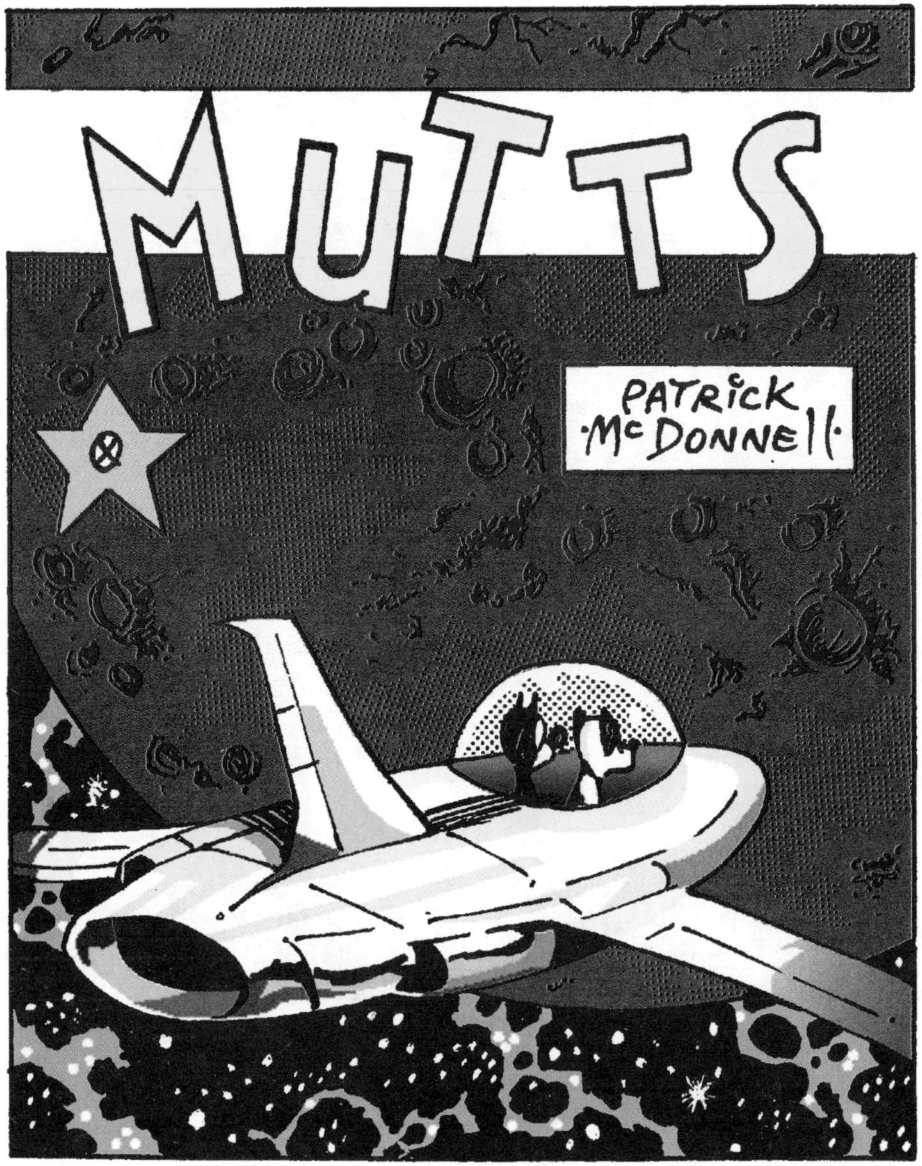
MUTTS
PATRICK McDONNELL

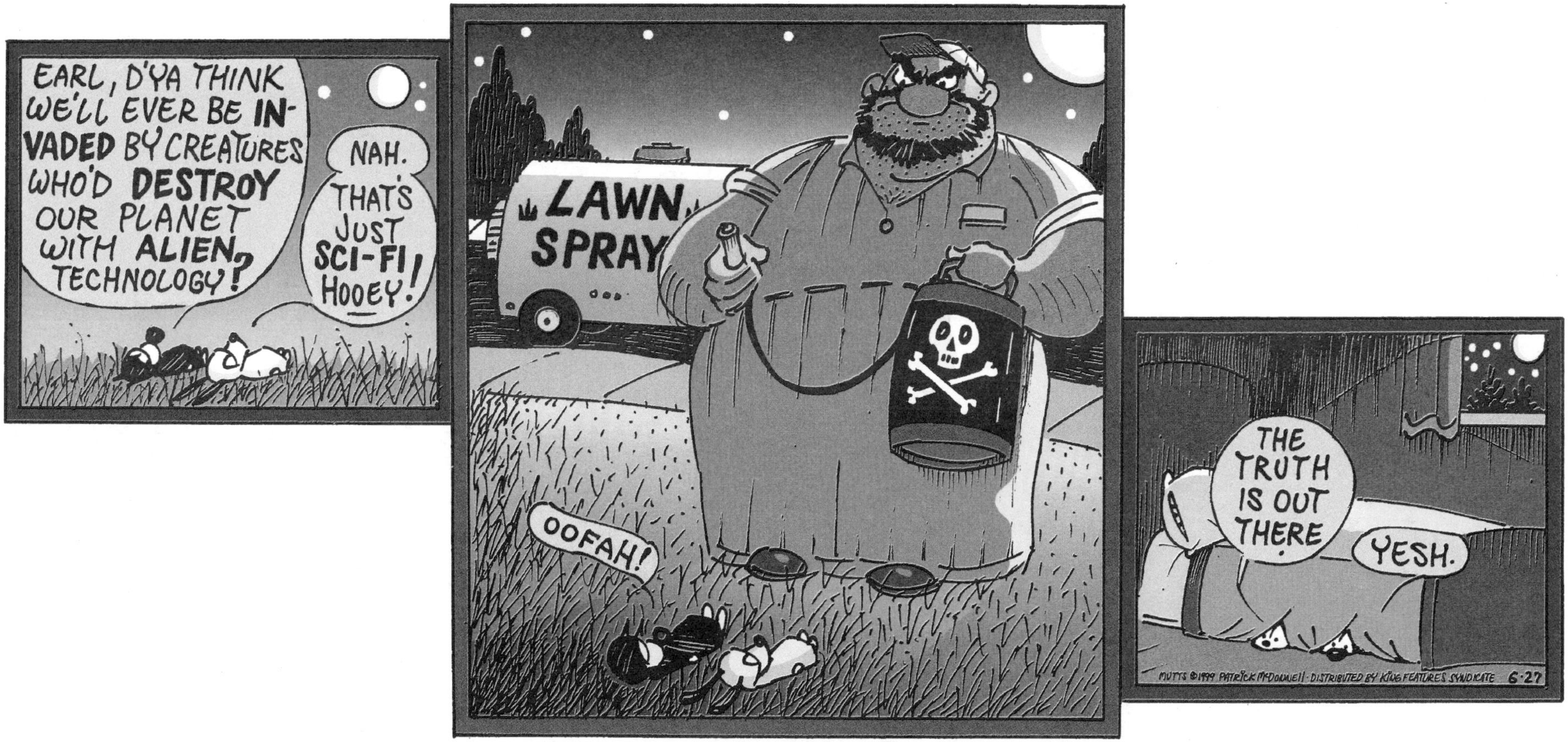
EARL, D'YA THINK WE'LL EVER BE **INVADED** BY CREATURES WHO'D **DESTROY** OUR PLANET WITH **ALIEN** TECHNOLOGY?
NAH. THAT'S JUST **SCI-FI** HOOEY!
LAWN SPRAY
OOFAH!
THE TRUTH IS OUT THERE.
YESH.
MUTTS ©1999 PATRICK McDONNELL · DISTRIBUTED BY KING FEATURES SYNDICATE 6·27

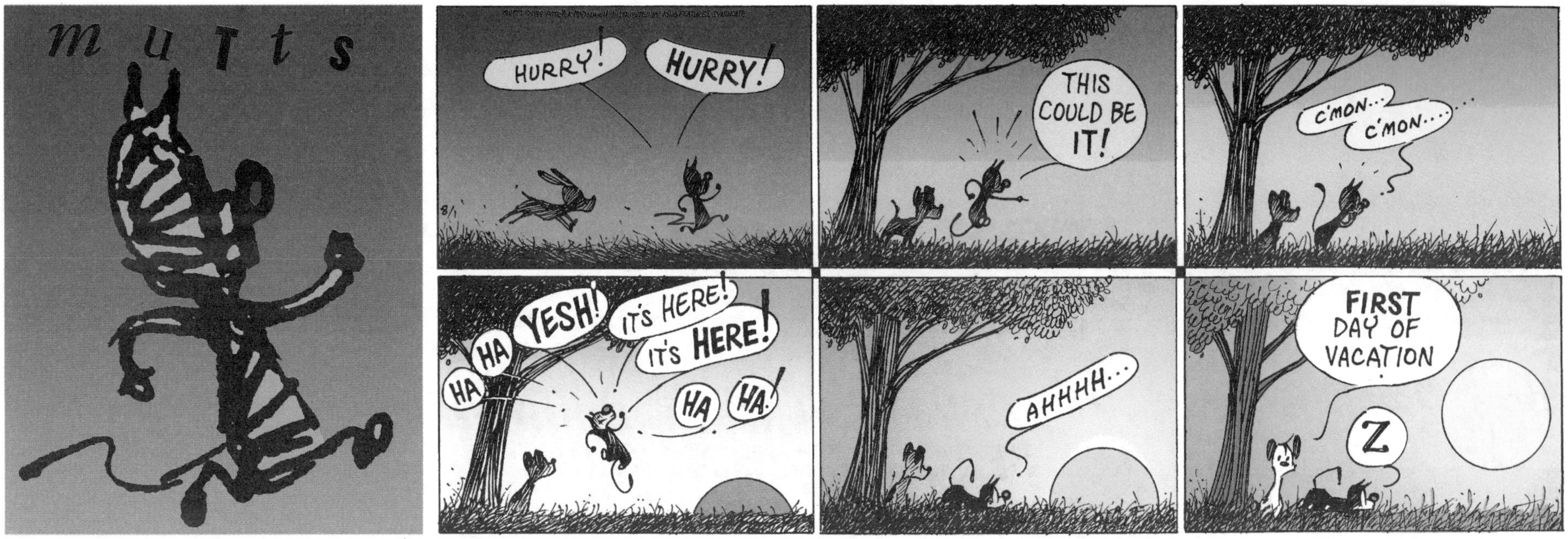
mutts
HURRY!
HURRY!
THIS COULD BE IT!
C'MON...
C'MON....
HA
HA
YESH!
IT'S HERE!
IT'S HERE!
HA
HA!
AHHHH...
FIRST DAY OF VACATION
Z

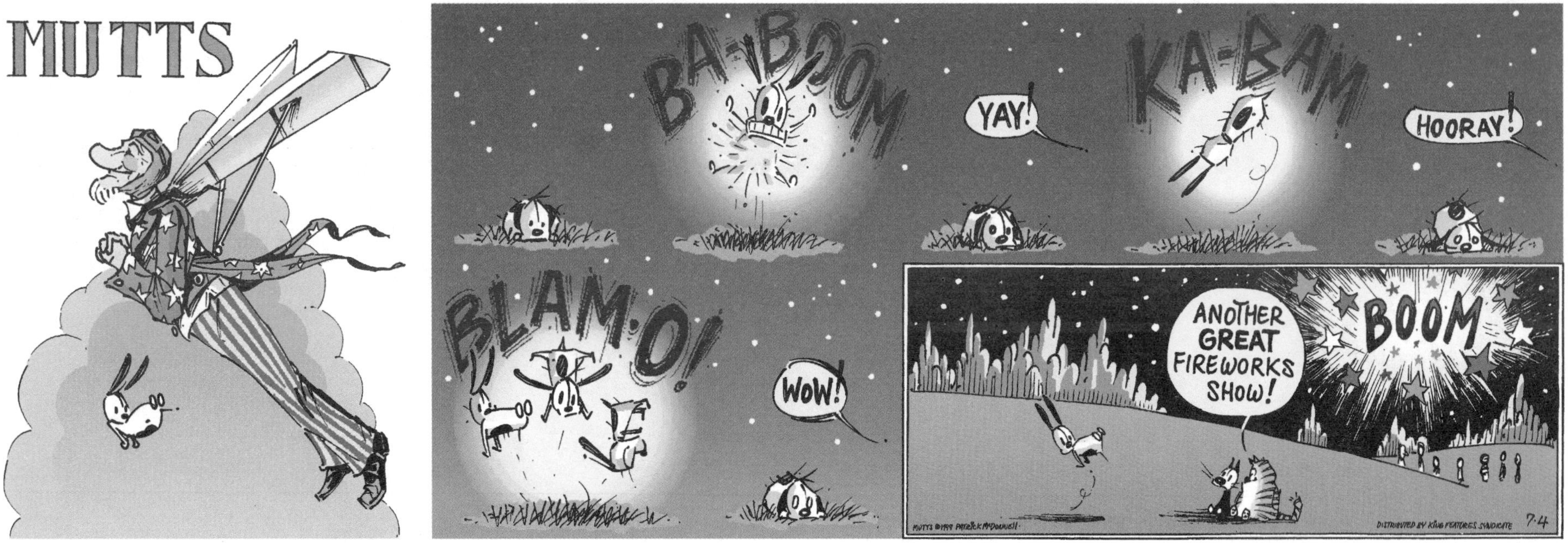
MUTTS
BA-BOOM
YAY!
KA-BAM
HOORAY!
BLAM-O!
WOW!
ANOTHER GREAT FIREWORKS SHOW!
BOOM

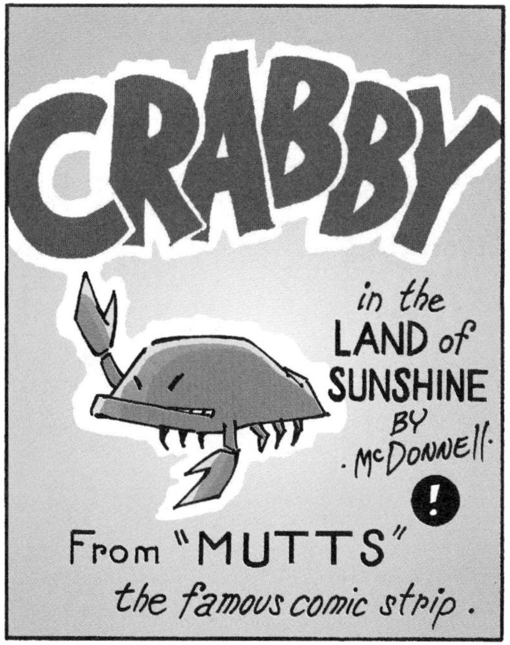
CRABBY
in the LAND of SUNSHINE
BY · McDONNELL ·
!
From "MUTTS" the famous comic strip.

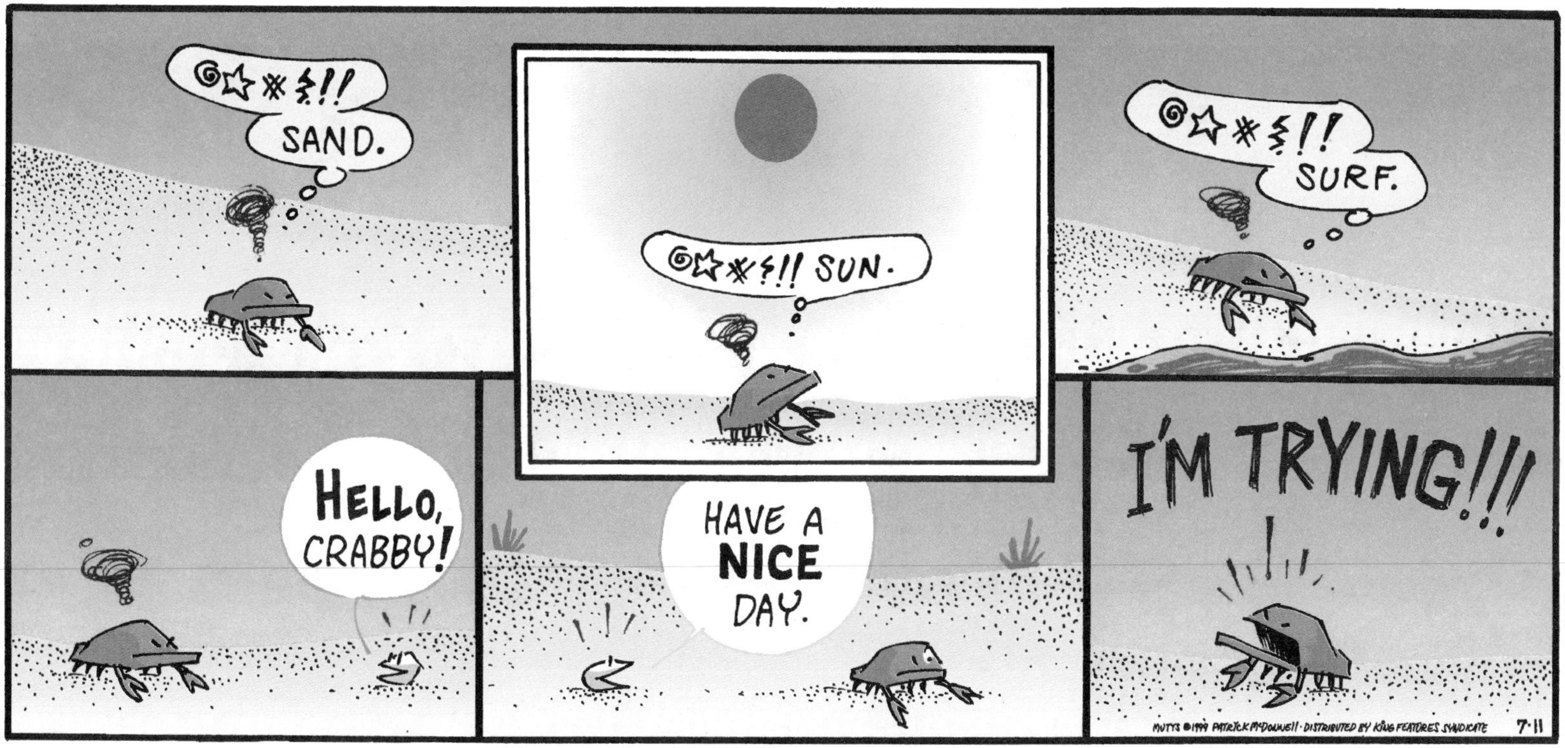
!! SAND.
!! SUN.
!! SURF.
HELLO, CRABBY!
HAVE A NICE DAY.
I'M TRYING!!!
MUTTS ©1999 PATRICK McDONNELL · DISTRIBUTED BY KING FEATURES SYNDICATE
7·11

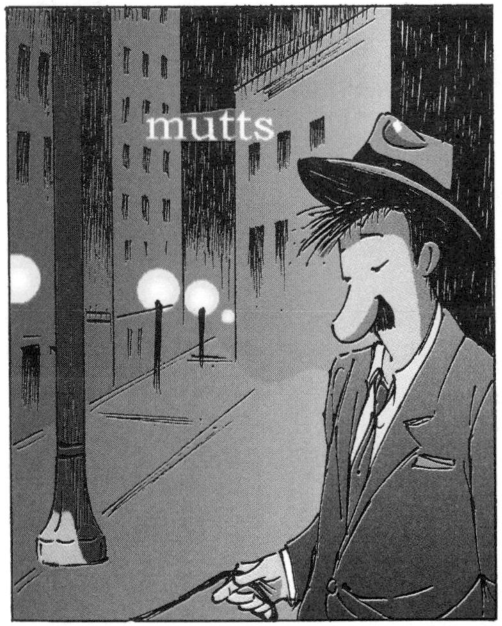
mutts

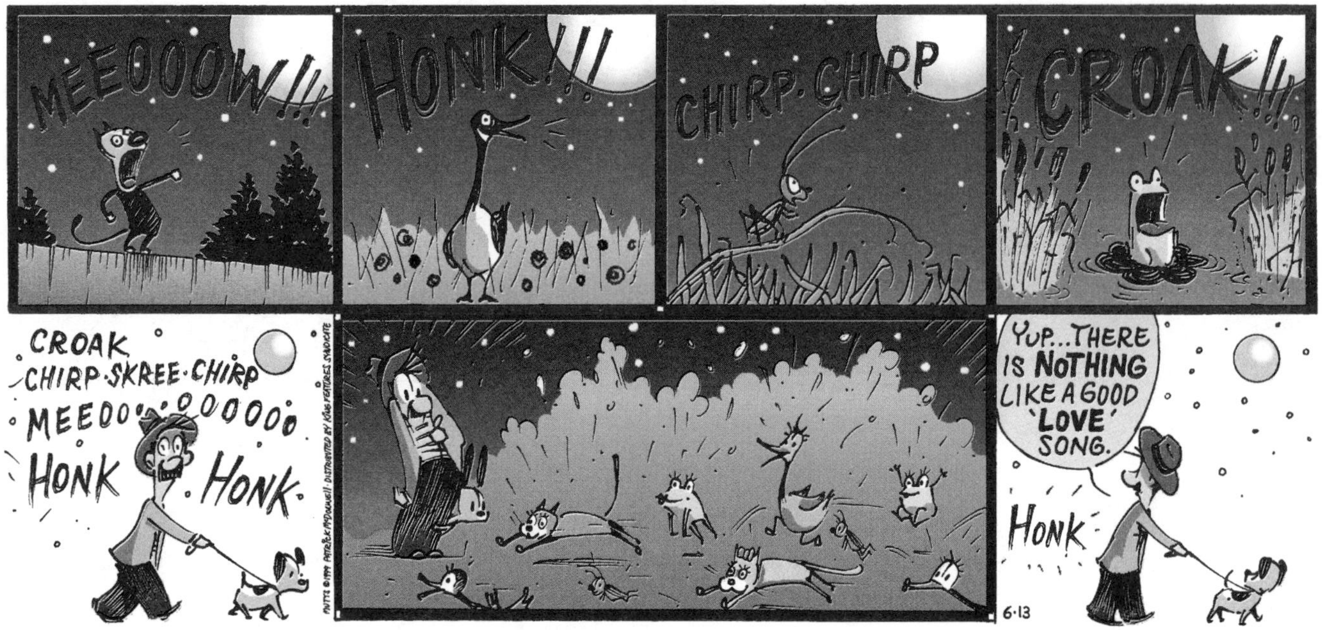
MEEOOOW!!!
HONK!!!
CHIRP·CHIRP
CROAK!!!
CROAK
CHIRP·SKREE·CHIRP
MEEOOOOOOOOO
HONK
HONK
MUTTS ©1999 PATRICK McDONNELL · DISTRIBUTED BY KING FEATURES SYNDICATE
YUP...THERE IS NOTHING LIKE A GOOD 'LOVE' SONG.
HONK
6·13

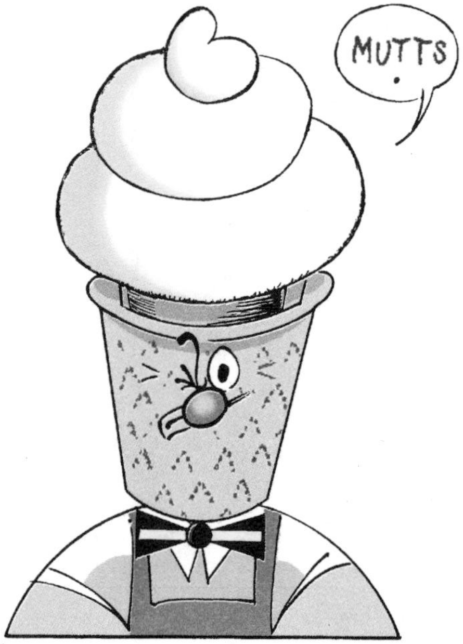
MUTTS

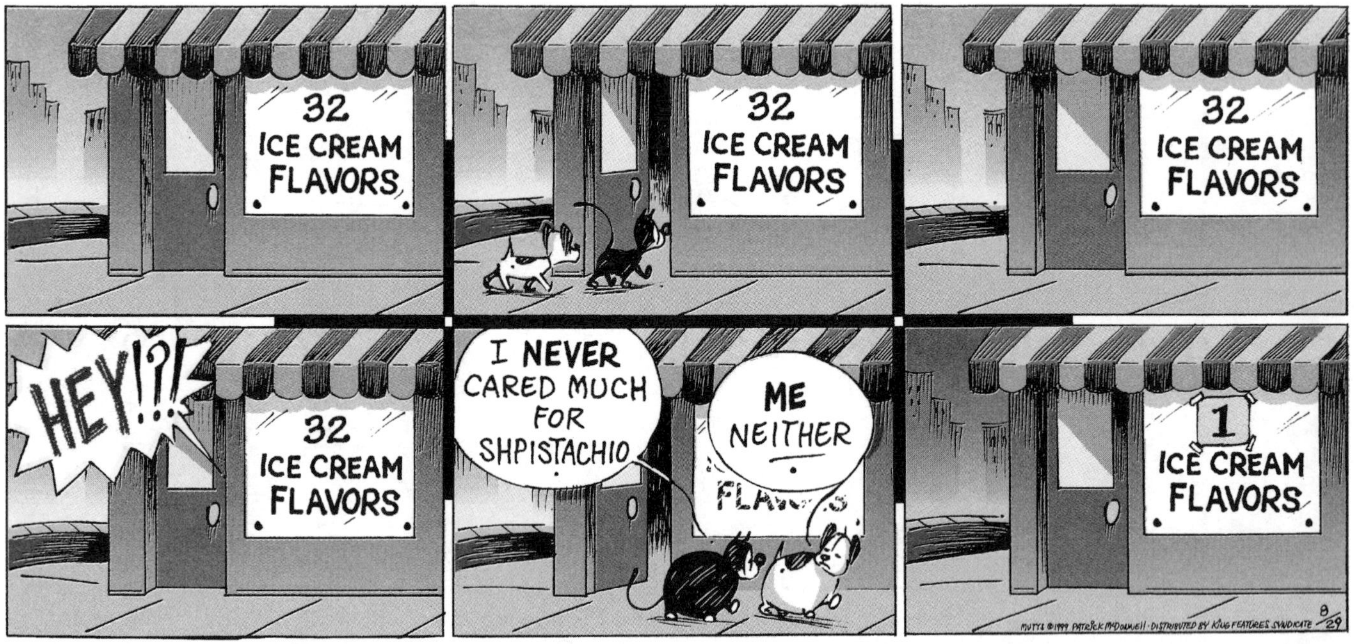
32 ICE CREAM FLAVORS
32 ICE CREAM FLAVORS
32 ICE CREAM FLAVORS
HEY!?!
32 ICE CREAM FLAVORS
I NEVER CARED MUCH FOR SHPISTACHIO
ME NEITHER
1 ICE CREAM FLAVORS
MUTTS ©1999 PATRICK McDONNELL · DISTRIBUTED BY KING FEATURES SYNDICATE
8/29

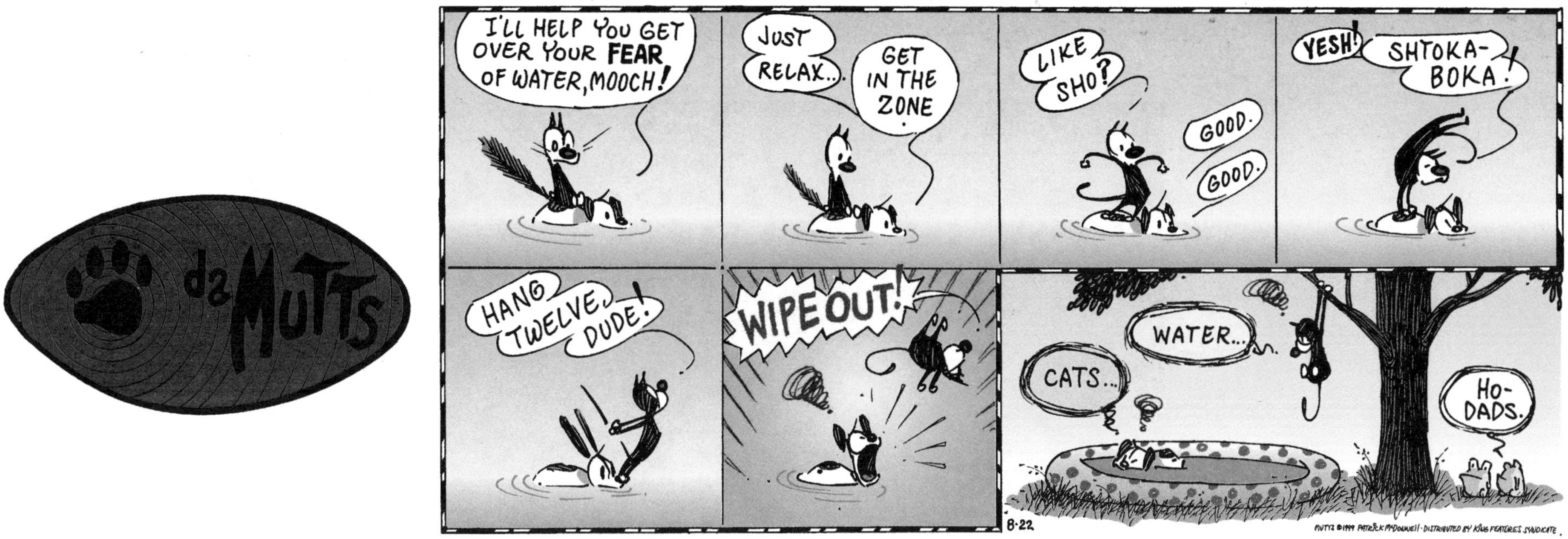
da MUTTS
I'LL HELP YOU GET OVER YOUR FEAR OF WATER, MOOCH!
JUST RELAX...
GET IN THE ZONE.
LIKE SHO?
GOOD.
GOOD.
YESH!
SHTOKA-BOKA!
HANG TWELVE, DUDE!
WIPE OUT!
WATER...
CATS...
HO-DADS.
8-22
MUTTS ©1999 PATRICK McDONNELL · DISTRIBUTED BY KING FEATURES SYNDICATE.

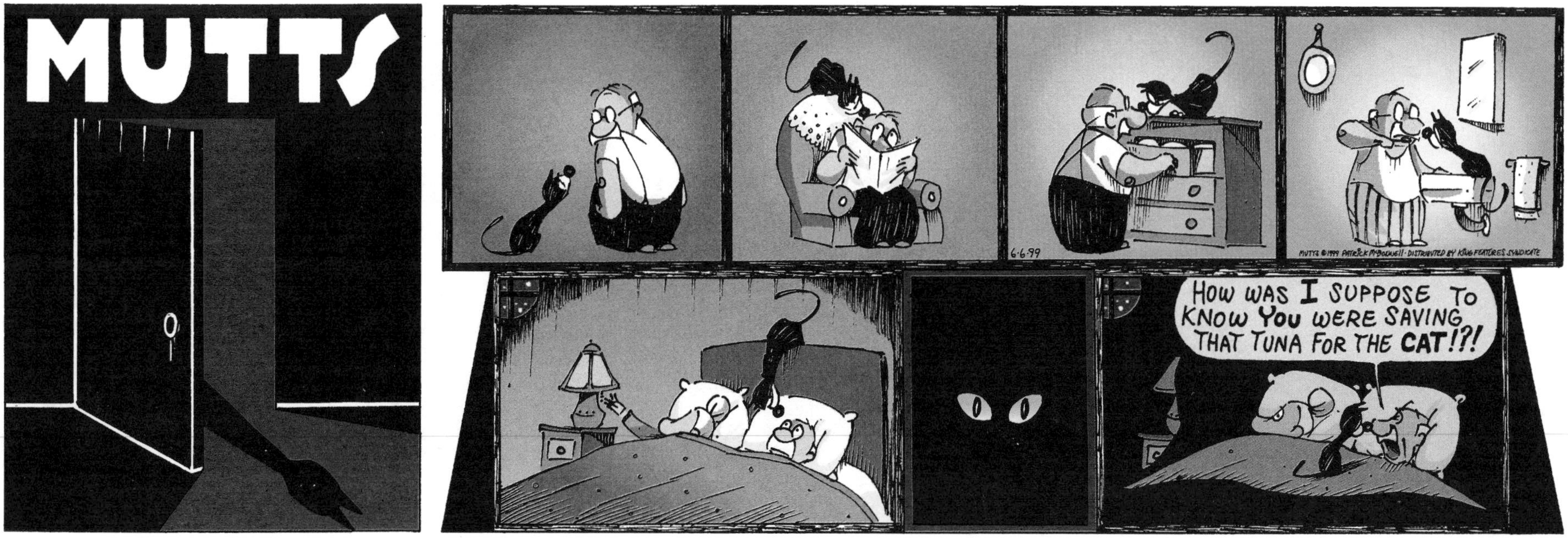
MUTTS
6-6-99
MUTTS ©1999 PATRICK McDONNELL · DISTRIBUTED BY KING FEATURES SYNDICATE
HOW WAS I SUPPOSE TO KNOW YOU WERE SAVING THAT TUNA FOR THE CAT!?!

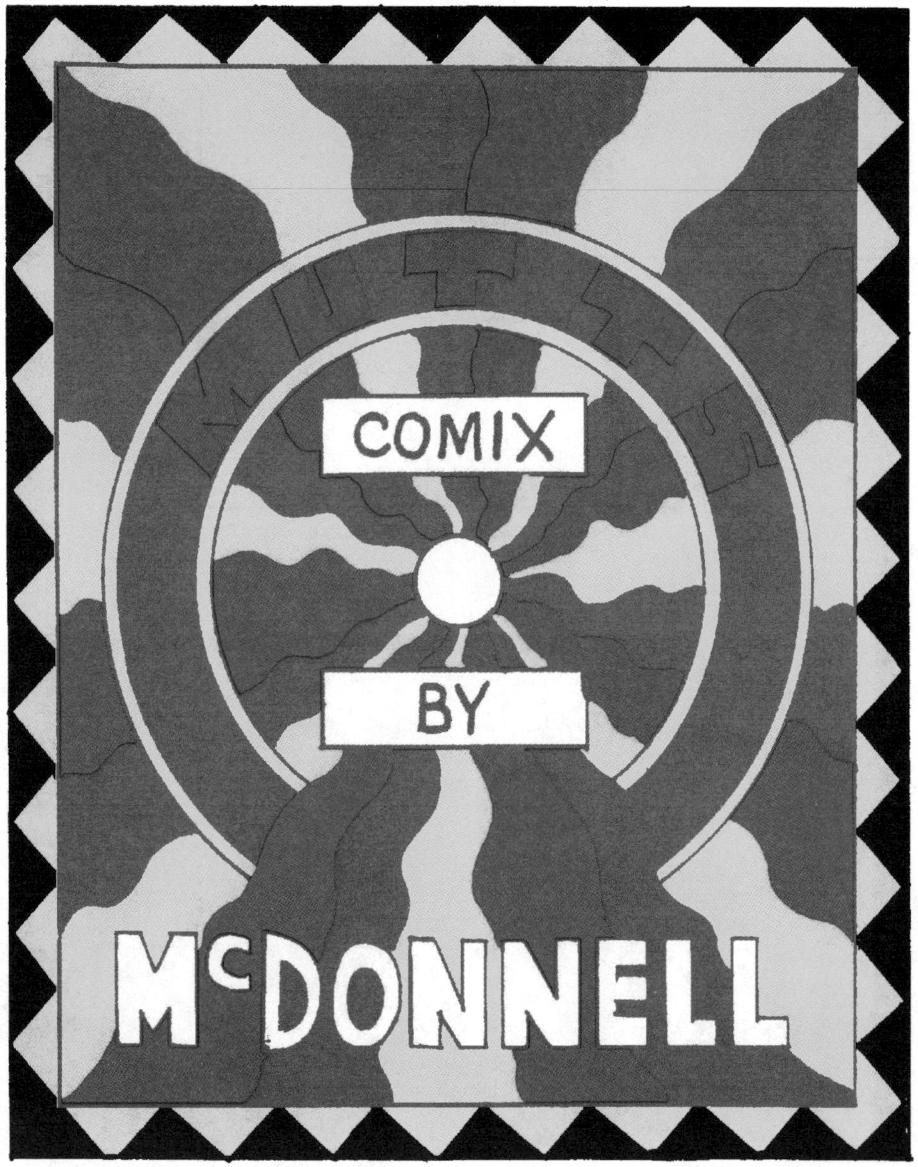
COMIX
BY
McDONNELL

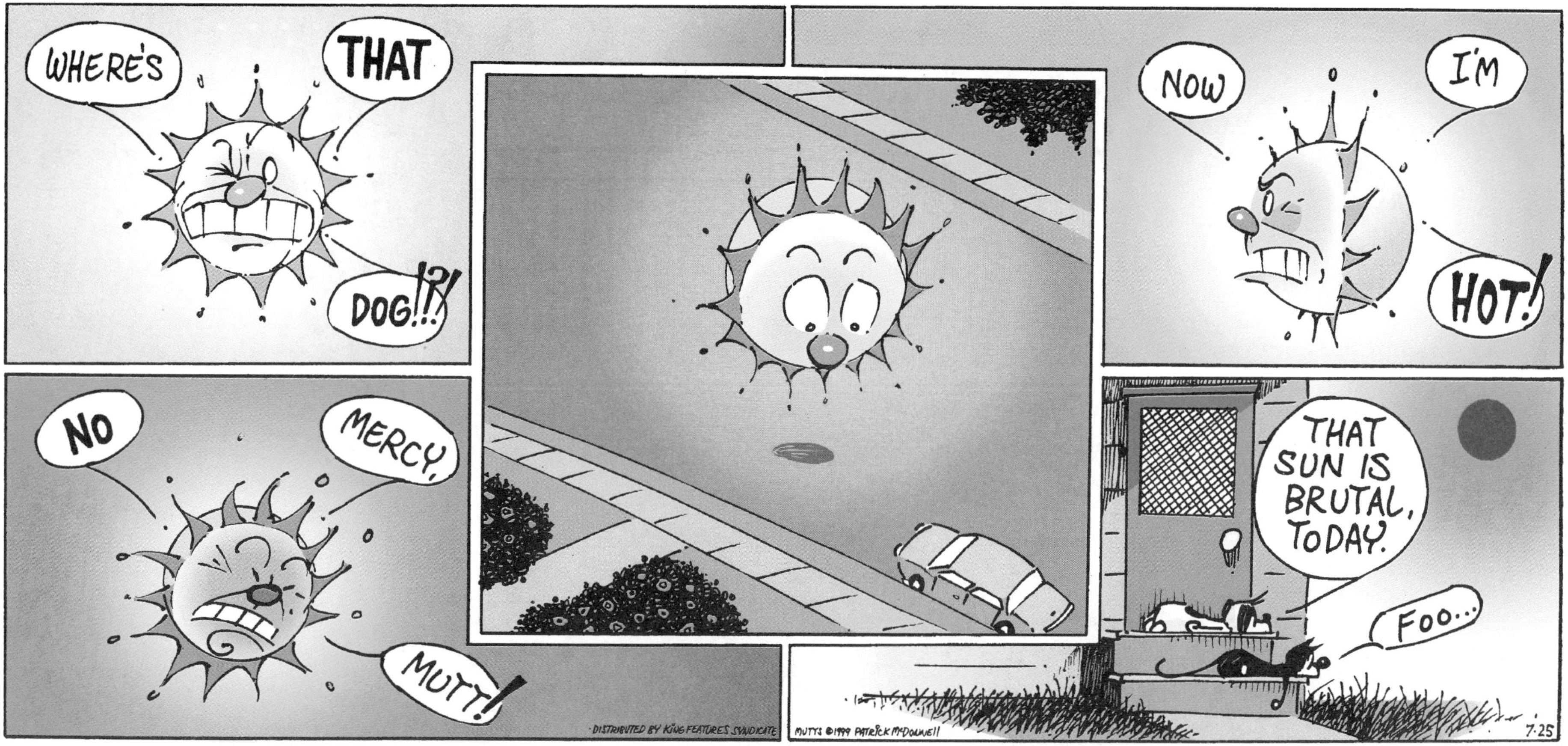
WHERE'S
THAT
DOG!?!
NO
MERCY,
MUTT!
NOW
I'M
HOT!
THAT SUN IS BRUTAL, TODAY.
FOO...
DISTRIBUTED BY KING FEATURES SYNDICATE
MUTTS ©1999 PATRICK McDONNELL
7·25

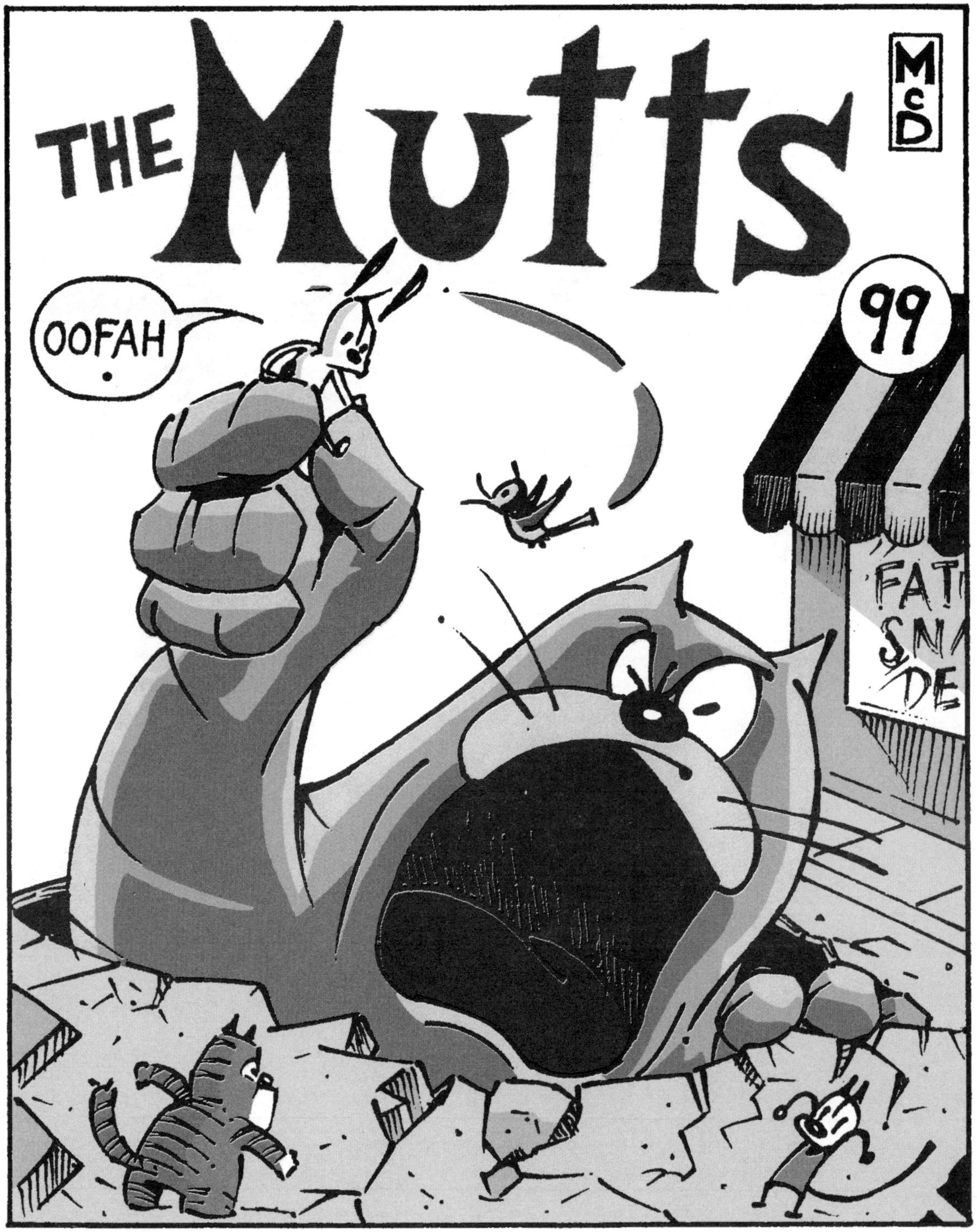
THE Mutts
McD
99
OOFAH

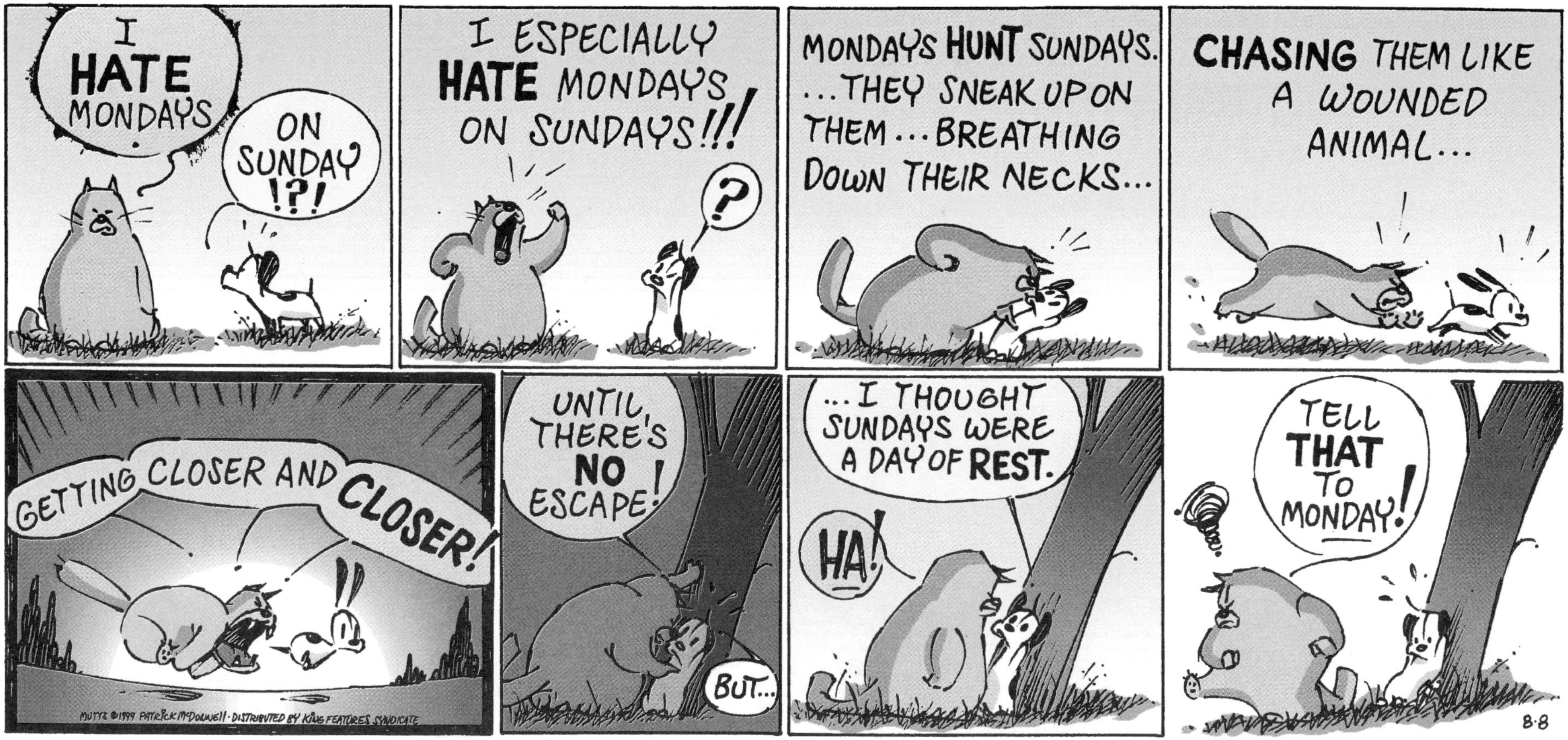
I HATE MONDAYS.
ON SUNDAY !?!
I ESPECIALLY HATE MONDAYS ON SUNDAYS!!!
?
MONDAYS HUNT SUNDAYS. ...THEY SNEAK UP ON THEM ... BREATHING DOWN THEIR NECKS...
CHASING THEM LIKE A WOUNDED ANIMAL...
GETTING CLOSER AND CLOSER!
MUTTS ©1999 PATRICK McDONNELL · DISTRIBUTED BY KING FEATURES SYNDICATE
UNTIL THERE'S NO ESCAPE!
BUT...
HA!
... I THOUGHT SUNDAYS WERE A DAY OF REST.
TELL THAT TO MONDAY!
8·8

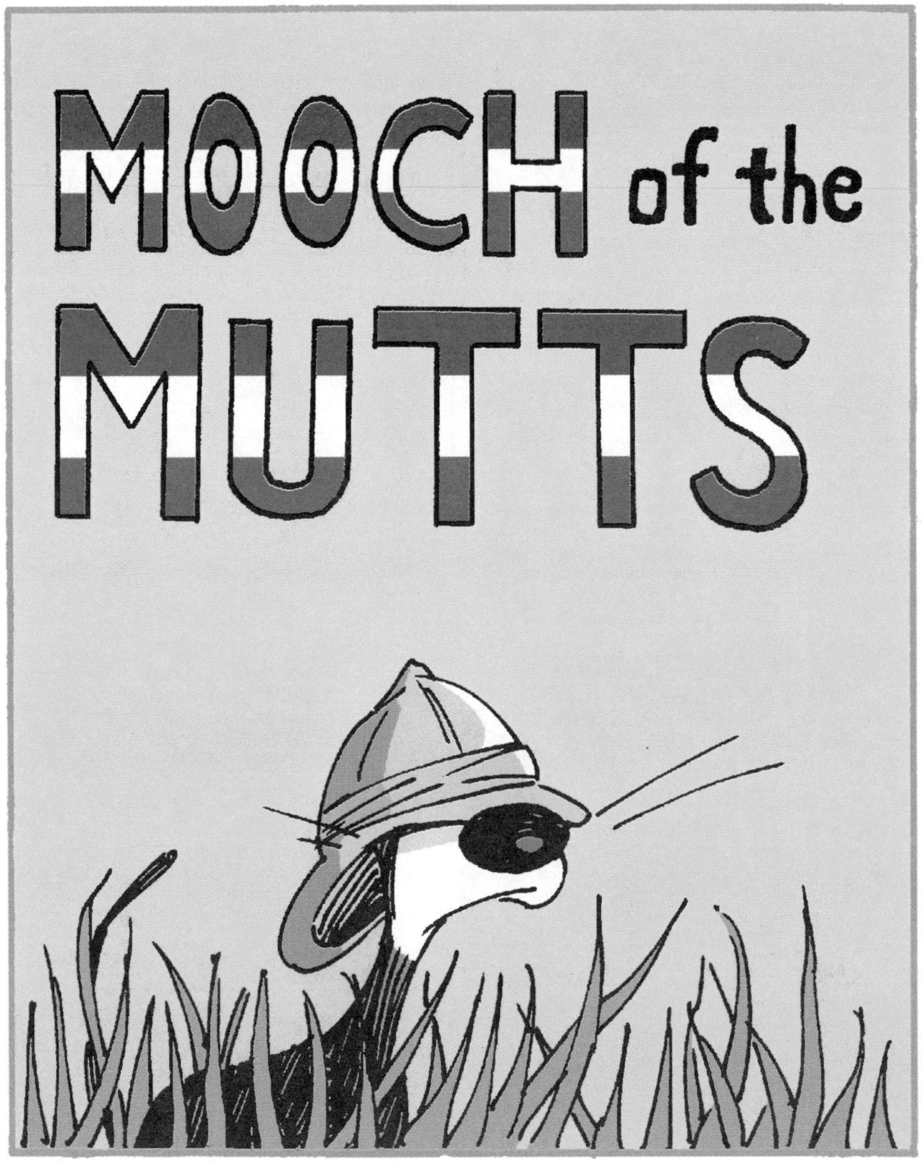
MOOCH of the
MUTTS

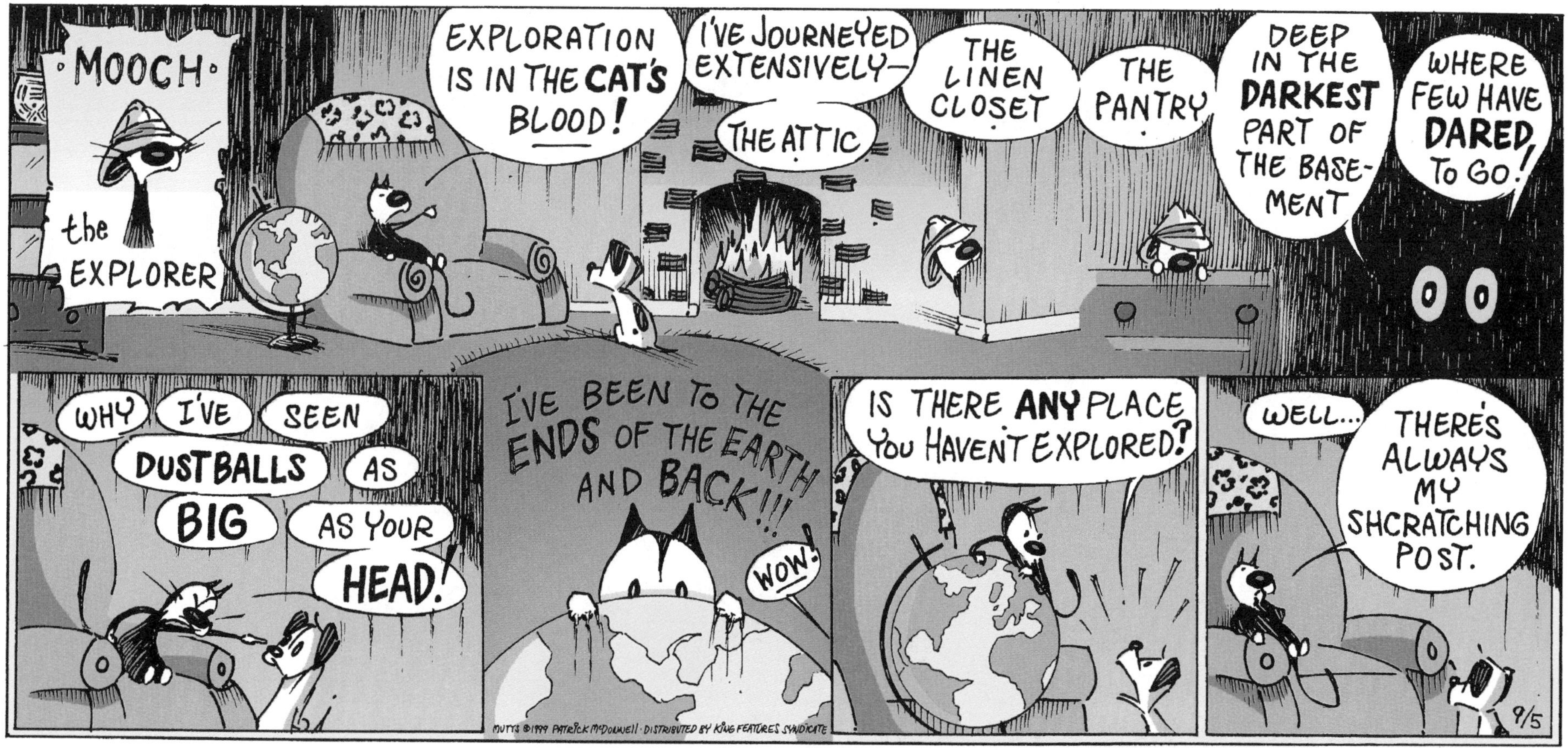
MOOCH the EXPLORER
EXPLORATION IS IN THE CAT'S BLOOD!
I'VE JOURNEYED EXTENSIVELY—
THE ATTIC
THE LINEN CLOSET
THE PANTRY
DEEP IN THE DARKEST PART OF THE BASE-MENT
WHERE FEW HAVE DARED TO GO!
WHY I'VE SEEN DUSTBALLS AS BIG AS YOUR HEAD!
I'VE BEEN TO THE ENDS OF THE EARTH AND BACK!!!
WOW!
IS THERE ANY PLACE YOU HAVEN'T EXPLORED?
WELL...
THERE'S ALWAYS MY SHCRATCHING POST.
MUTTS ©1999 PATRICK McDONNELL · DISTRIBUTED BY KING FEATURES SYNDICATE
9/5

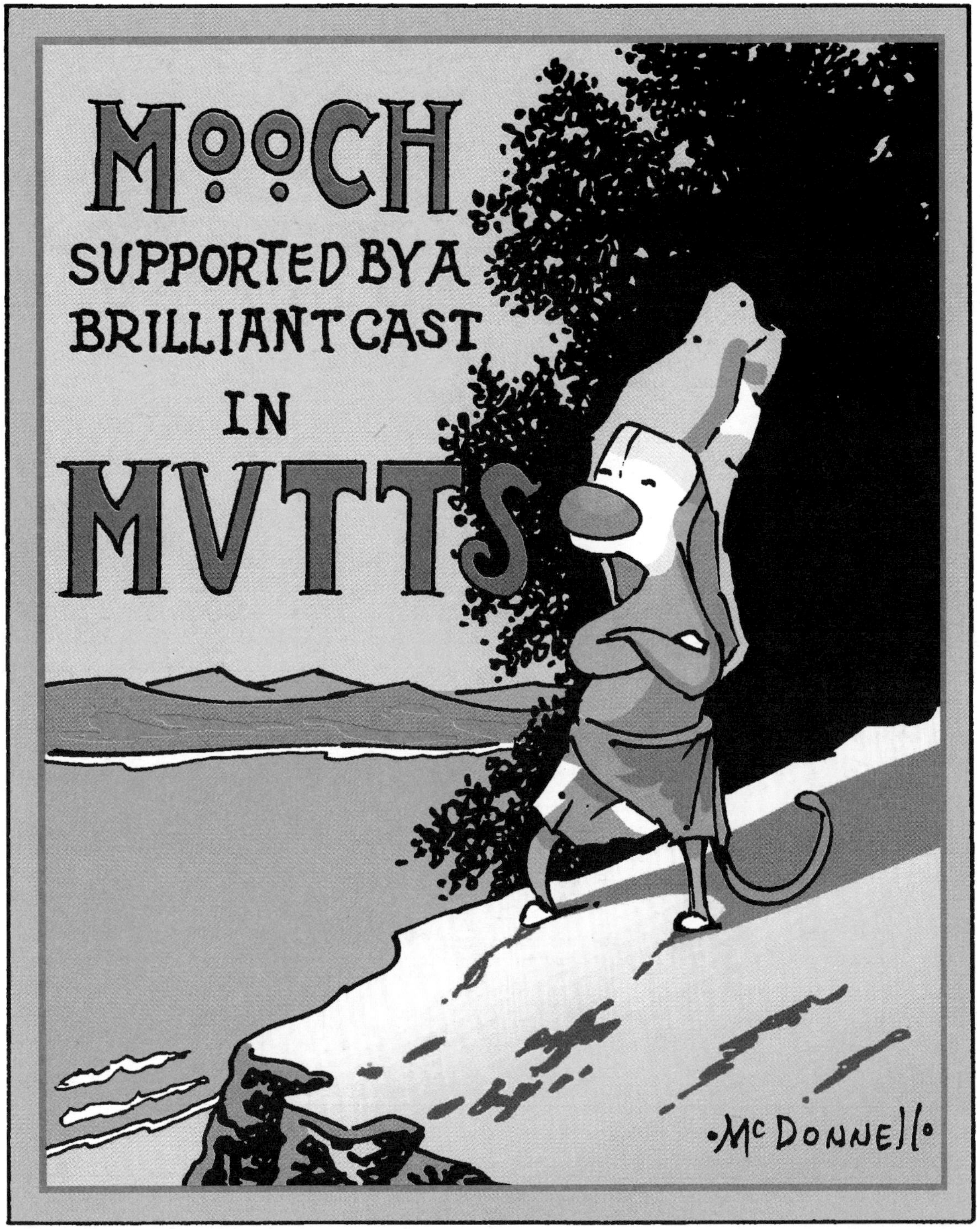
MOOCH
SUPPORTED BY A
BRILLIANT CAST
IN
MUTTS
McDONNELL

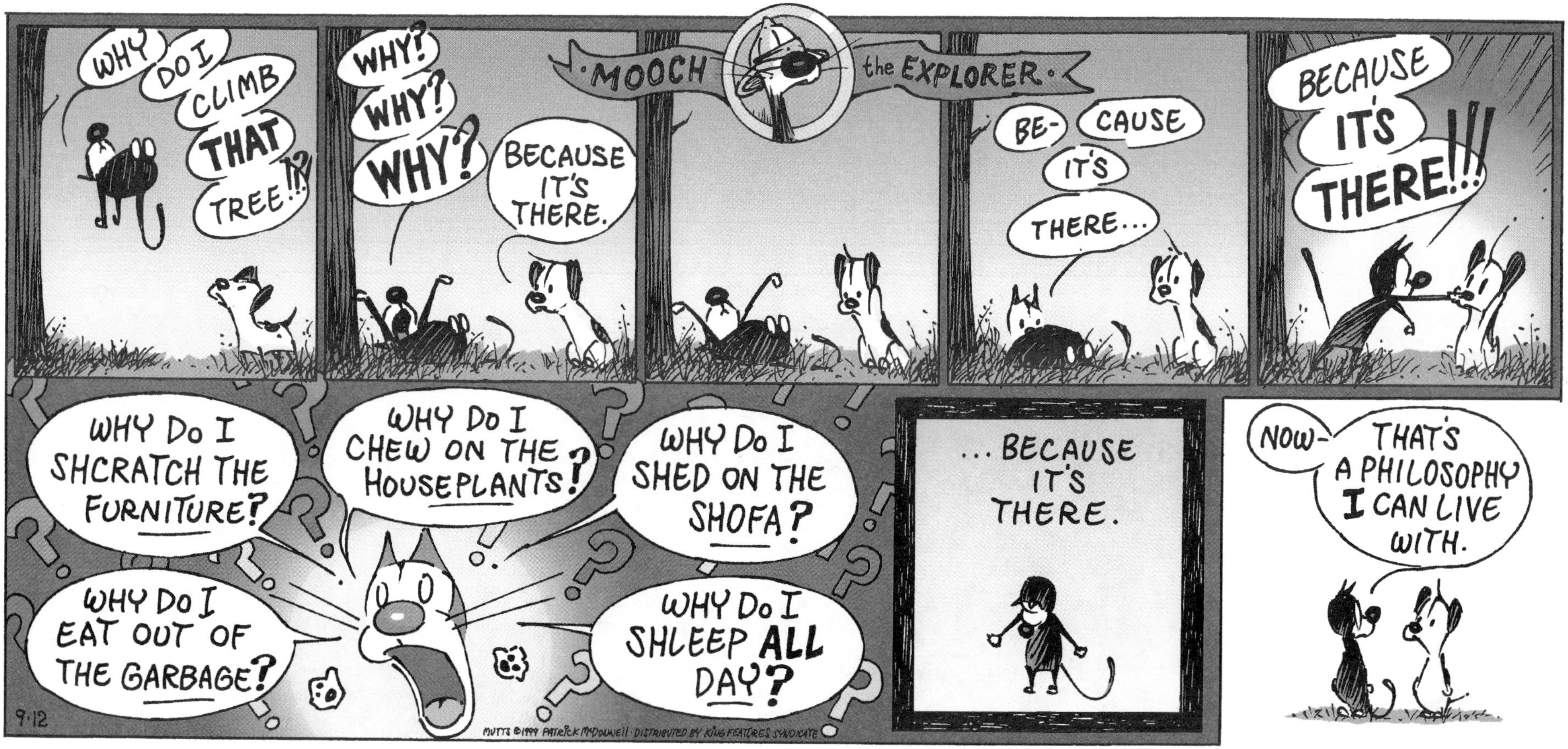

WHY DO I CLIMB THAT TREE!?!
WHY? WHY? WHY?
BECAUSE IT'S THERE.
MOOCH the EXPLORER
BE- CAUSE IT'S THERE...
BECAUSE IT'S THERE!!!
WHY DO I SHCRATCH THE FURNITURE?
WHY DO I CHEW ON THE HOUSEPLANTS?
WHY DO I SHED ON THE SHOFA?
WHY DO I EAT OUT OF THE GARBAGE?
WHY DO I SHLEEP ALL DAY?
9.12
MUTTS ©1999 PATRICK McDONNELL · DISTRIBUTED BY KING FEATURES SYNDICATE
... BECAUSE IT'S THERE.
NOW- THAT'S A PHILOSOPHY I CAN LIVE WITH.

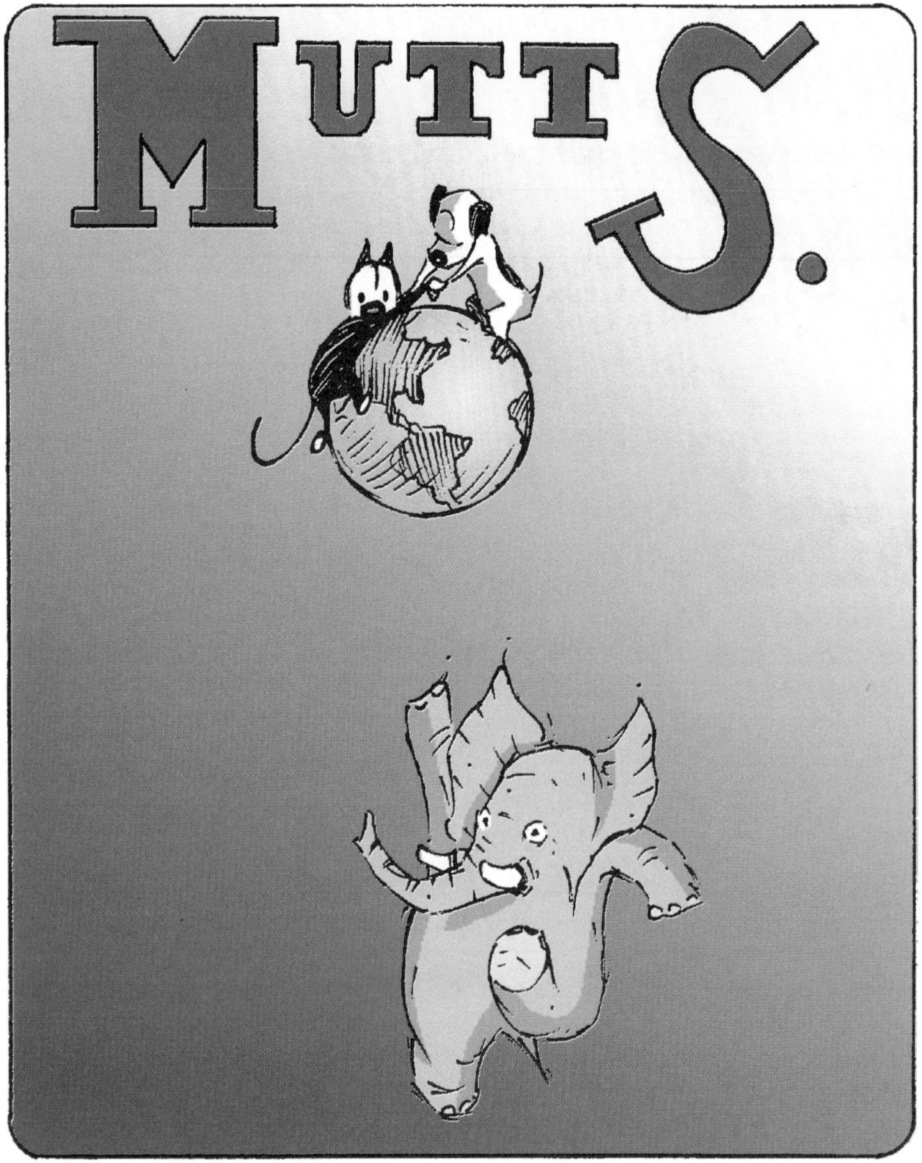
MUTTS.

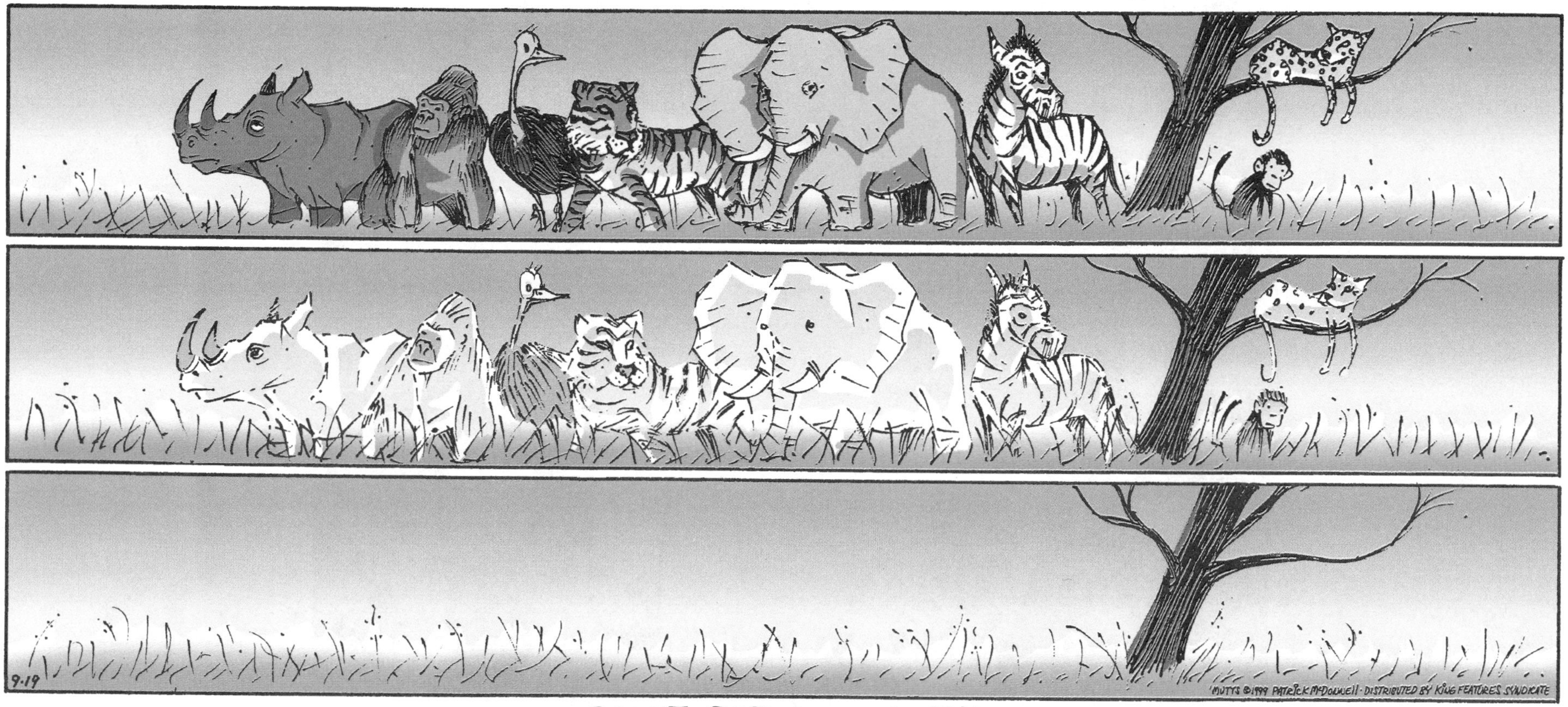
9-19
MUTTS ©1999 PATRICK McDONNELL · DISTRIBUTED BY KING FEATURES SYNDICATE

... RIGHT BEFORE OUR EYES...

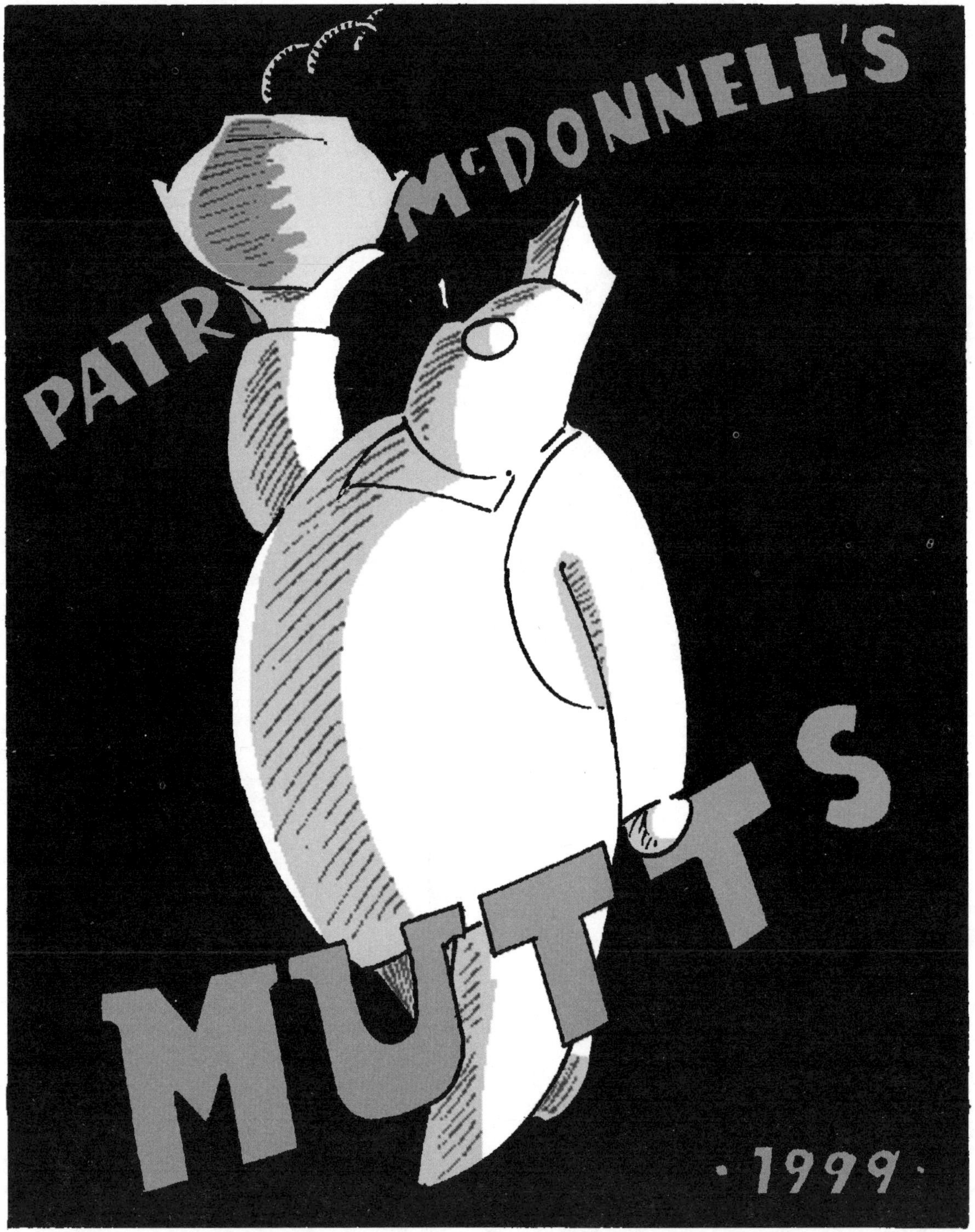
PATR
McDONNELL'S
MUTTS
·1999·

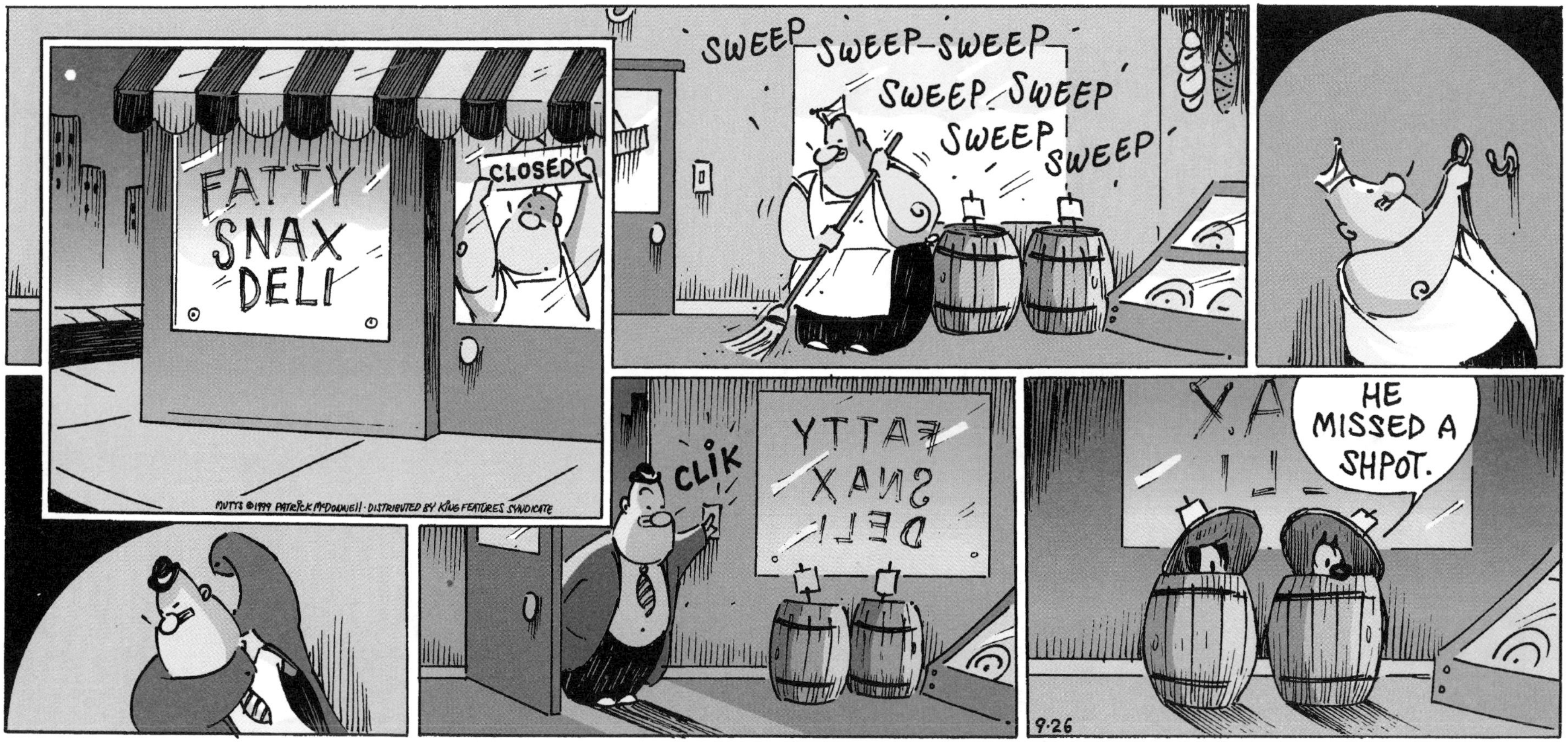
FATTY SNAX DELI
CLOSED
MUTTS ©1999 PATRICK McDONNELL · DISTRIBUTED BY KING FEATURES SYNDICATE
SWEEP SWEEP SWEEP
SWEEP SWEEP
SWEEP
SWEEP
CLIK
HE MISSED A SHPOT.
9·26

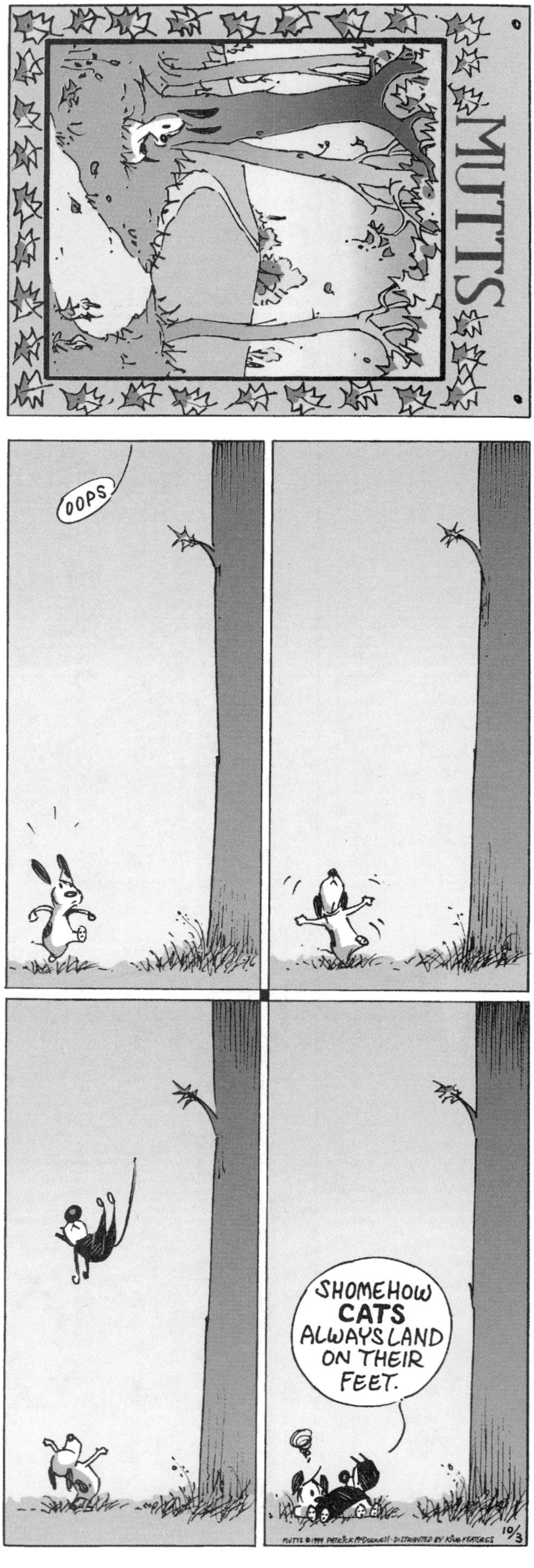
MUTTS
OOPS
SHOMEHOW CATS ALWAYS LAND ON THEIR FEET.
MUTTS ©1999 PATRICK McDONNELL · DISTRIBUTED BY KING FEATURES
10/3

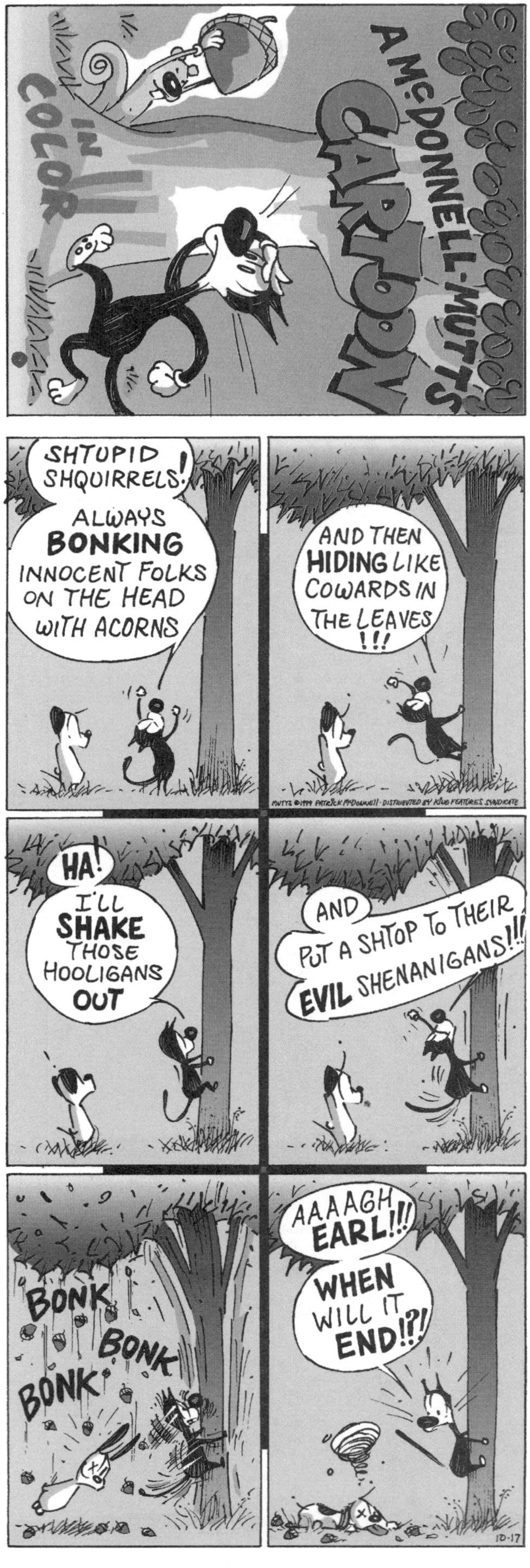
A McDONNELL-MUTTS CARTOON
IN COLOR
SHTUPID SHQUIRRELS!
ALWAYS BONKING INNOCENT FOLKS ON THE HEAD WITH ACORNS
AND THEN HIDING LIKE COWARDS IN THE LEAVES !!!
MUTTS ©1999 PATRICK McDONNELL · DISTRIBUTED BY KING FEATURES SYNDICATE
HA!
I'LL SHAKE THOSE HOOLIGANS OUT
AND
PUT A SHTOP TO THEIR EVIL SHENANIGANS!!!
BONK
BONK
BONK
AAAAGH EARL!!!
WHEN WILL IT END!?!
10-17

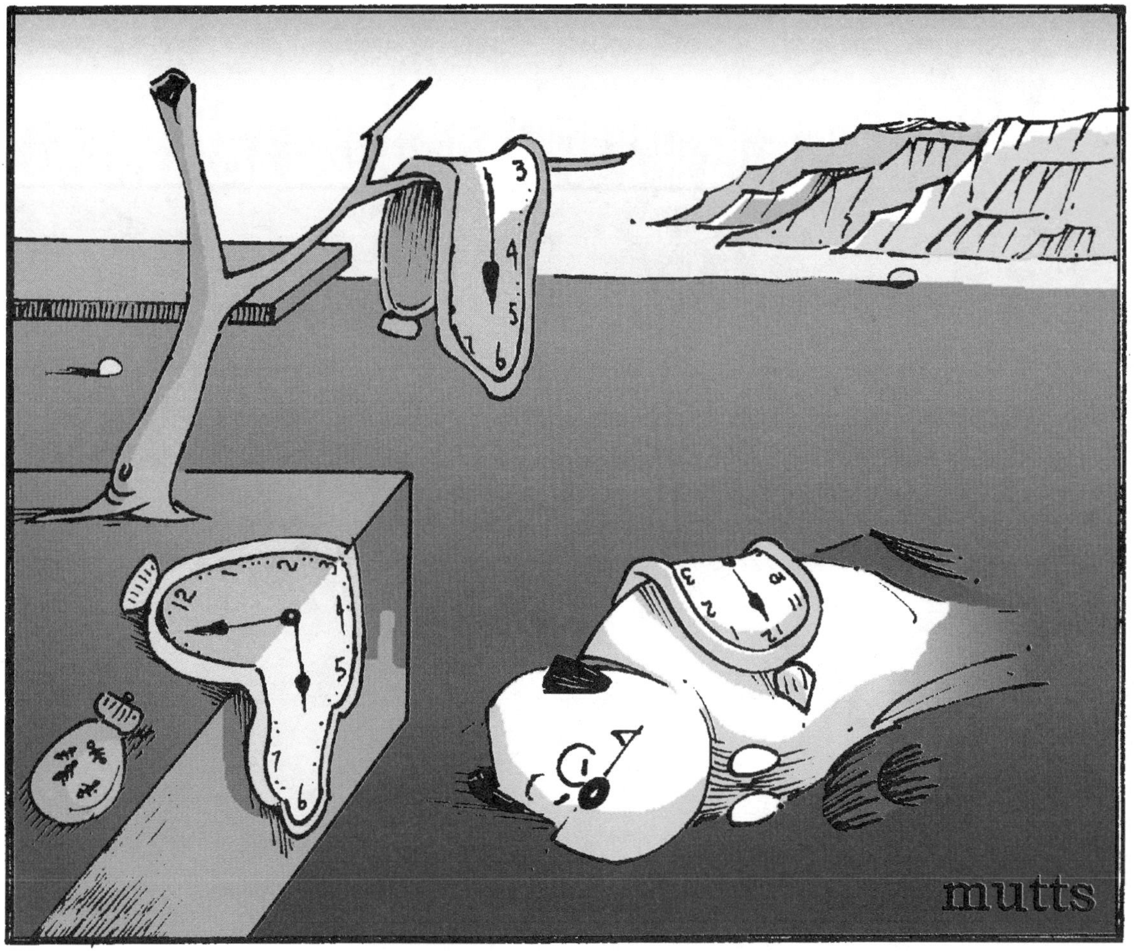
mutts

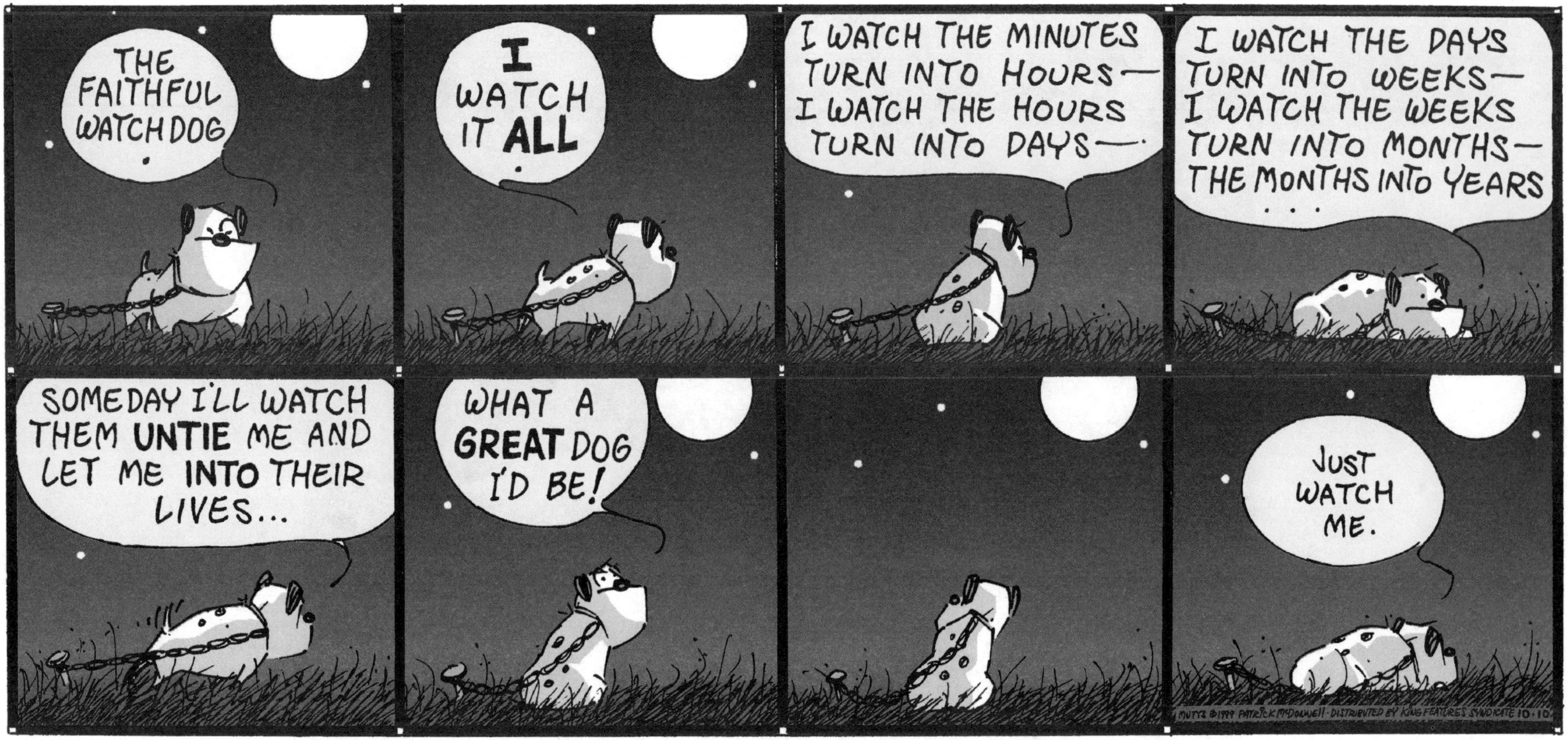
THE FAITHFUL WATCHDOG.
I WATCH IT ALL.
I WATCH THE MINUTES TURN INTO HOURS— I WATCH THE HOURS TURN INTO DAYS—.
I WATCH THE DAYS TURN INTO WEEKS— I WATCH THE WEEKS TURN INTO MONTHS— THE MONTHS INTO YEARS . . .
SOMEDAY I'LL WATCH THEM UNTIE ME AND LET ME INTO THEIR LIVES...
WHAT A GREAT DOG I'D BE!
JUST WATCH ME.
MUTTS ©1999 PATRICK McDONNELL · DISTRIBUTED BY KING FEATURES SYNDICATE 10·10

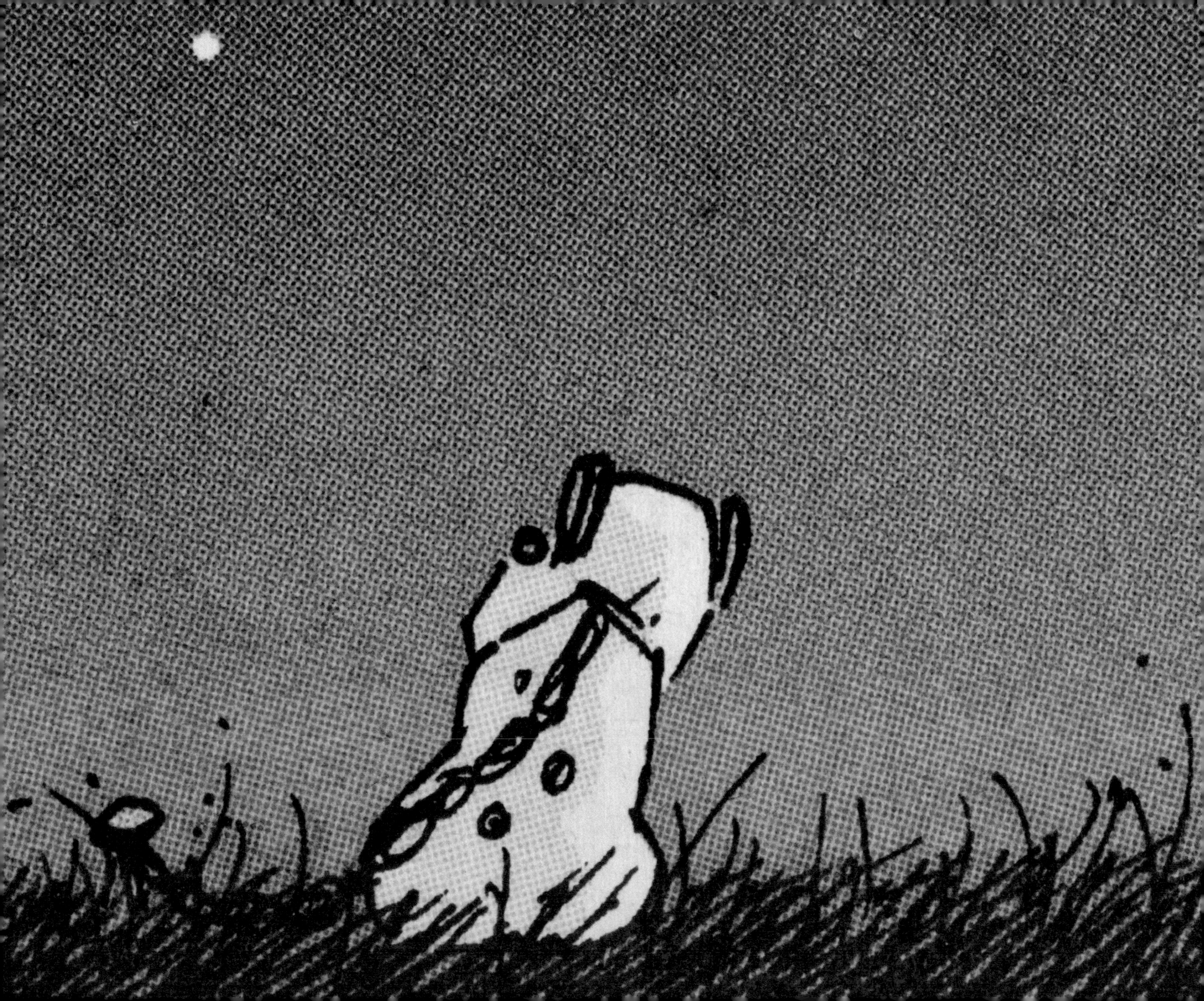

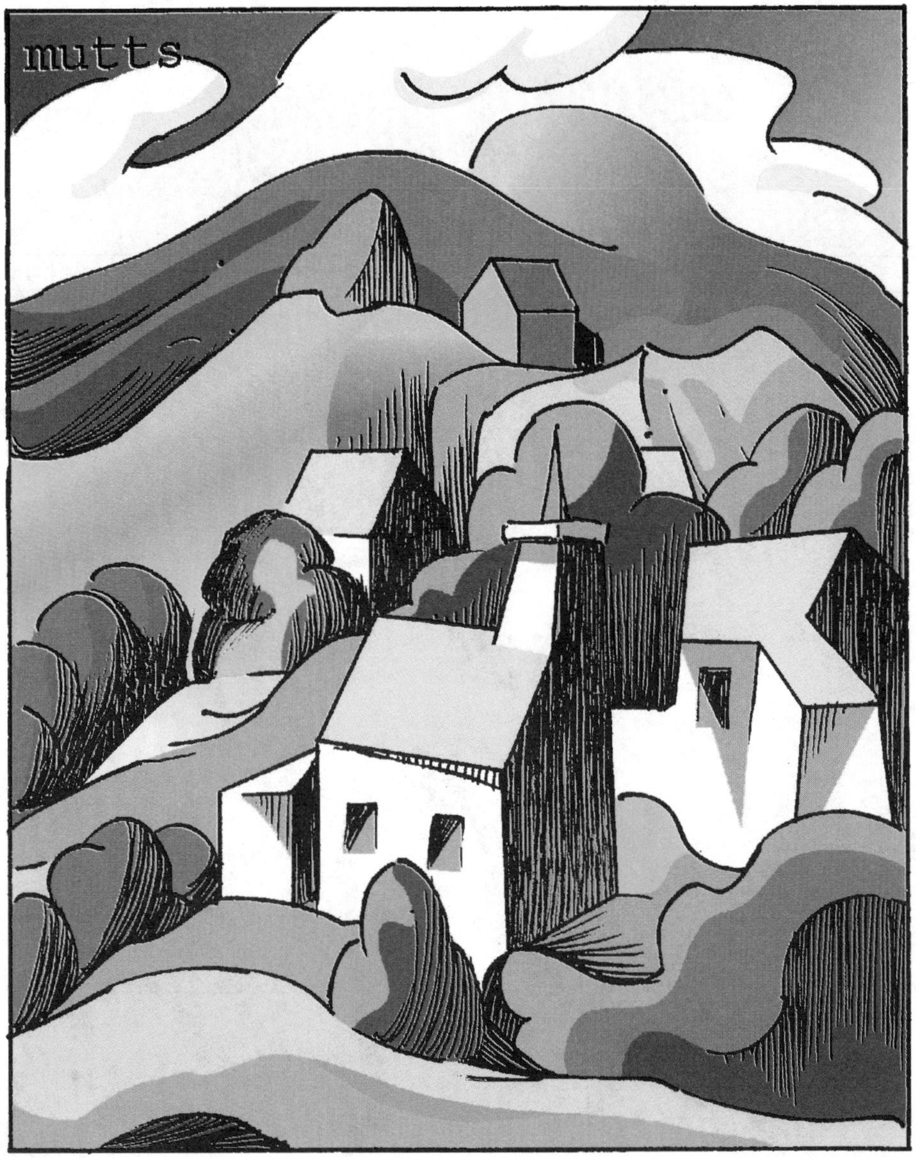
mutts

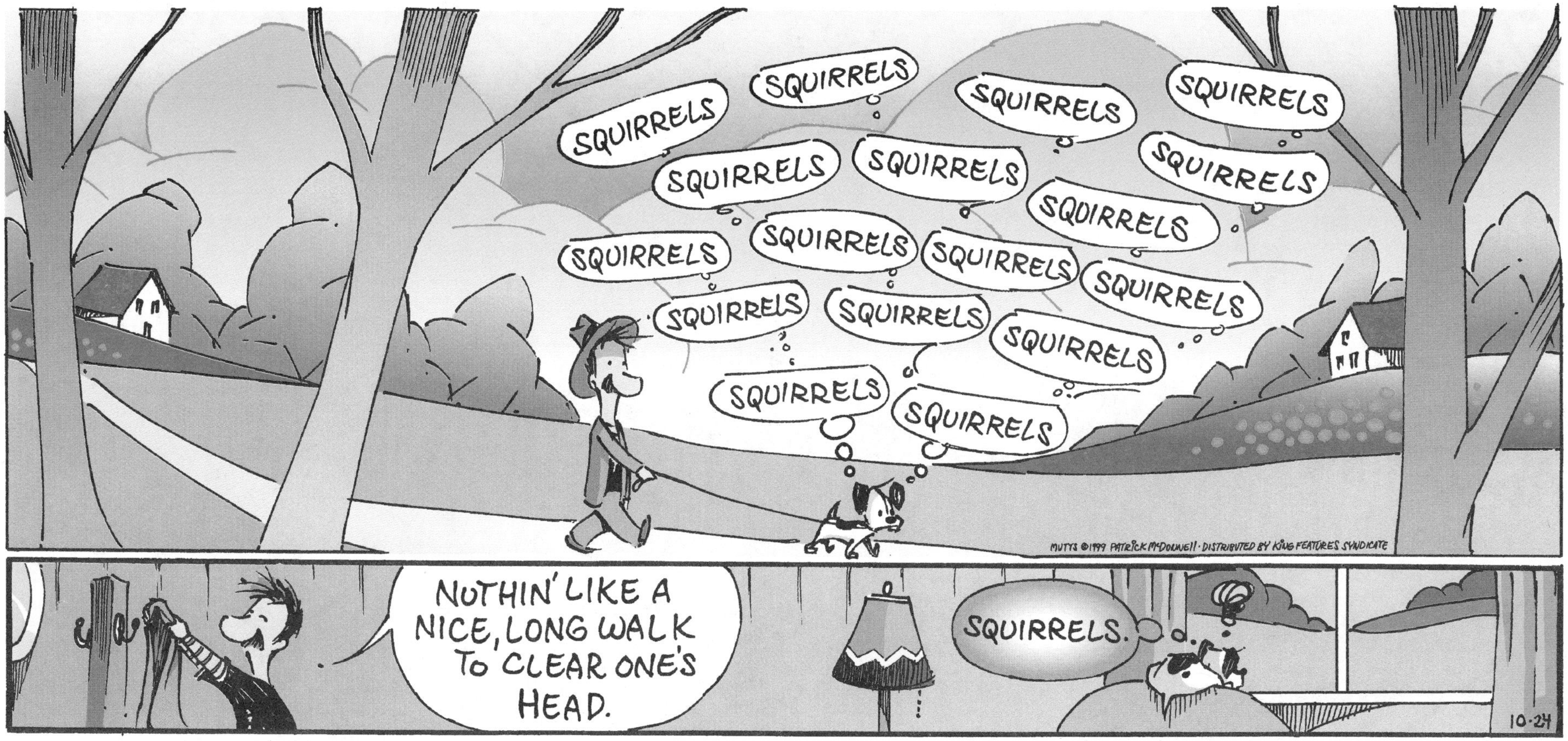
SQUIRRELS
SQUIRRELS
SQUIRRELS
SQUIRRELS
SQUIRRELS
SQUIRRELS
SQUIRRELS
SQUIRRELS
SQUIRRELS
SQUIRRELS
SQUIRRELS
SQUIRRELS
SQUIRRELS
SQUIRRELS
SQUIRRELS
SQUIRRELS
SQUIRRELS
MUTTS ©1999 PATRICK McDONNELL · DISTRIBUTED BY KING FEATURES SYNDICATE
NUTHIN' LIKE A NICE, LONG WALK TO CLEAR ONE'S HEAD.
SQUIRRELS.
10·24

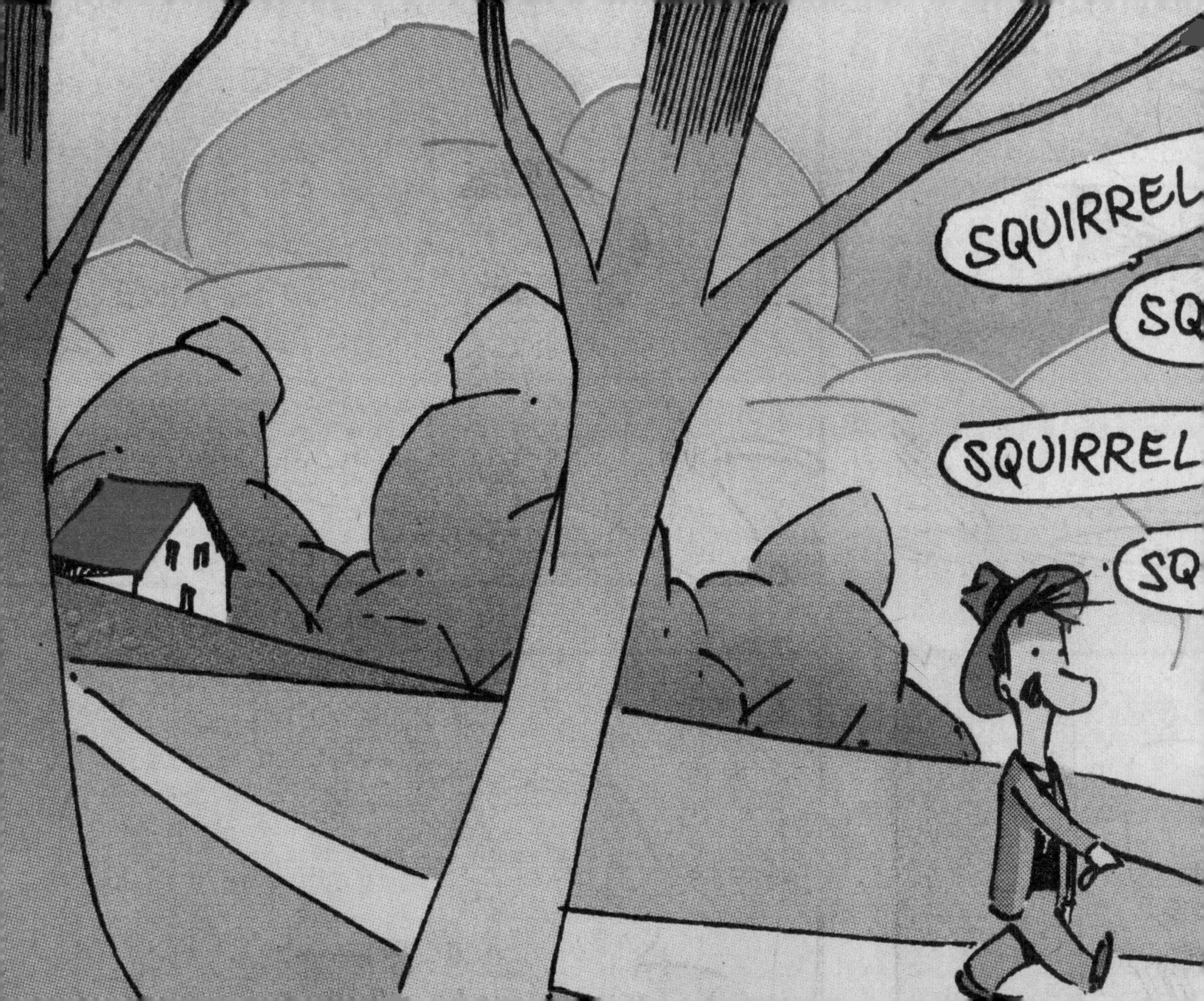

SQUIRREL
SQ
SQUIRREL
SQ

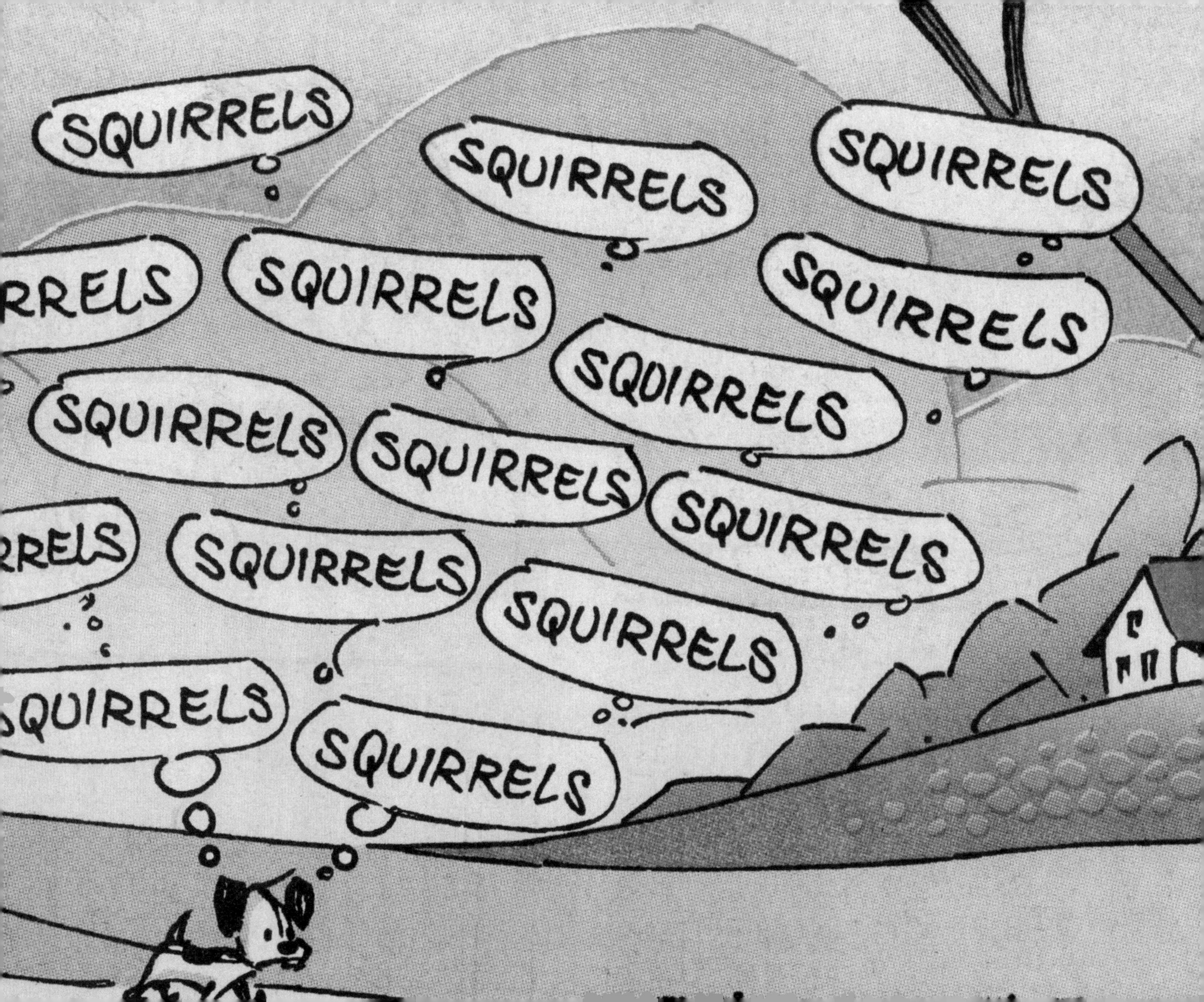
SQUIRRELS
SQUIRRELS
SQUIRRELS
RRELS
SQUIRRELS
SQUIRRELS
SQUIRRELS
SQUIRRELS
SQUIRRELS
RELS
SQUIRRELS
SQUIRRELS
SQUIRRELS
QUIRRELS
SQUIRRELS

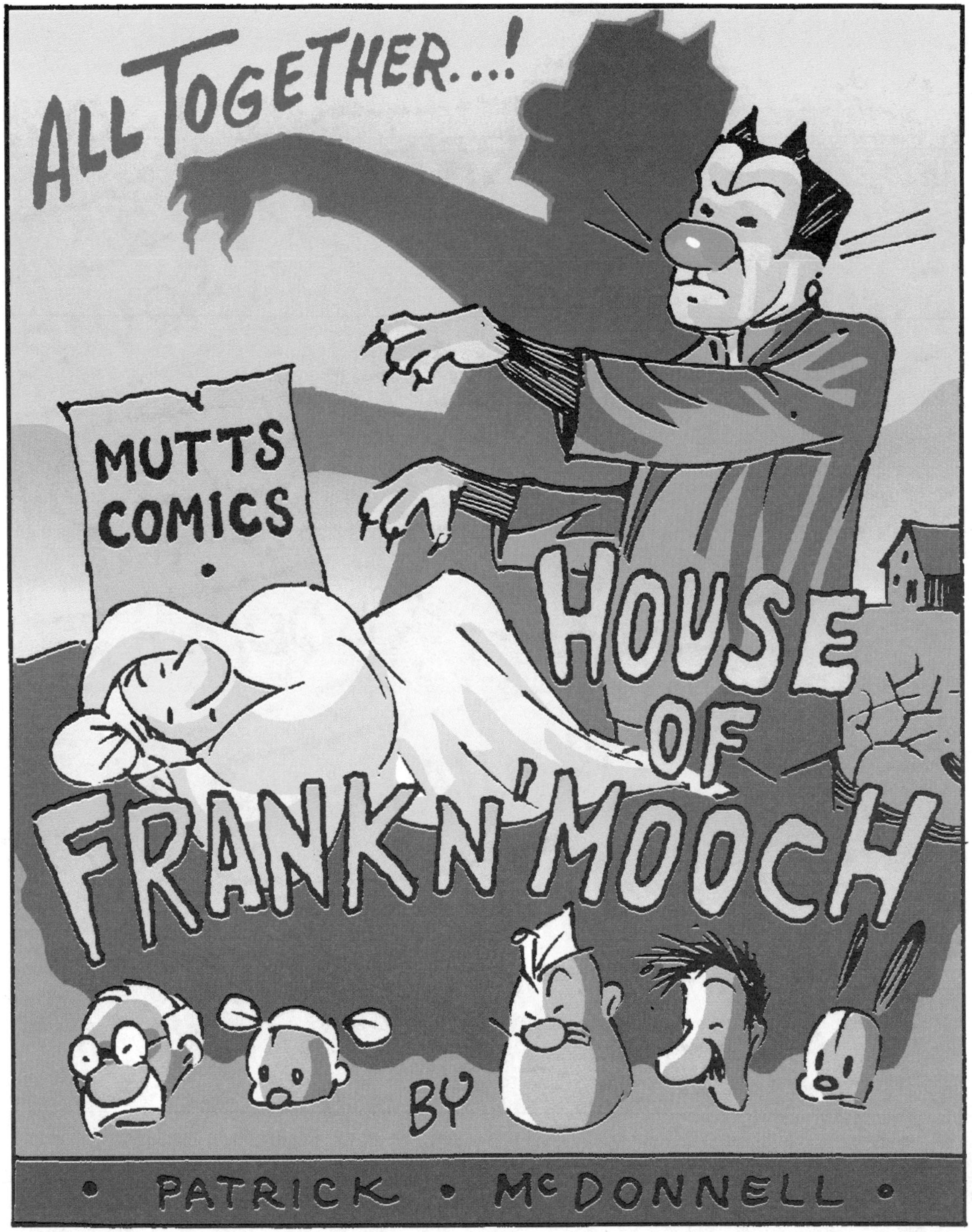
ALL TOGETHER...!
MUTTS COMICS
HOUSE OF FRANK N' MOOCH
BY
• PATRICK • McDONNELL •

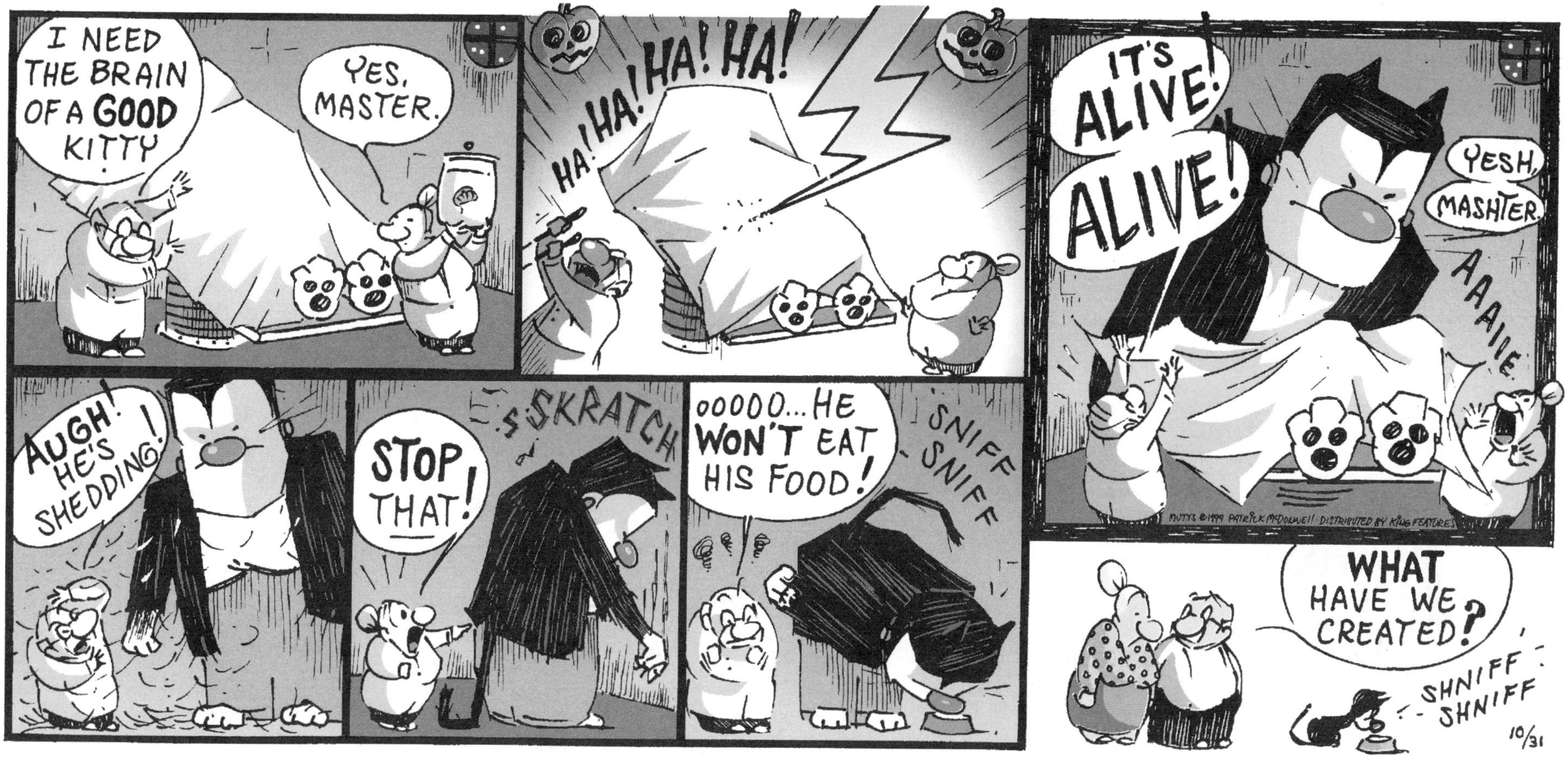

I NEED THE BRAIN OF A GOOD KITTY
YES, MASTER.
HA! HA! HA! HA! HA!
IT'S ALIVE!
ALIVE!
YESH, MASHTER.
AAAIIE.
NUTTS ©1999 PATRICK McDONNELL DISTRIBUTED BY KING FEATURES
AUGH! HE'S SHEDDING!
STOP THAT!
SKRATCH
OOOOO... HE WON'T EAT HIS FOOD!
SNIFF SNIFF
WHAT HAVE WE CREATED?
SHNIFF SHNIFF
10/31

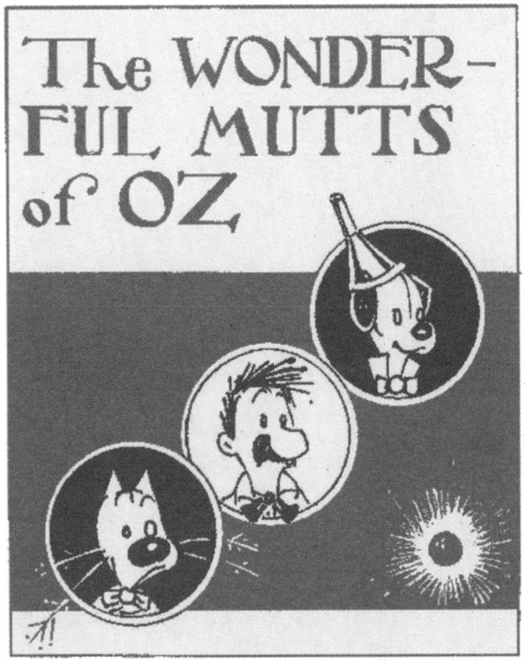
The WONDER-
FUL MUTTS
of OZ

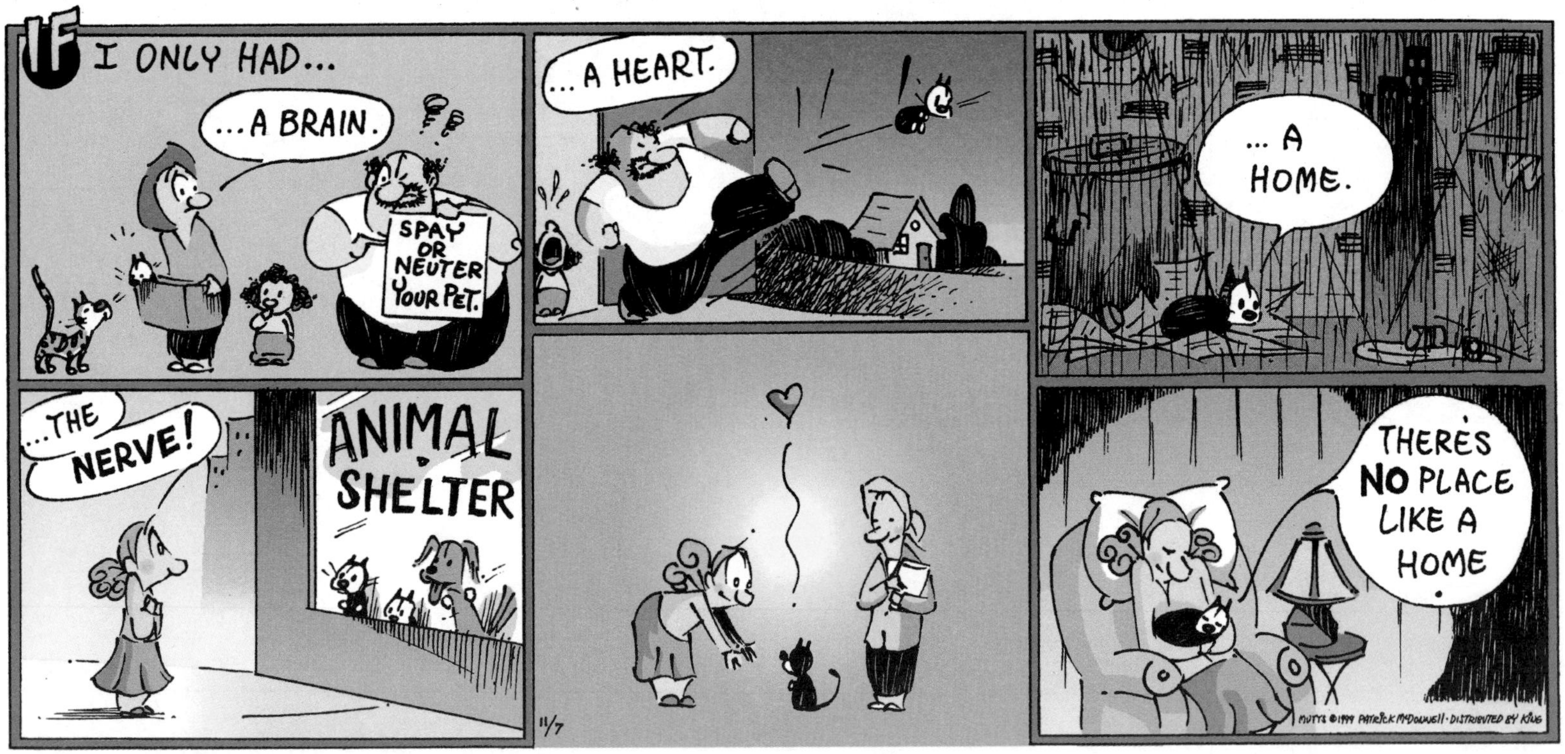
IF I ONLY HAD...
...A BRAIN.
SPAY OR NEUTER YOUR PET.
...A HEART.
... A HOME.
...THE NERVE!
ANIMAL SHELTER
THERE'S NO PLACE LIKE A HOME.
11/7
MUTTS © 1999 PATRICK McDONNELL · DISTRIBUTED BY KING

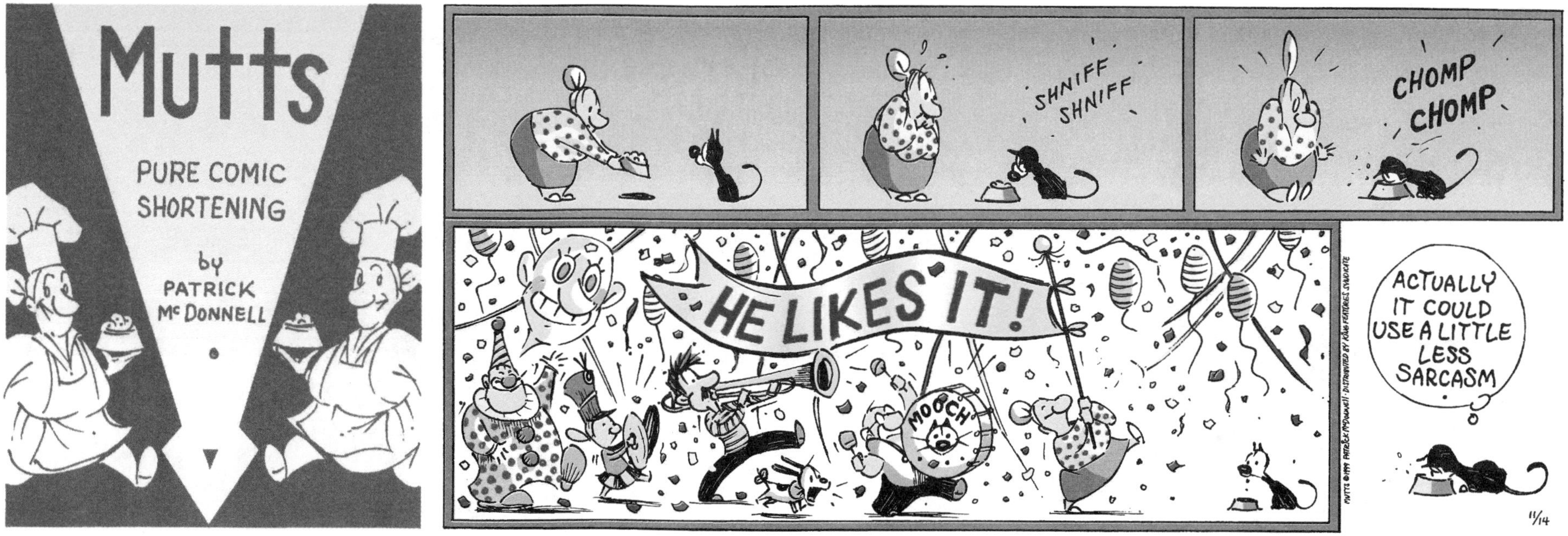
Mutts
PURE COMIC SHORTENING
by PATRICK McDONNELL
SHNIFF SHNIFF
CHOMP CHOMP
HE LIKES IT!
MOOCH
ACTUALLY IT COULD USE A LITTLE LESS SARCASM
11/14

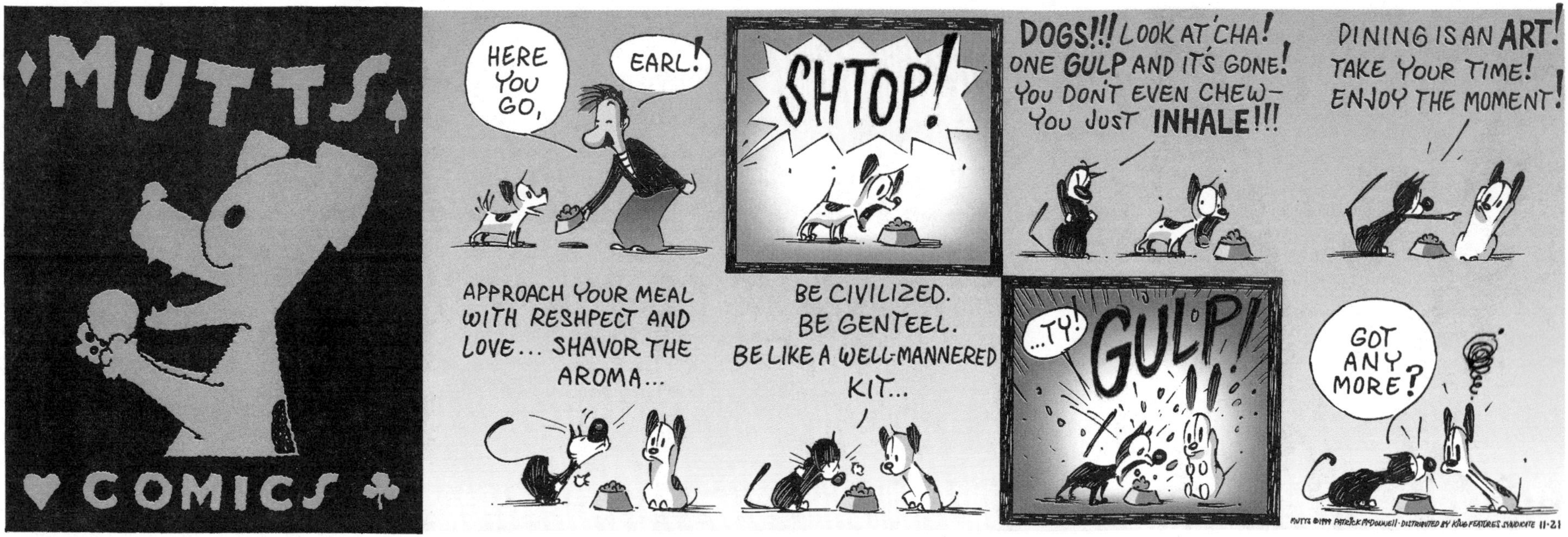
MUTTS
COMICS
HERE YOU GO,
EARL!
SHTOP!
DOGS!!! LOOK AT 'CHA! ONE GULP AND IT'S GONE! YOU DON'T EVEN CHEW– YOU JUST INHALE!!!
DINING IS AN ART! TAKE YOUR TIME! ENJOY THE MOMENT!
APPROACH YOUR MEAL WITH RESHPECT AND LOVE... SHAVOR THE AROMA...
BE CIVILIZED. BE GENTEEL. BE LIKE A WELL-MANNERED KIT...
...TY!
GULP!
GOT ANY MORE?
MUTTS ©1999 PATRICK McDONNELL · DISTRIBUTED BY KING FEATURES SYNDICATE 11·21

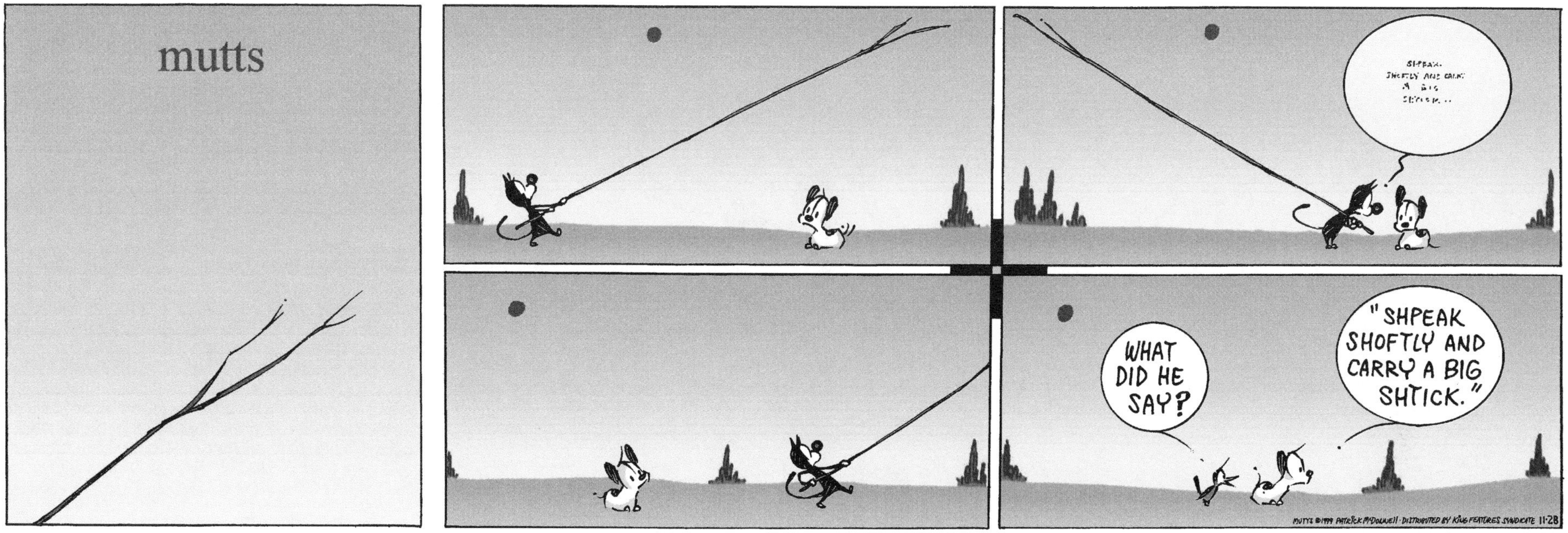
mutts
WHAT DID HE SAY?
"SHPEAK SHOFTLY AND CARRY A BIG SHTICK."
MUTTS ©1999 PATRICK McDONNELL · DISTRIBUTED BY KING FEATURES SYNDICATE 11·28

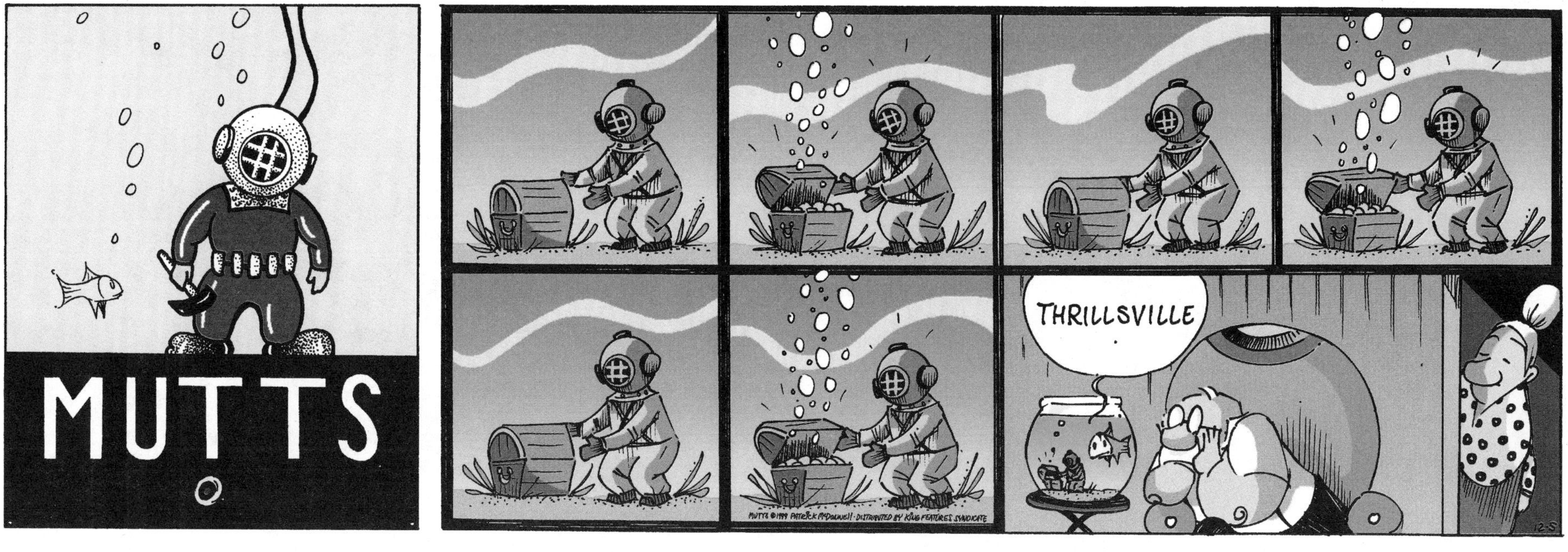
MUTTS
MUTTS ©1999 PATRICK McDONNELL · DISTRIBUTED BY KING FEATURES SYNDICATE
THRILLSVILLE
12·5

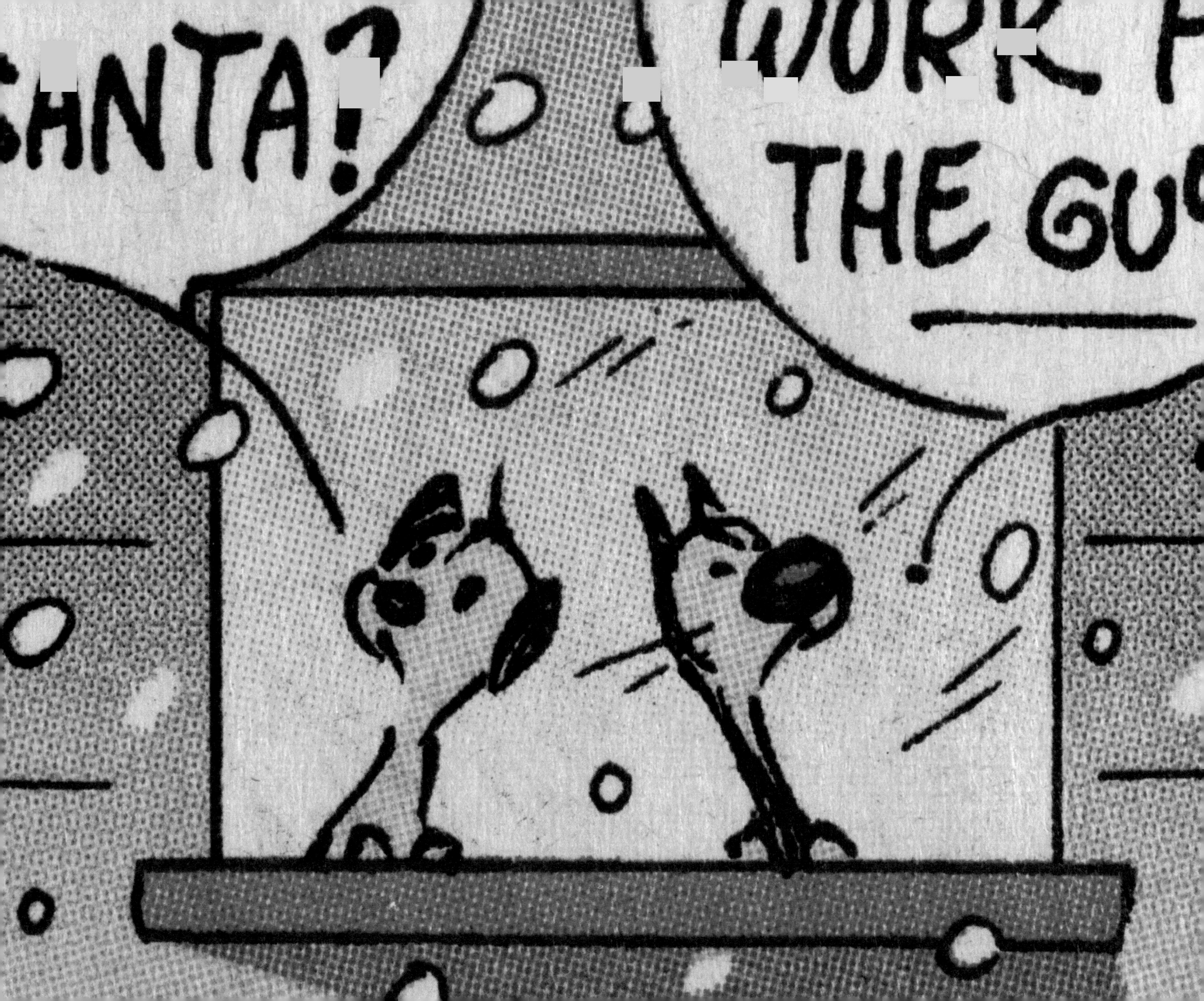
SANTA?
WORK
THE

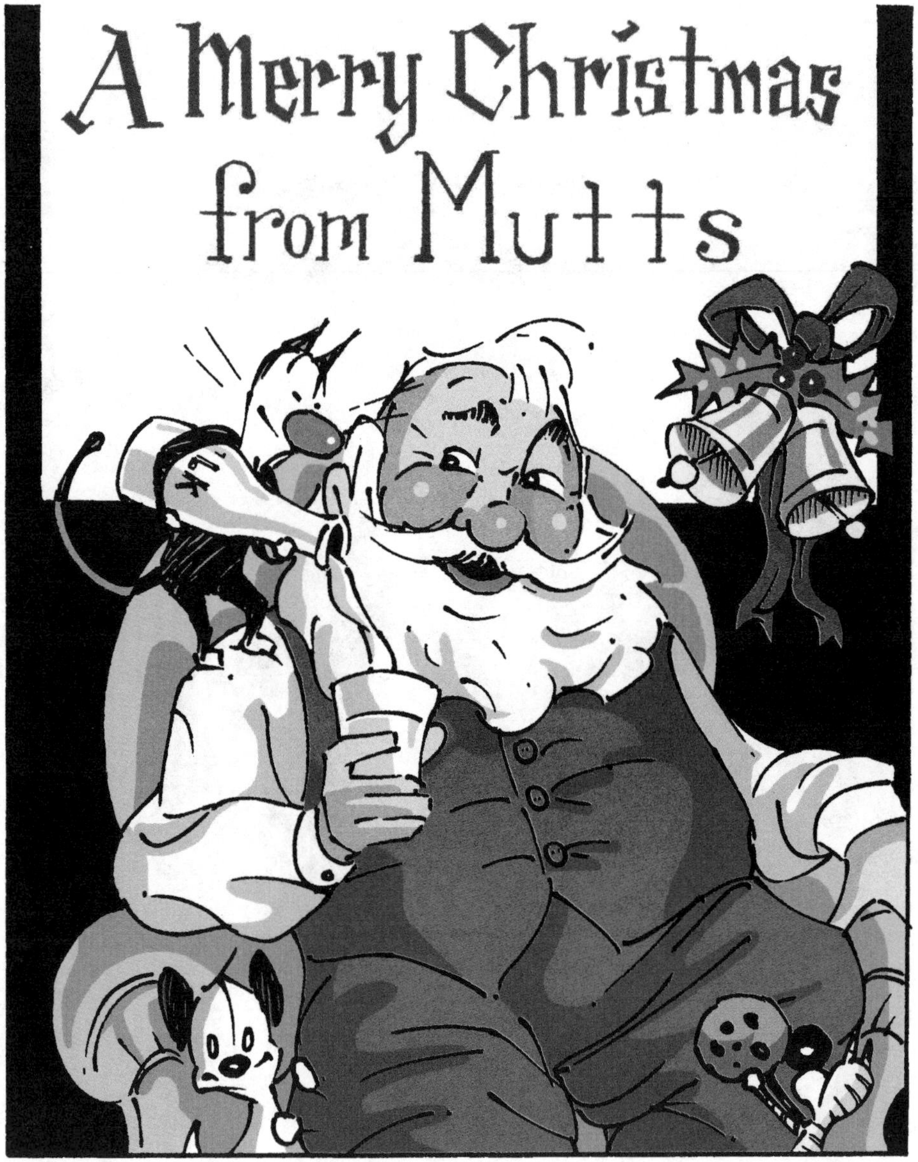
A Merry Christmas
from Mutts

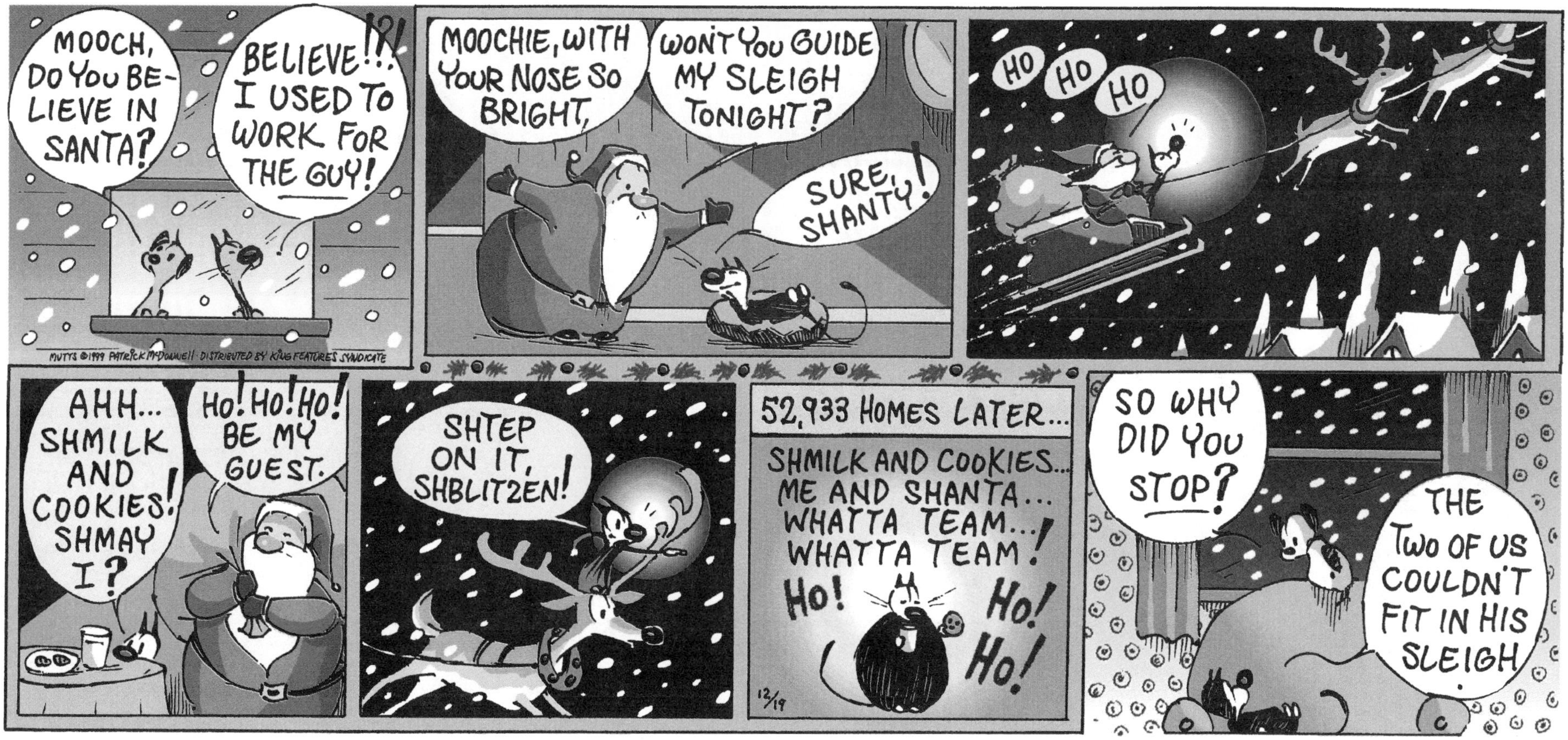
MOOCH, DO YOU BE-LIEVE IN SANTA?
BELIEVE!?! I USED TO WORK FOR THE GUY!
MUTTS ©1999 PATRICK McDONNELL · DISTRIBUTED BY KING FEATURES SYNDICATE
MOOCHIE, WITH YOUR NOSE SO BRIGHT,
WON'T YOU GUIDE MY SLEIGH TONIGHT?
SURE, SHANTY!
HO
HO
HO
AHH... SHMILK AND COOKIES! SHMAY I?
HO! HO! HO! BE MY GUEST.
SHTEP ON IT, SHBLITZEN!
52,933 HOMES LATER...
SHMILK AND COOKIES... ME AND SHANTA... WHATTA TEAM... WHATTA TEAM!
HO! HO! HO!
12/19
SO WHY DID YOU STOP?
THE TWO OF US COULDN'T FIT IN HIS SLEIGH.

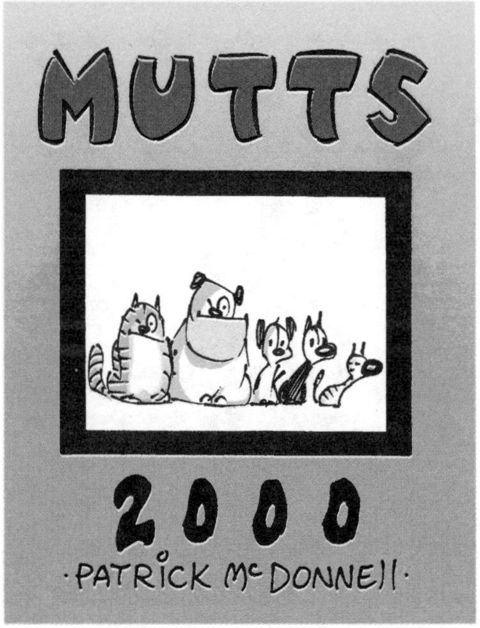
MUTTS
2000
·PATRICK McDONNELL·

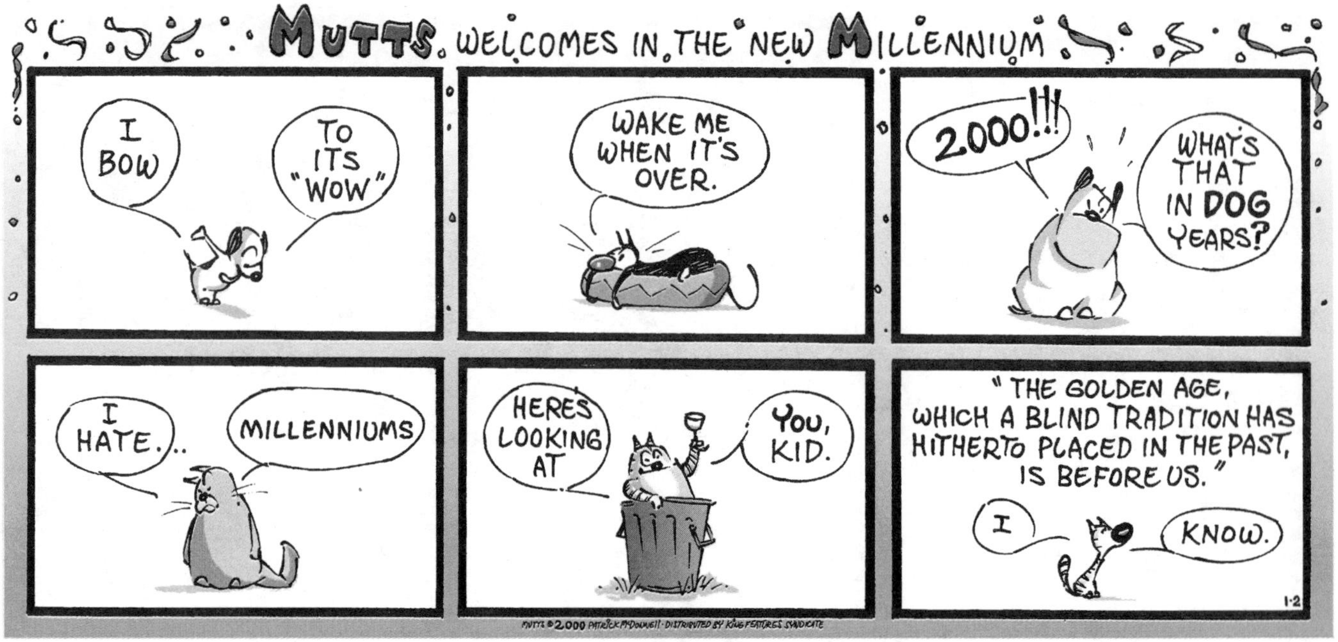
MUTTS WELCOMES IN THE NEW MILLENNIUM
I BOW
TO ITS "WOW"
WAKE ME WHEN IT'S OVER.
2000!!!
WHAT'S THAT IN DOG YEARS?
I HATE...
MILLENNIUMS
HERES LOOKING AT
YOU, KID.
"THE GOLDEN AGE, WHICH A BLIND TRADITION HAS HITHERTO PLACED IN THE PAST, IS BEFORE US."
I
KNOW.
1·2

mutts

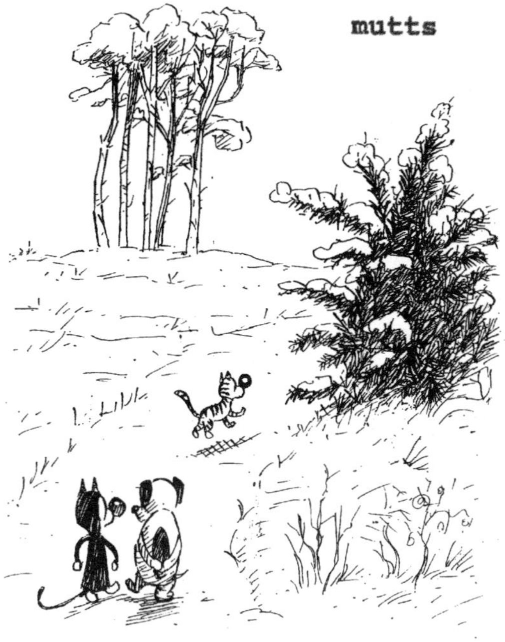

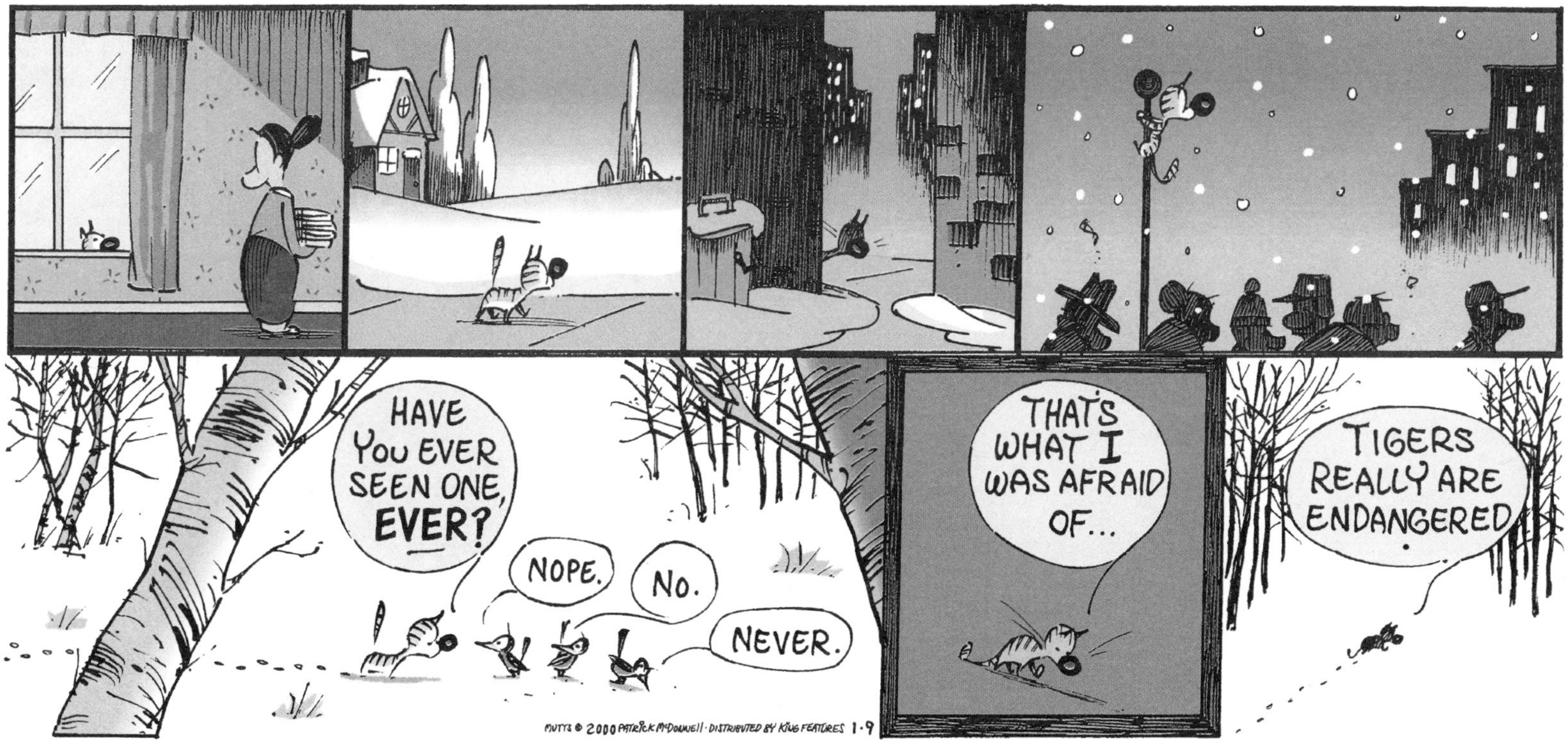
HAVE YOU EVER SEEN ONE, EVER?
NOPE.
NO.
NEVER.
THAT'S WHAT I WAS AFRAID OF...
TIGERS REALLY ARE ENDANGERED.
MUTTS © 2000 PATRICK McDONNELL · DISTRIBUTED BY KING FEATURES 1·9

ORIGINAL-SHTUFF-McDONNELL
Mutts

YOU HIBERNATE IN THERE !?!
YOU GOT SOME PLACE BETTER?
WALK THIS WAY..
WELL?
TOO SOFT.
BEARS.
CATS!
1·16
I'M BEAT.
LET'S GO RIGHT TO BED.
!
I THINK IT'S TIME SOMEONE CHANGED HIS PAJAMAS
MUTTS © 2000 PATRICK McDONNELL · DISTRIBUTED BY KING FEATURES SYNDICATE

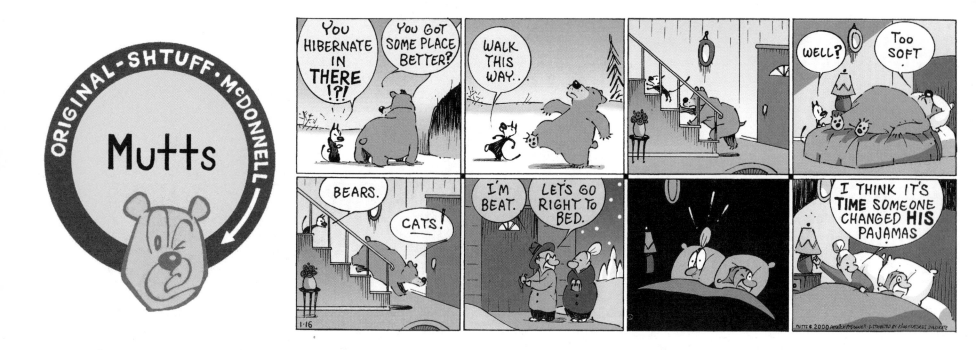

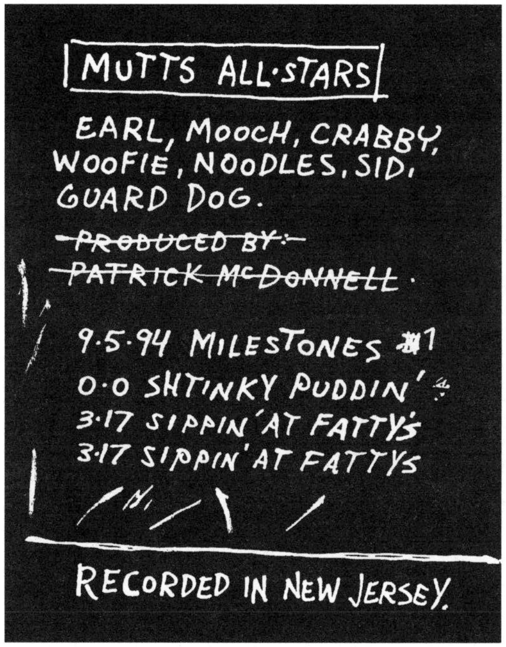

MUTTS ALL·STARS
EARL, MOOCH, CRABBY, WOOFIE, NOODLES, SID, GUARD DOG.
PRODUCED BY: PATRICK McDONNELL.
9·5·94 MILESTONES #1
0·0 SHTINKY PUDDIN'
3·17 SIPPIN' AT FATTY'S
3·17 SIPPIN' AT FATTYS
RECORDED IN NEW JERSEY.

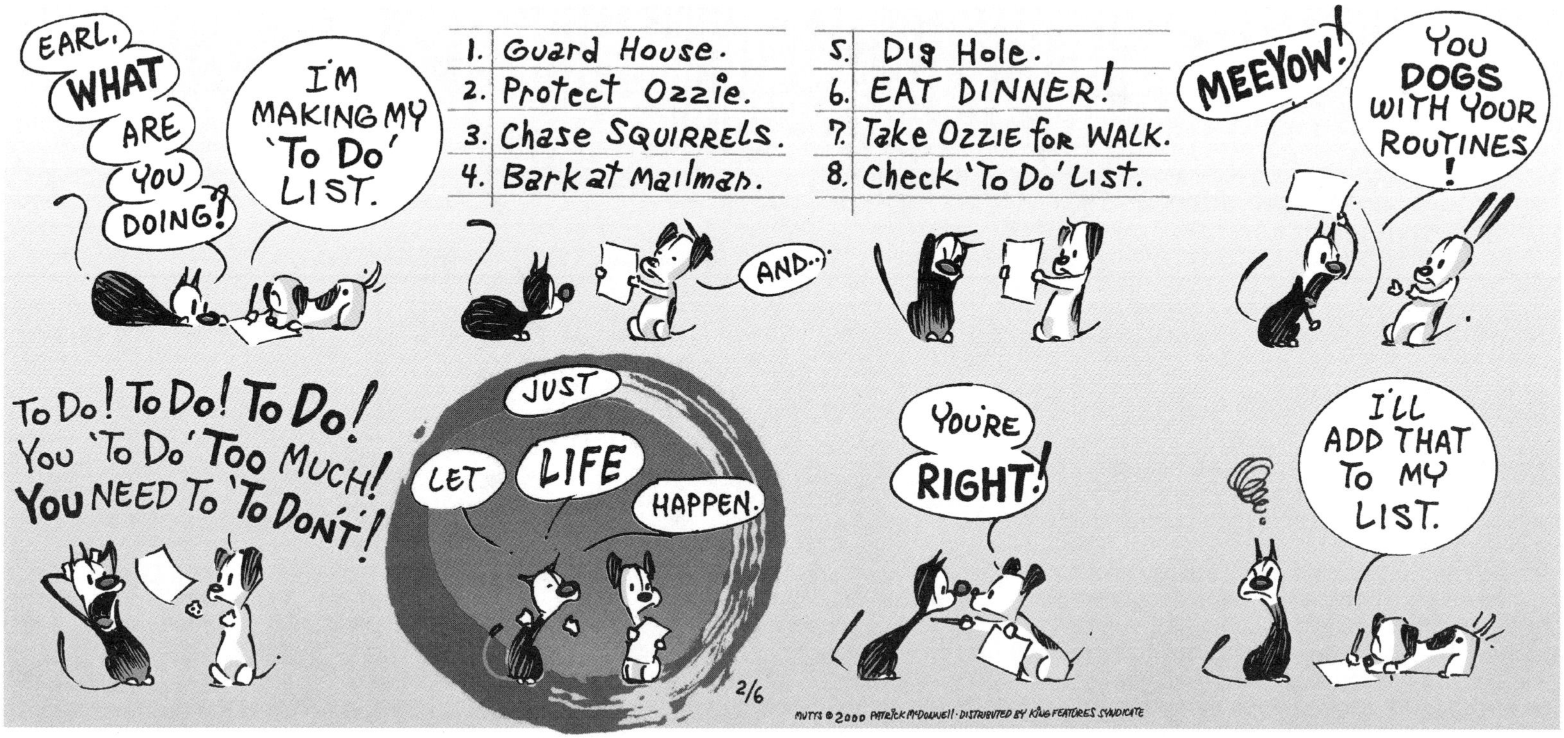

EARL, WHAT ARE YOU DOING?
I'M MAKING MY 'TO DO' LIST.
1. Guard House.
2. Protect Ozzie.
3. Chase SQUIRRELS.
4. Bark at Mailman.
AND...
5. Dig Hole.
6. EAT DINNER!
7. Take Ozzie for WALK.
8. Check 'To Do' List.
MEEYOW!
YOU DOGS WITH YOUR ROUTINES!
To Do! To Do! To Do! You 'To Do' Too MUCH! You NEED To 'To DON'T'!
JUST LET LIFE HAPPEN.
YOU'RE RIGHT!
I'LL ADD THAT TO MY LIST.
2/6
MUTTS © 2000 PATRICK McDONNELL · DISTRIBUTED BY KING FEATURES SYNDICATE

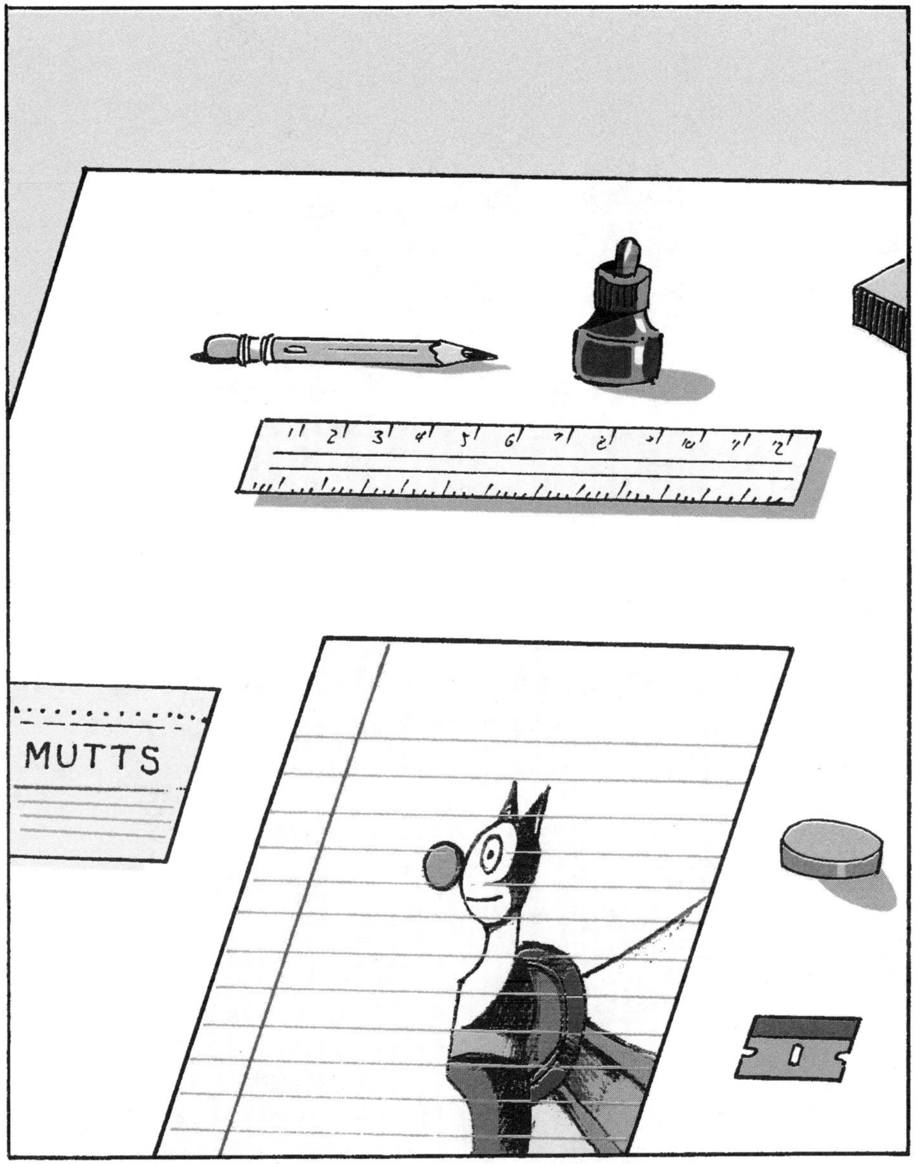
MUTTS

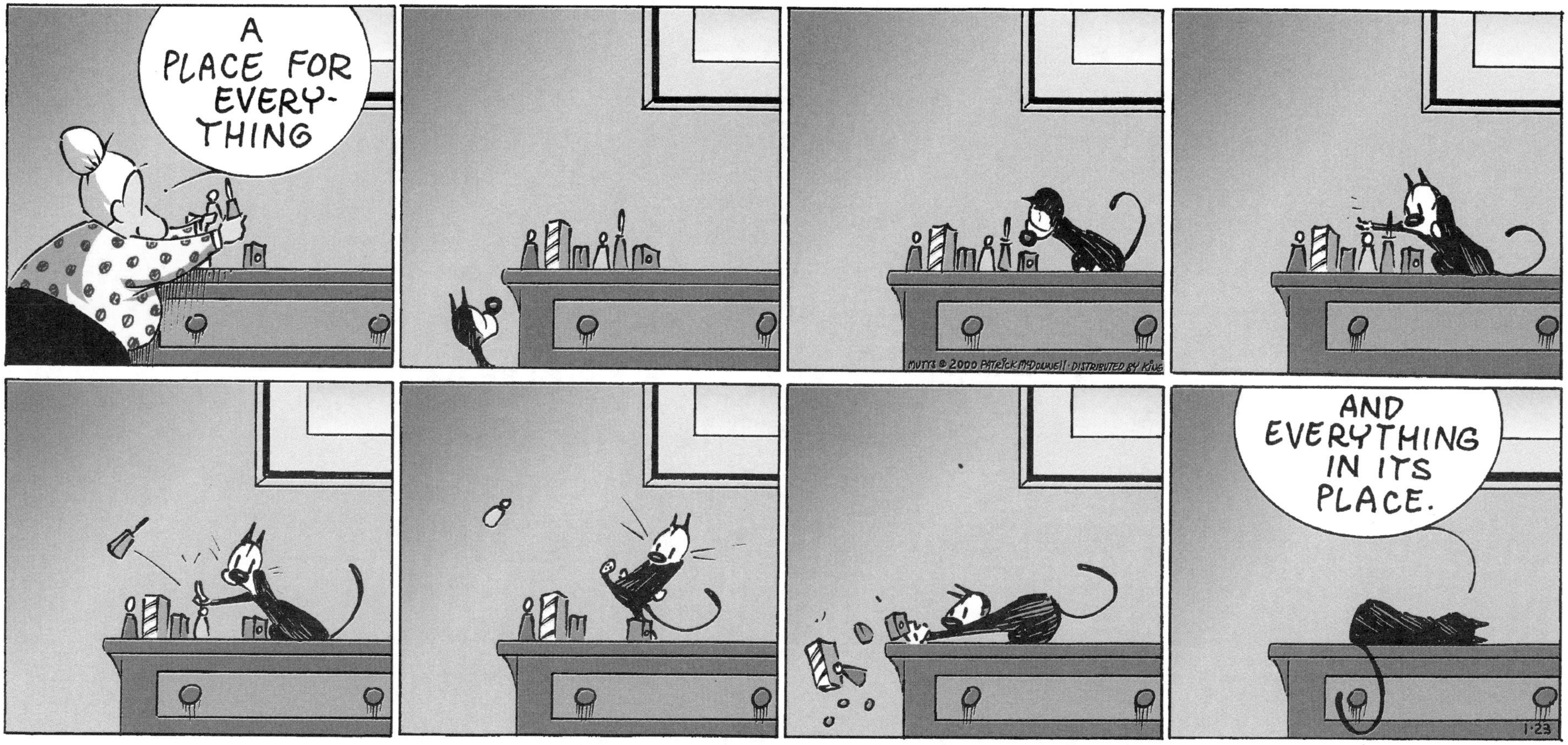
A PLACE FOR EVERY-THING
MUTTS © 2000 PATRICK McDONNELL · DISTRIBUTED BY KING
AND EVERYTHING IN ITS PLACE.
1·23

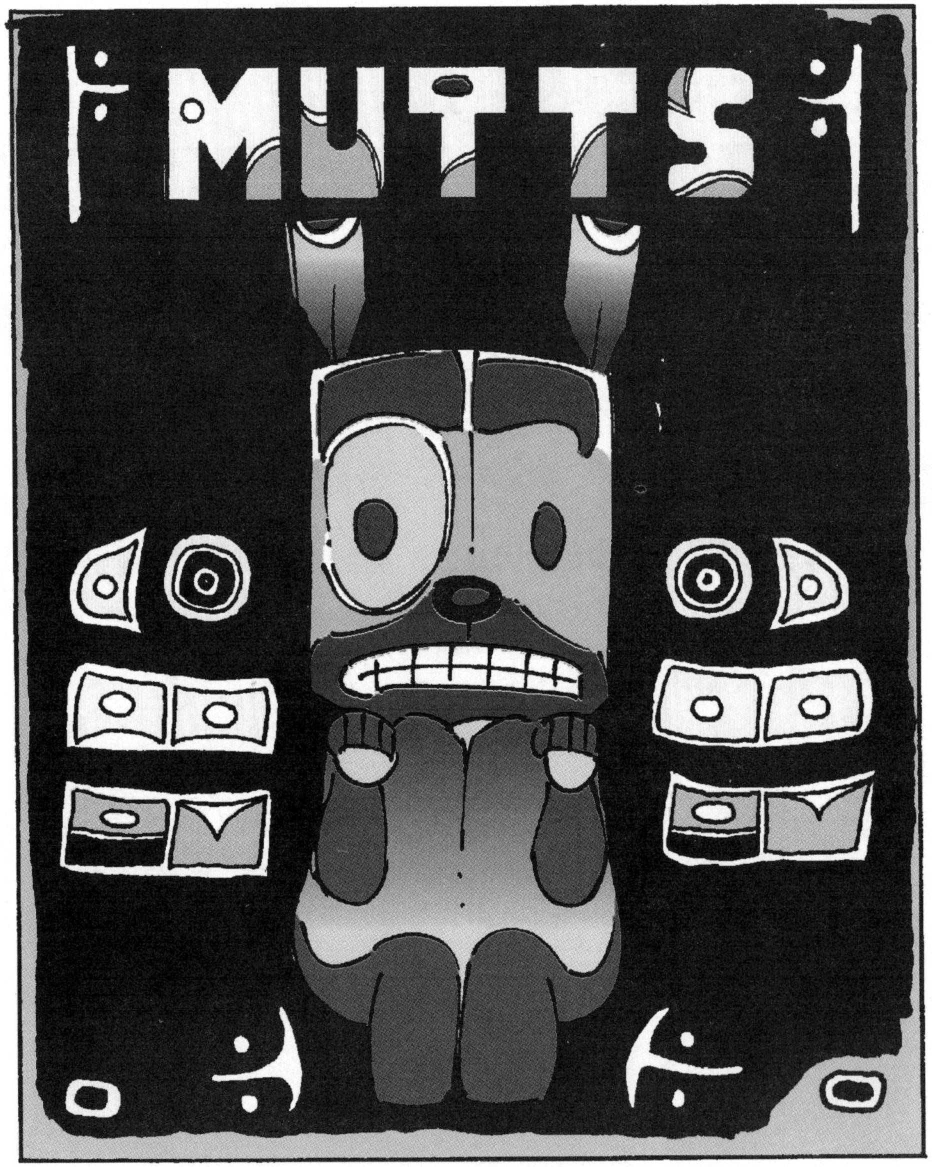
MUTTS

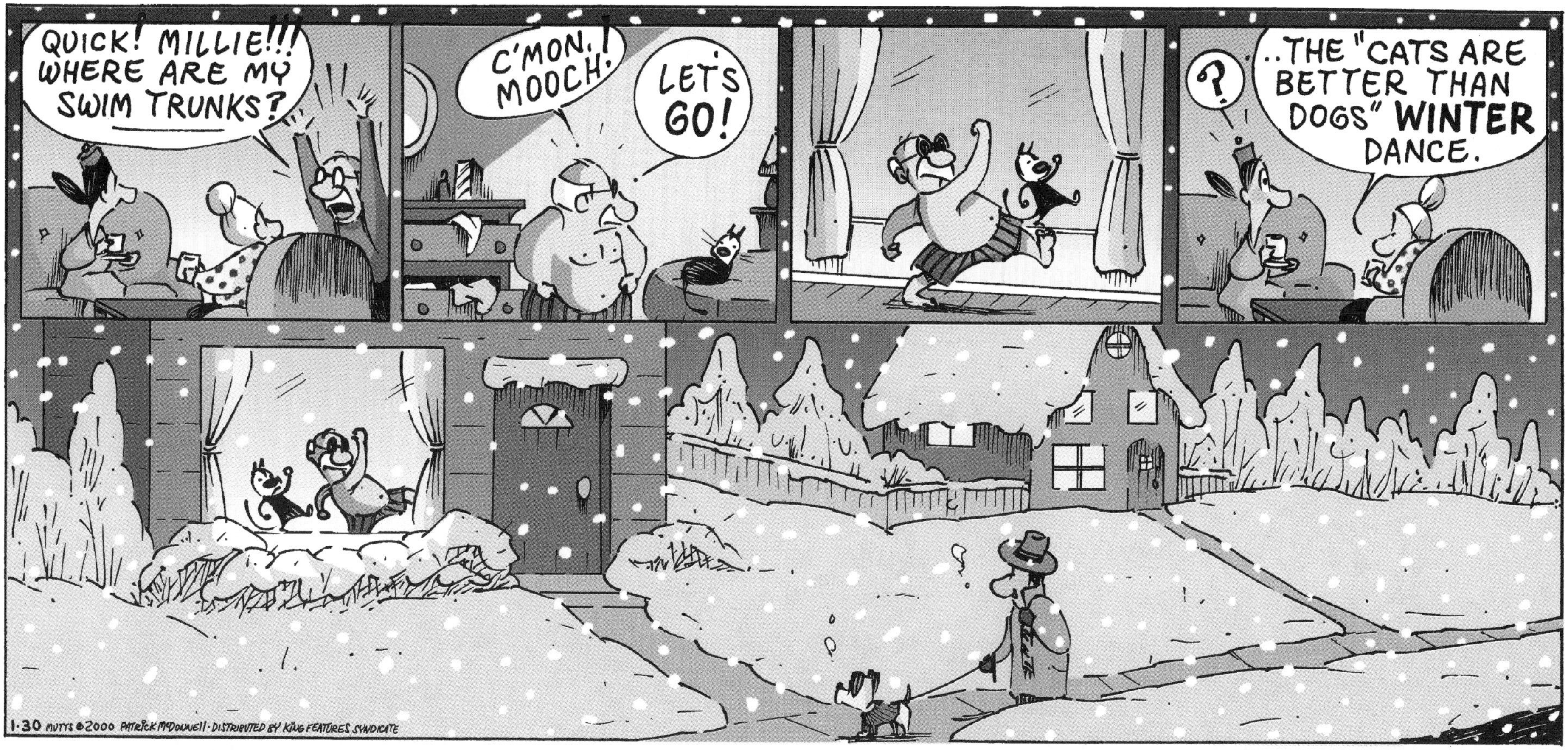
QUICK! MILLIE!!! WHERE ARE MY SWIM TRUNKS?
C'MON, MOOCH!
LET'S GO!
?
..THE "CATS ARE BETTER THAN DOGS" WINTER DANCE.
1·30 MUTTS ©2000 PATRICK McDONNELL · DISTRIBUTED BY KING FEATURES SYNDICATE

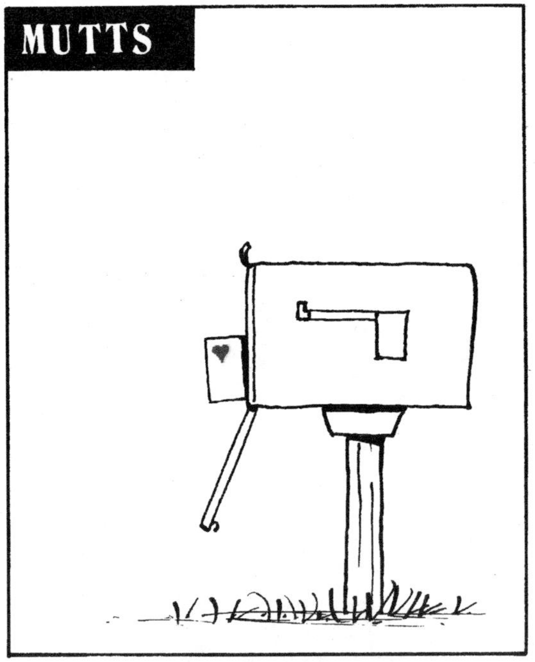
MUTTS

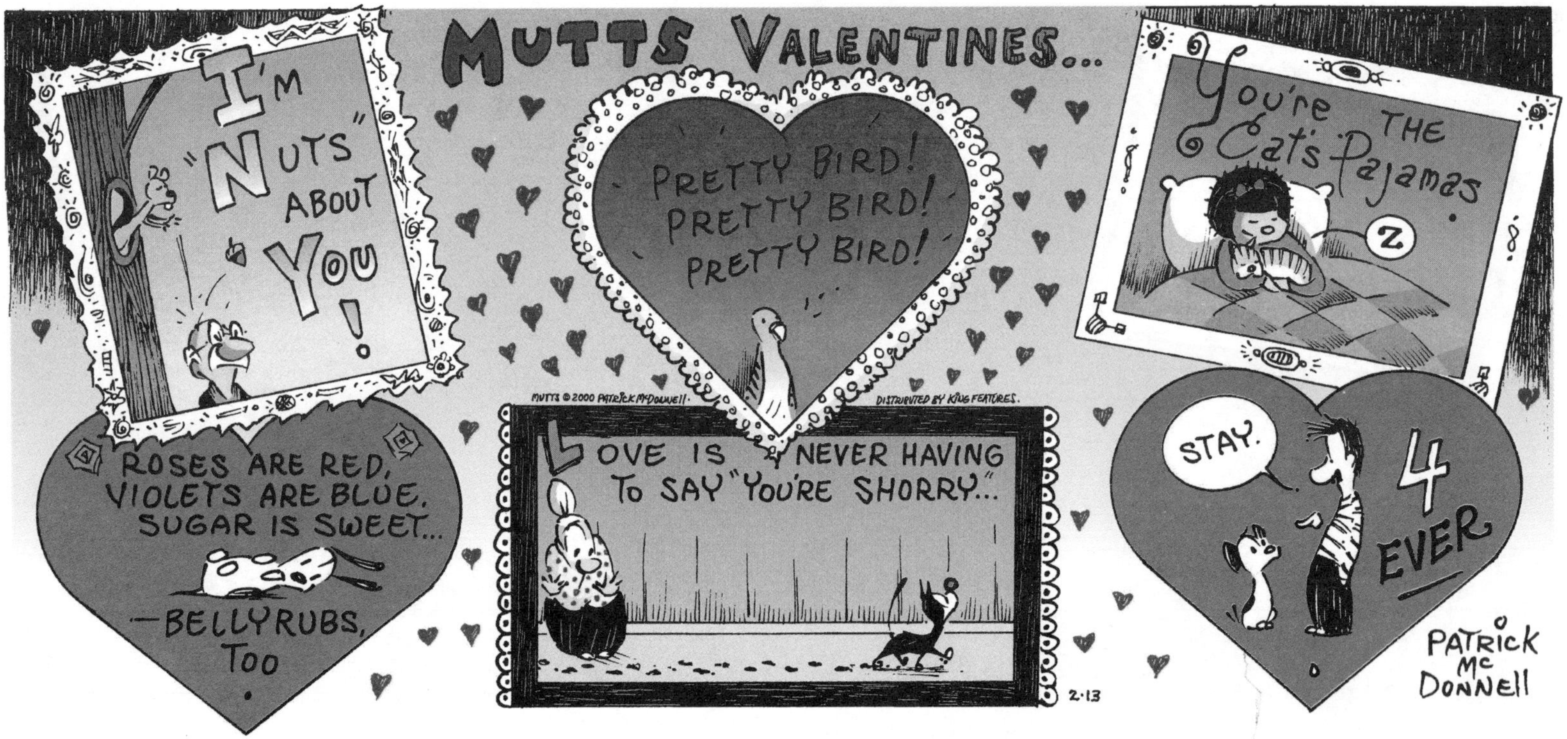
MUTTS VALENTINES...
I'M "NUTS" ABOUT YOU!
PRETTY BIRD! PRETTY BIRD! PRETTY BIRD!
You're THE Cat's Pajamas.
Z
ROSES ARE RED, VIOLETS ARE BLUE. SUGAR IS SWEET... —BELLYRUBS, TOO
MUTTS © 2000 PATRICK McDONNELL
DISTRIBUTED BY KING FEATURES
LOVE IS NEVER HAVING TO SAY "YOU'RE SHORRY"...
STAY.
4 EVER
PATRICK Mc DONNELL
2-13

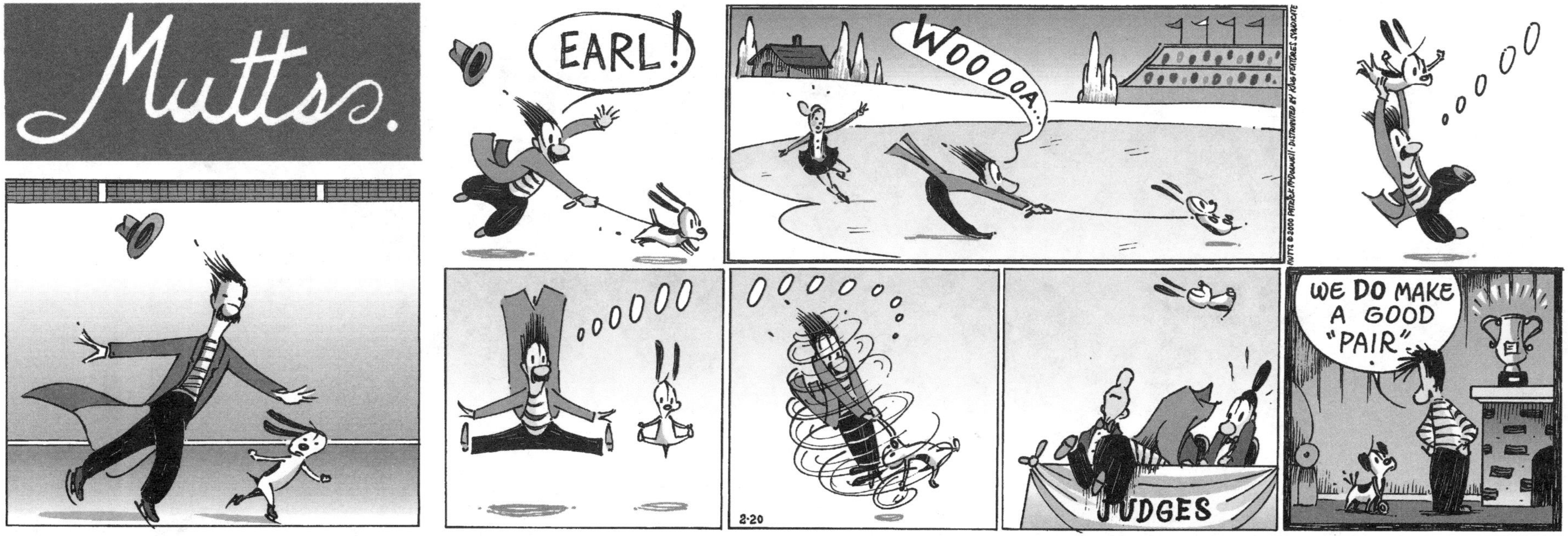
Mutts.
EARL!
WOOOOA...
MUTTS © 2000 PATRICK McDONNELL · DISTRIBUTED BY KING FEATURES SYNDICATE
ooooo
oooooo
oooooooo
2·20
JUDGES
WE DO MAKE A GOOD "PAIR".

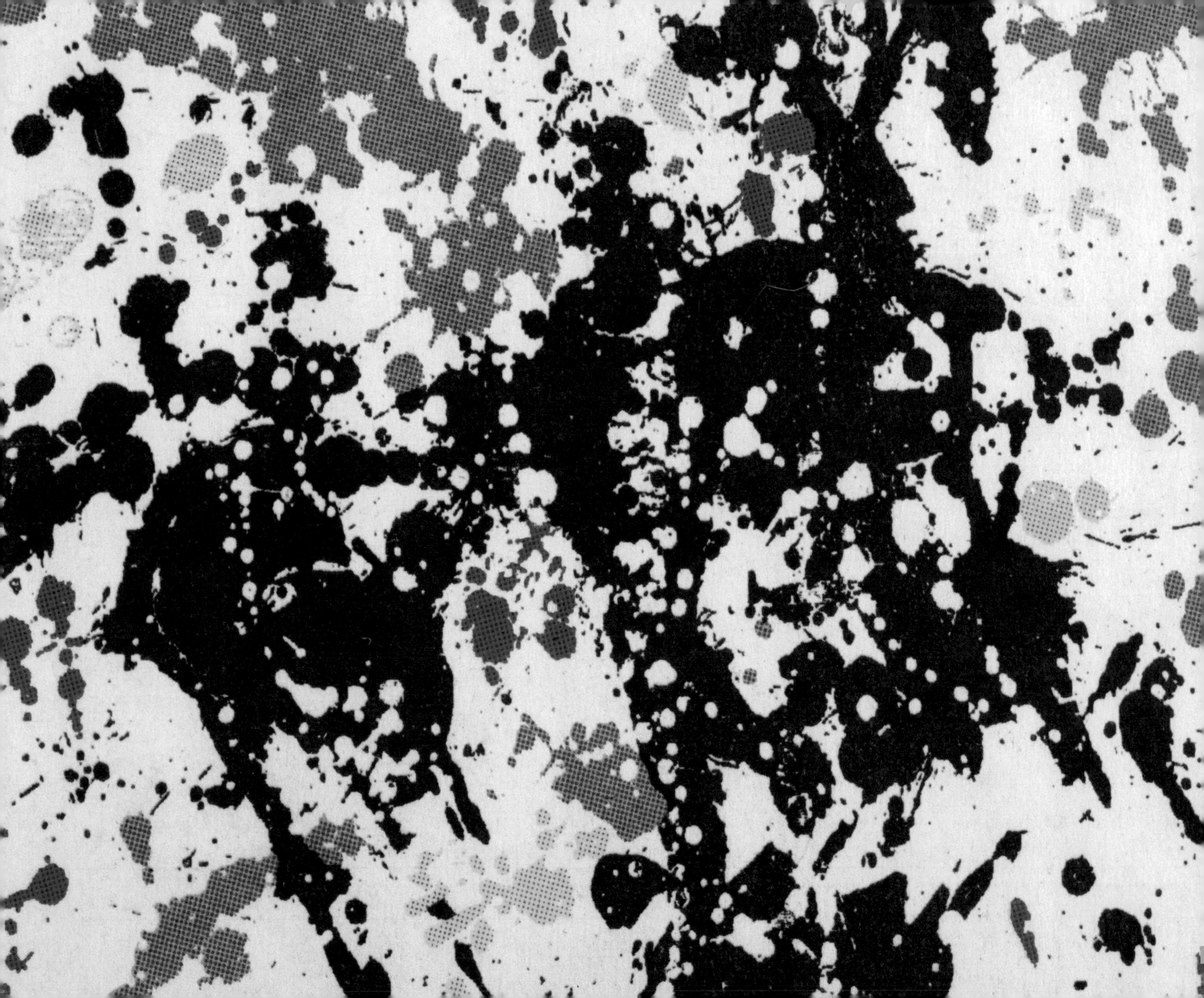

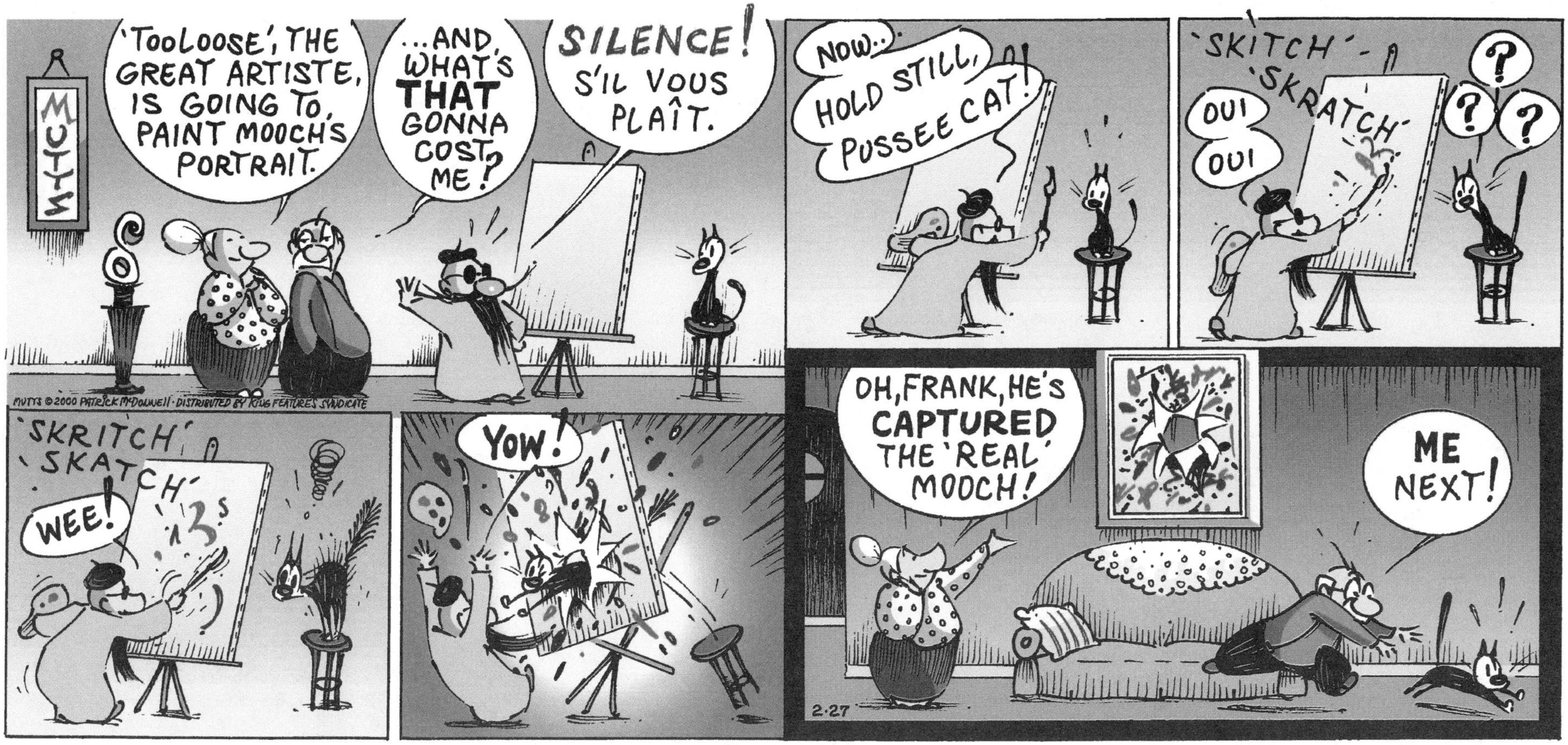
MUTTS
'TOOLOOSE', THE GREAT ARTISTE, IS GOING TO PAINT MOOCH'S PORTRAIT.
...AND, WHAT'S **THAT** GONNA COST ME?
SILENCE! S'IL VOUS PLAÎT.
MUTTS © 2000 PATRICK McDONNELL · DISTRIBUTED BY KING FEATURES SYNDICATE
NOW...
HOLD STILL, PUSSEE CAT!
'SKITCH' 'SKRATCH'
OUI OUI
?
? ?
'SKRITCH' 'SKATCH'
WEE!
YOW!
OH, FRANK, HE'S **CAPTURED** THE 'REAL' MOOCH!
ME NEXT!
2·27

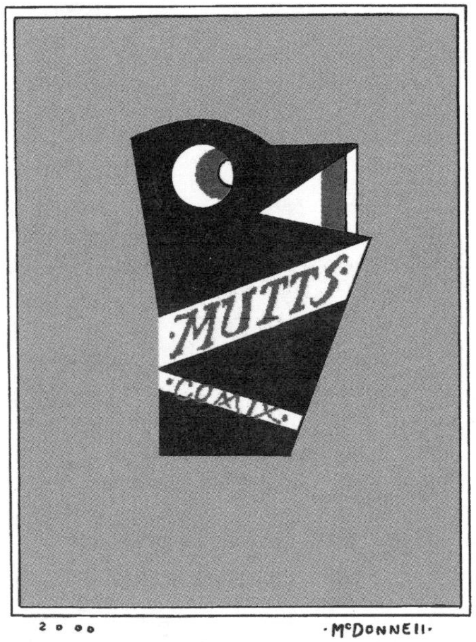

MUTTS
·CMXIX·
2000
·McDONNELL·

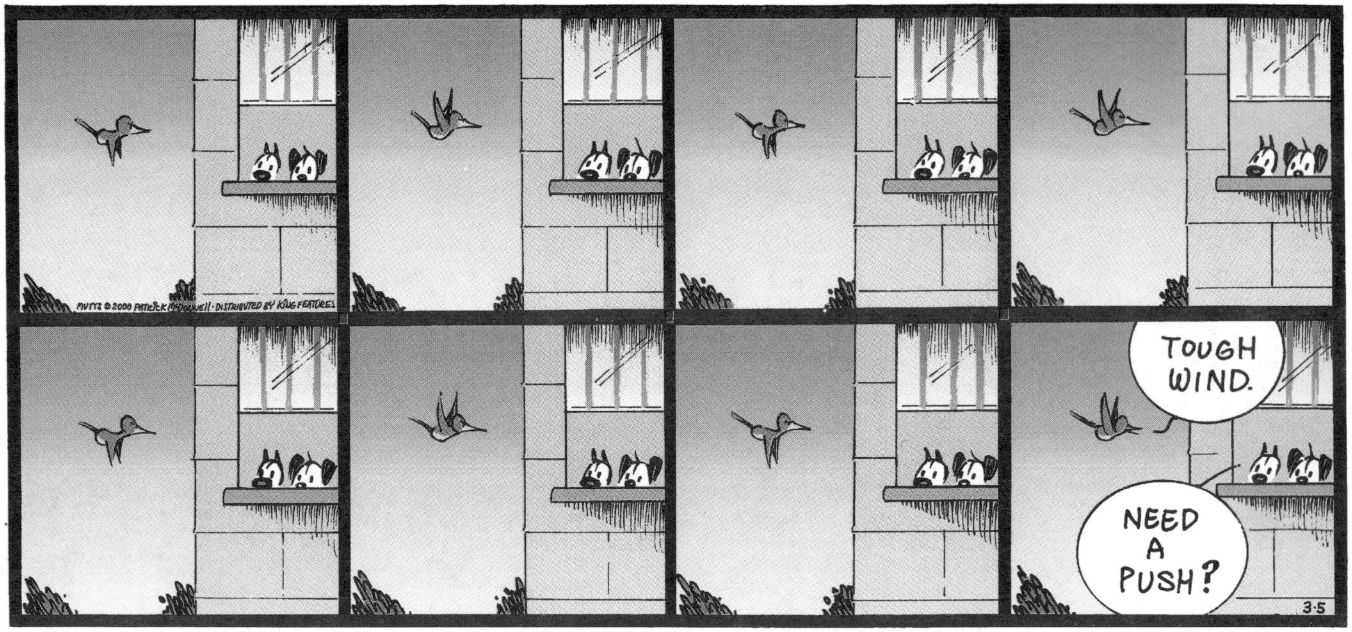

MUTTS © 2000 PATRICK McDONNELL · DISTRIBUTED BY KING FEATURES
TOUGH WIND.
NEED A PUSH?
3·5

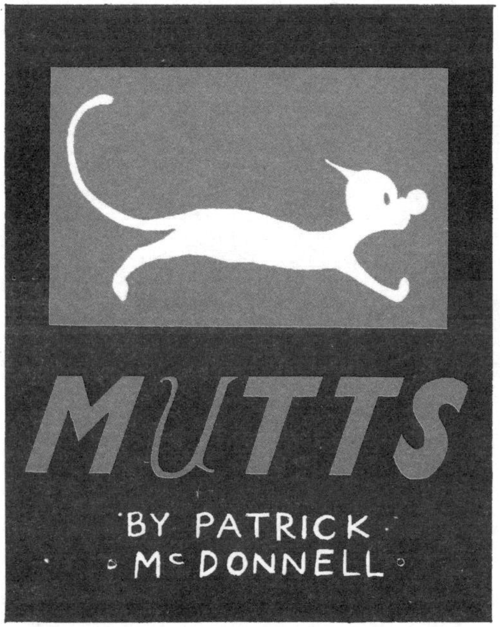

MUTTS
BY PATRICK McDONNELL

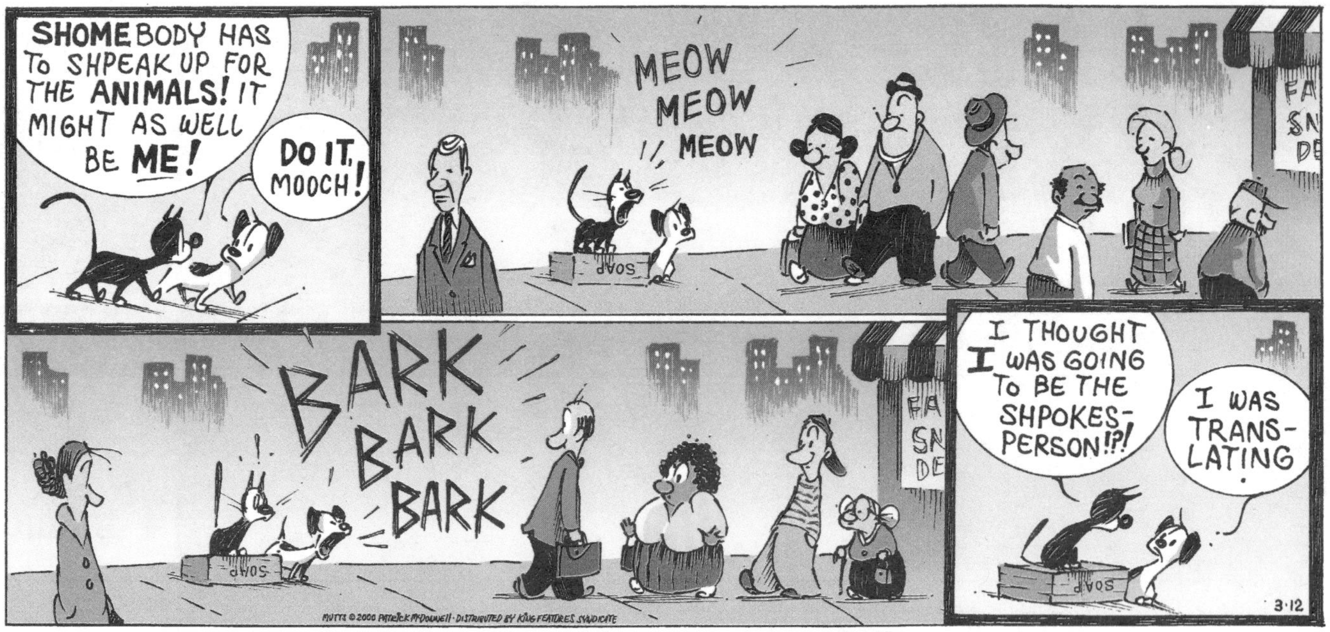

SHOMEBODY HAS TO SHPEAK UP FOR THE ANIMALS! IT MIGHT AS WELL BE ME!
DO IT, MOOCH!
MEOW MEOW MEOW
SOAP
BARK BARK BARK
I THOUGHT I WAS GOING TO BE THE SHPOKES-PERSON!?!
I WAS TRANS-LATING.
MUTTS © 2000 PATRICK McDONNELL · DISTRIBUTED BY KING FEATURES SYNDICATE
3·12

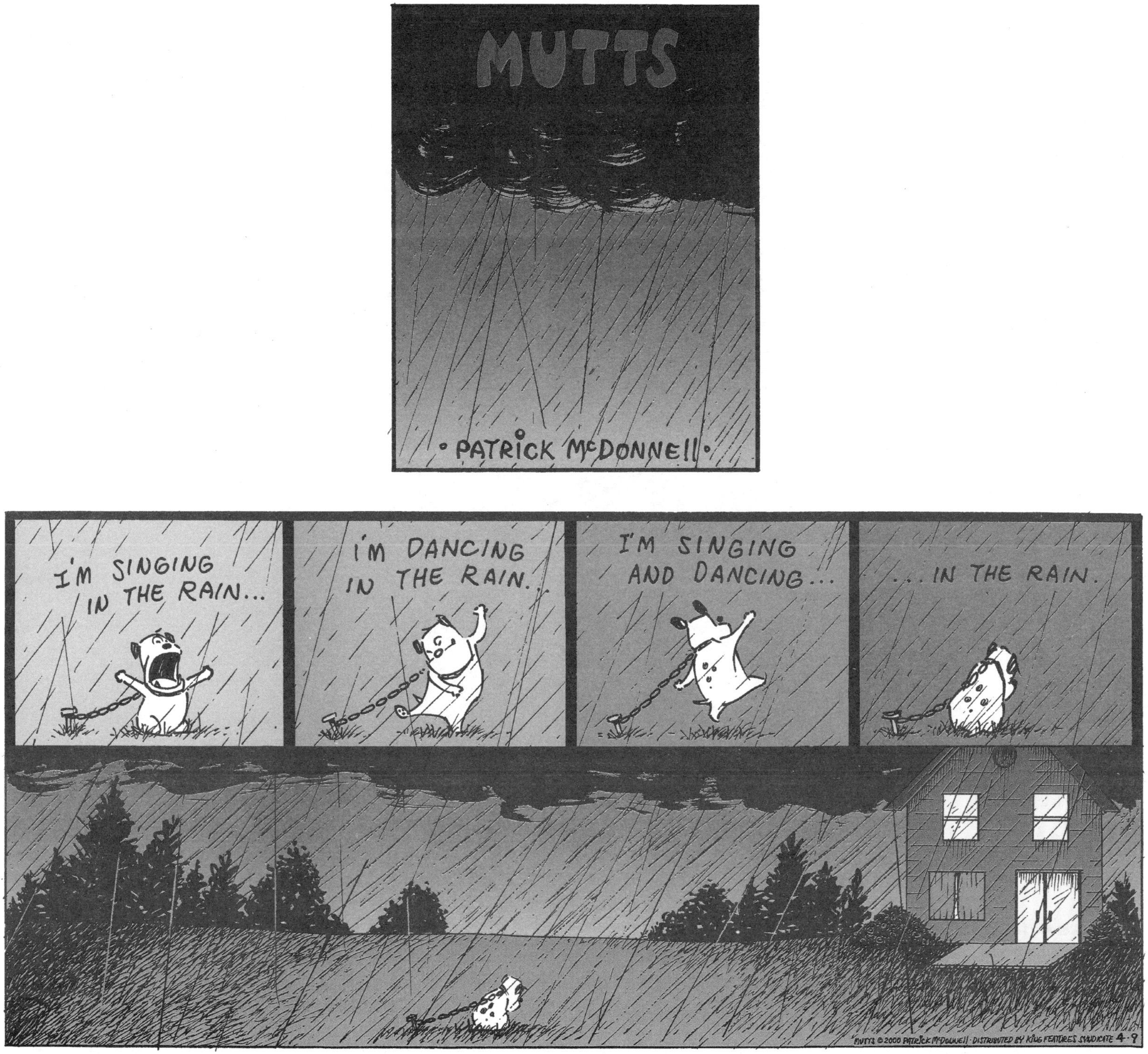
MUTTS
• PATRICK McDONNELL •
I'M SINGING IN THE RAIN...
I'M DANCING IN THE RAIN...
I'M SINGING AND DANCING...
...IN THE RAIN.
MUTTS © 2000 PATRICK McDONNELL · DISTRIBUTED BY KING FEATURES SYNDICATE 4·9

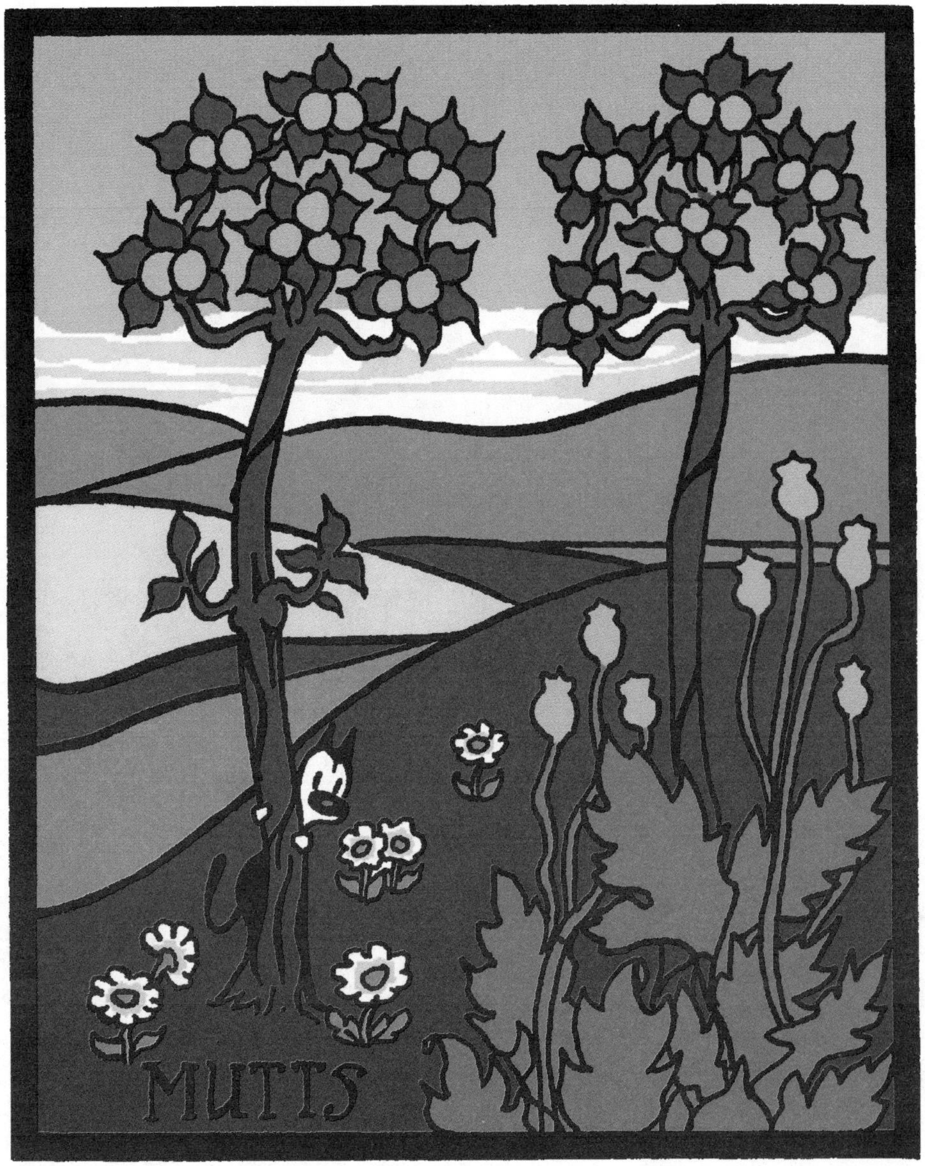
MUTTS

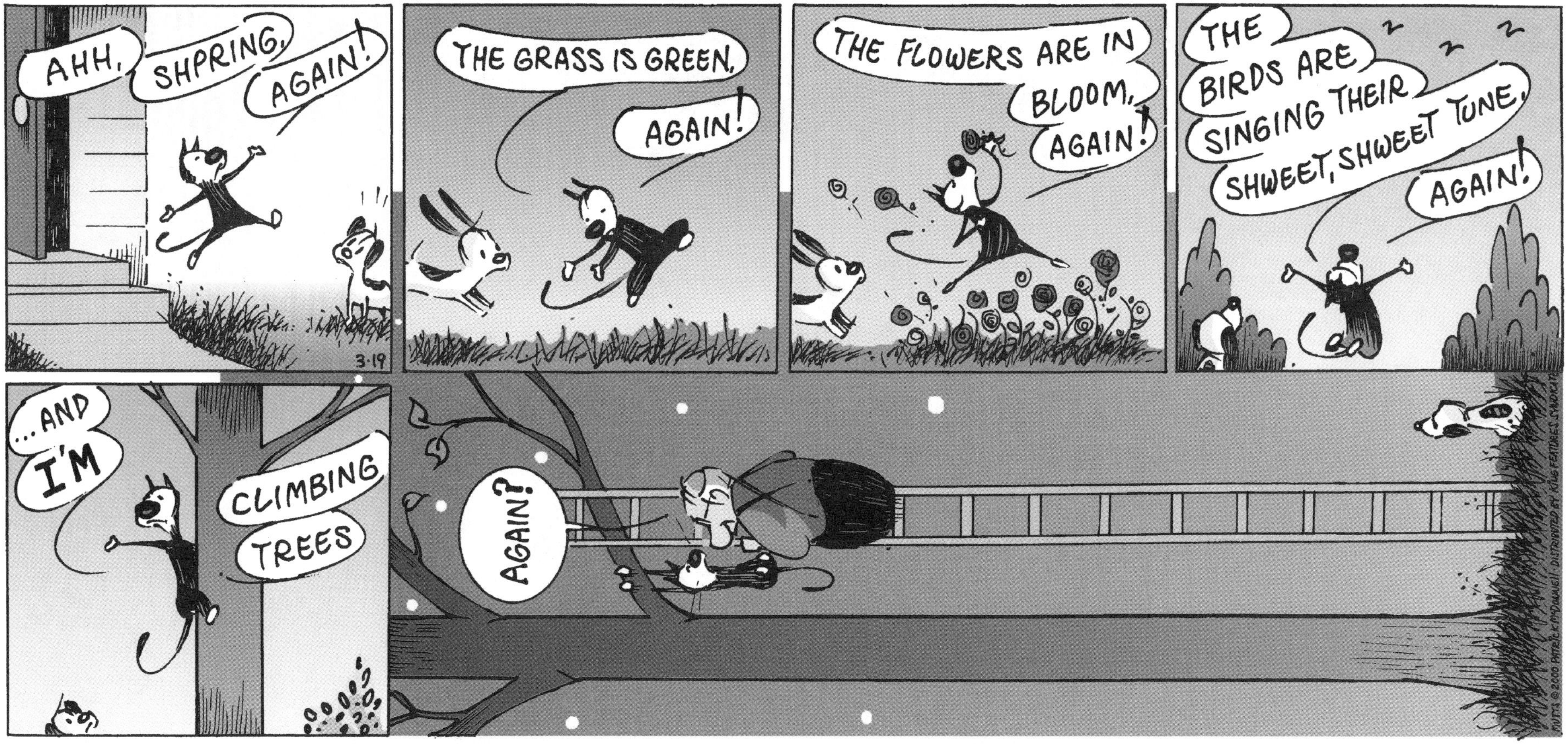
AHH,
SHPRING,
AGAIN!
3·19
THE GRASS IS GREEN,
AGAIN!
THE FLOWERS ARE IN
BLOOM,
AGAIN!
THE
BIRDS ARE
SINGING THEIR
SHWEET, SHWEET TUNE,
AGAIN!
...AND
I'M
CLIMBING
TREES
AGAIN?
MUTTS © 2000 PATRICK McDONNELL. DISTRIBUTED BY KING FEATURES SYNDICATE

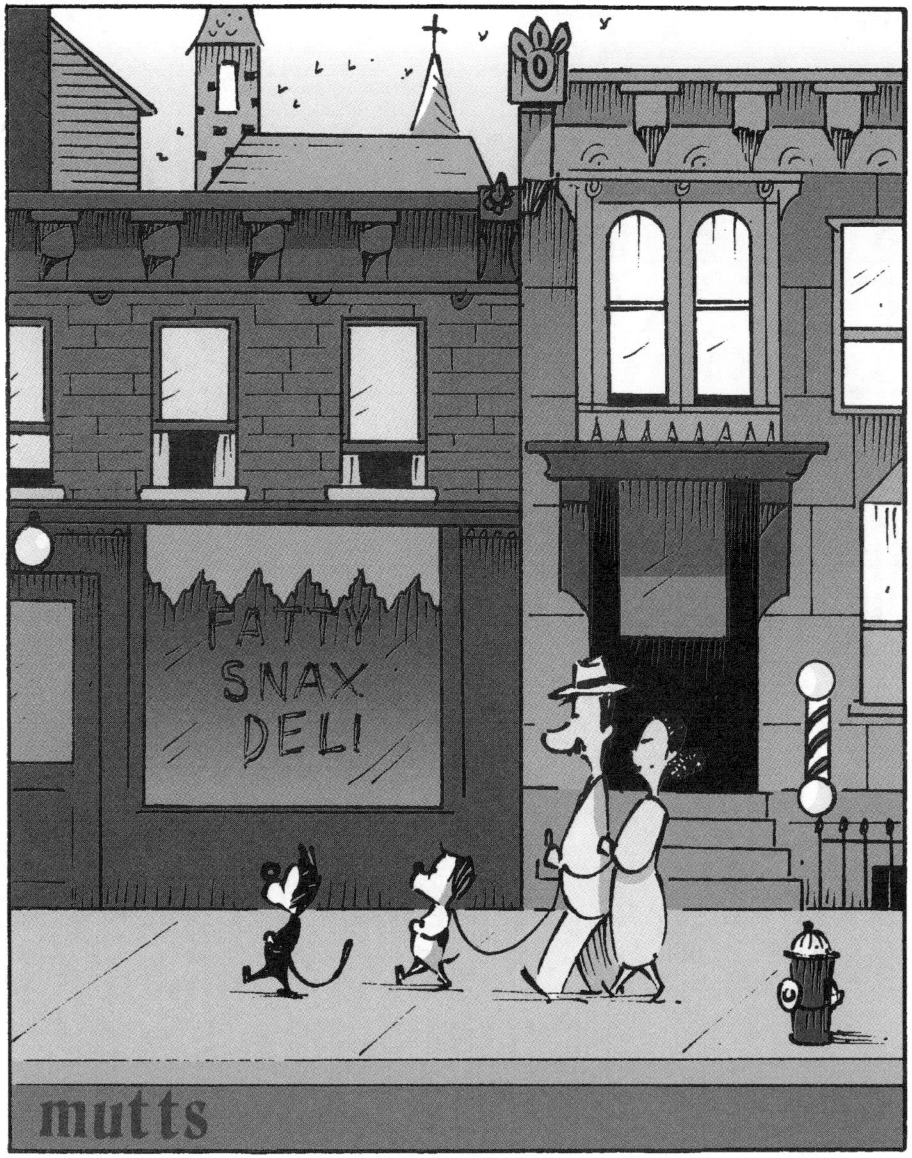
FATTY SNAX DELI
mutts

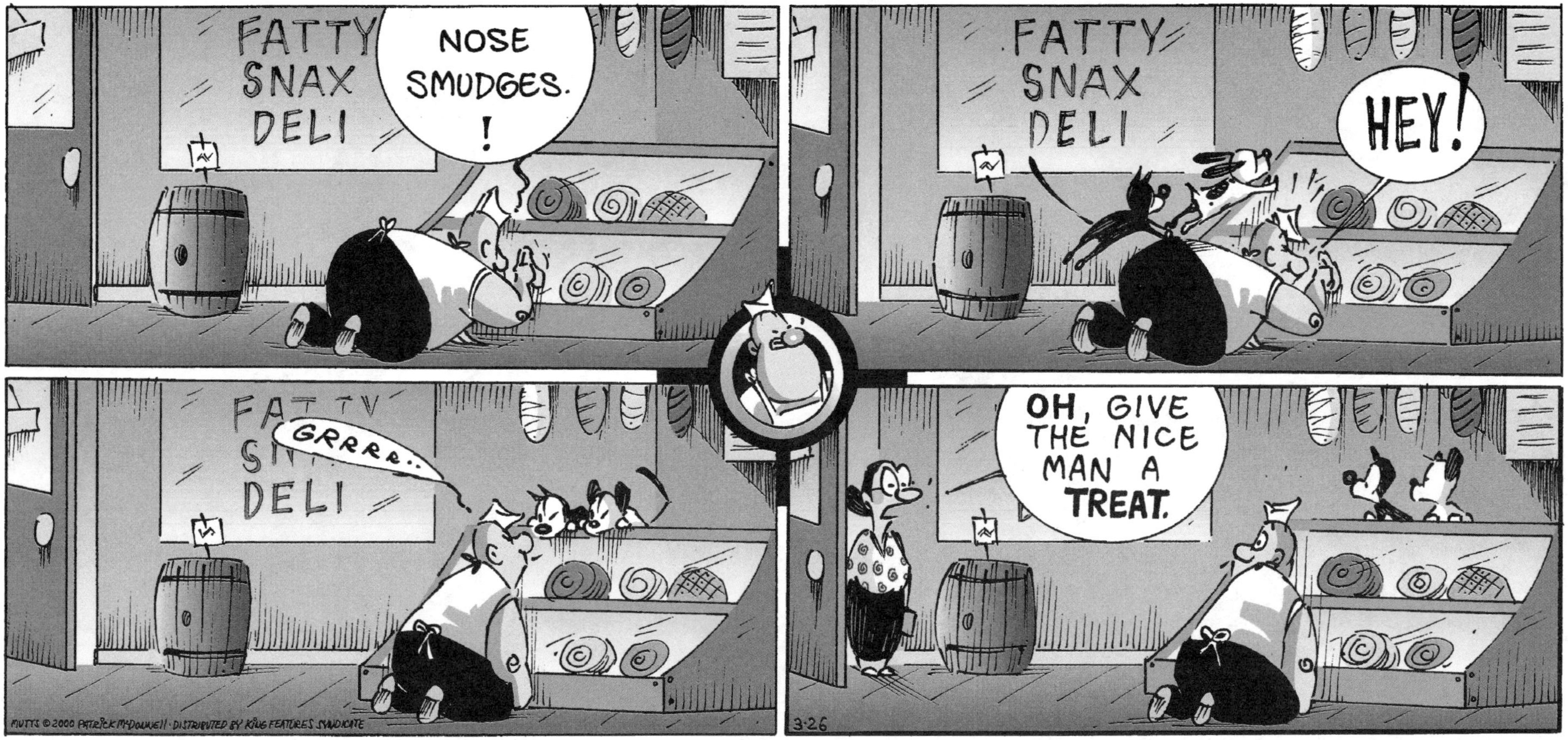
FATTY SNAX DELI
NOSE SMUDGES.
!
FATTY SNAX DELI
HEY!
DELI
GRRRR..
OH, GIVE THE NICE MAN A TREAT.
MUTTS © 2000 PATRICK McDONNELL · DISTRIBUTED BY KING FEATURES SYNDICATE
3·26

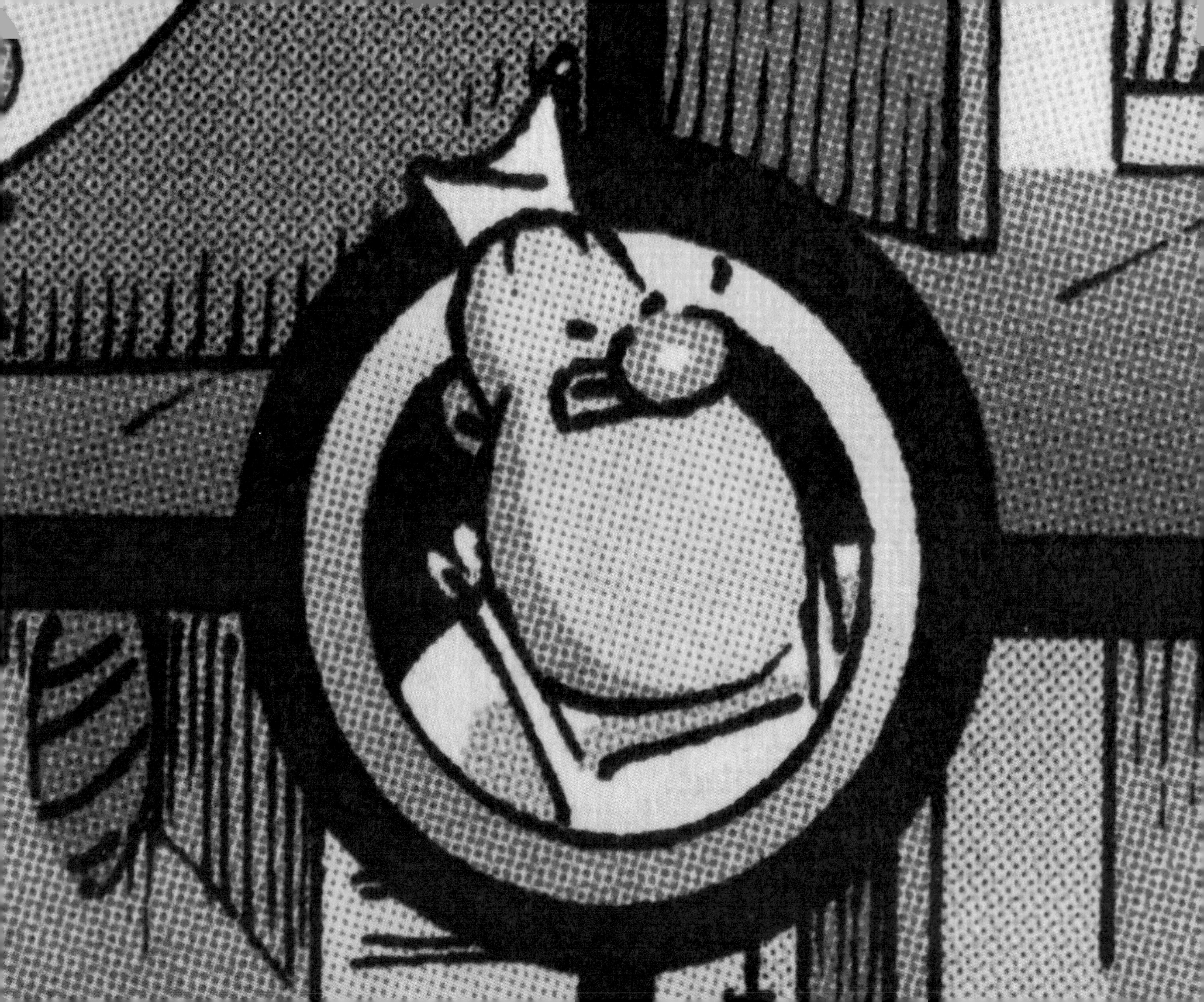

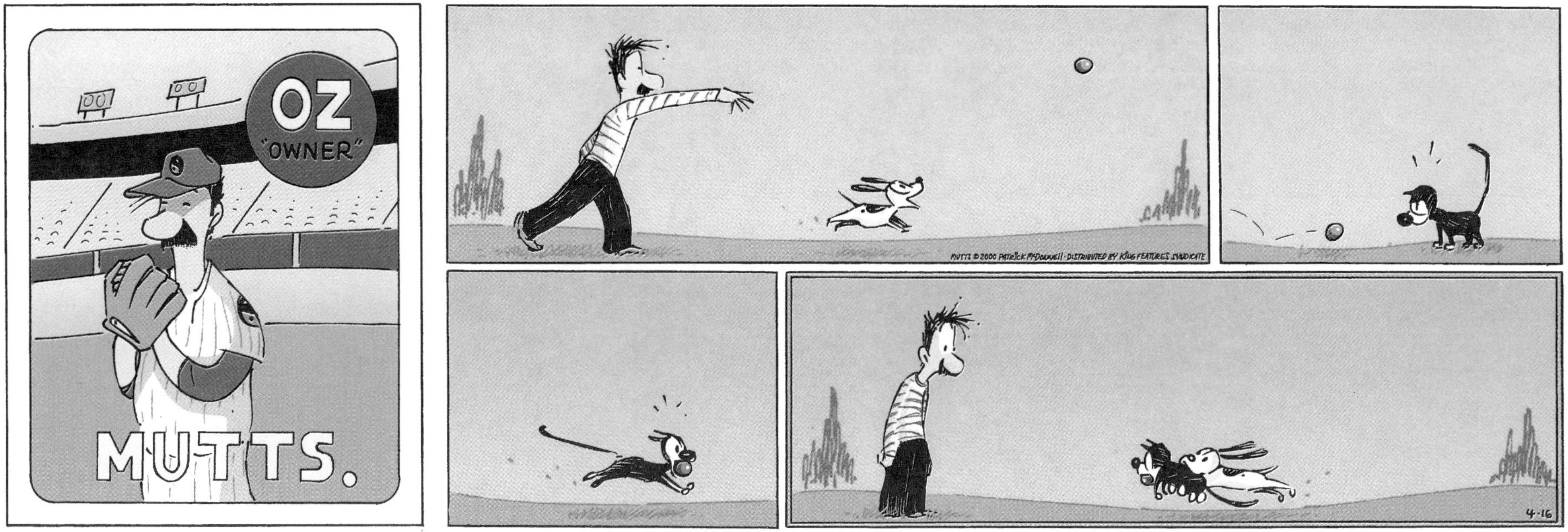
OZ
"OWNER"
MUTTS.
MUTTS © 2000 PATRICK McDONNELL · DISTRIBUTED BY KING FEATURES SYNDICATE
4·16

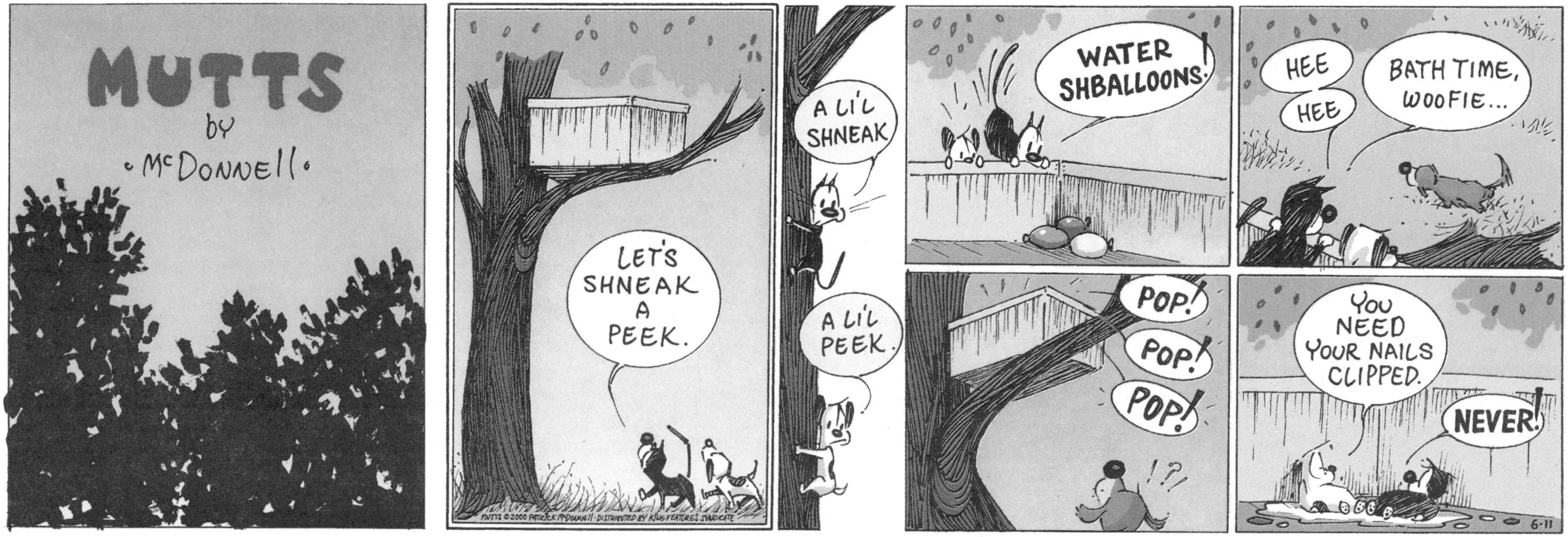
MUTTS
by
McDONNELL
LET'S SHNEAK A PEEK.
A LI'L SHNEAK
A LI'L PEEK.
WATER SHBALLOONS!
HEE
HEE
BATH TIME, WOOFIE...
POP!
POP!
POP!
!?
YOU NEED YOUR NAILS CLIPPED.
NEVER!
MUTTS © 2000 PATRICK McDONNELL · DISTRIBUTED BY KING FEATURES SYNDICATE
6·11

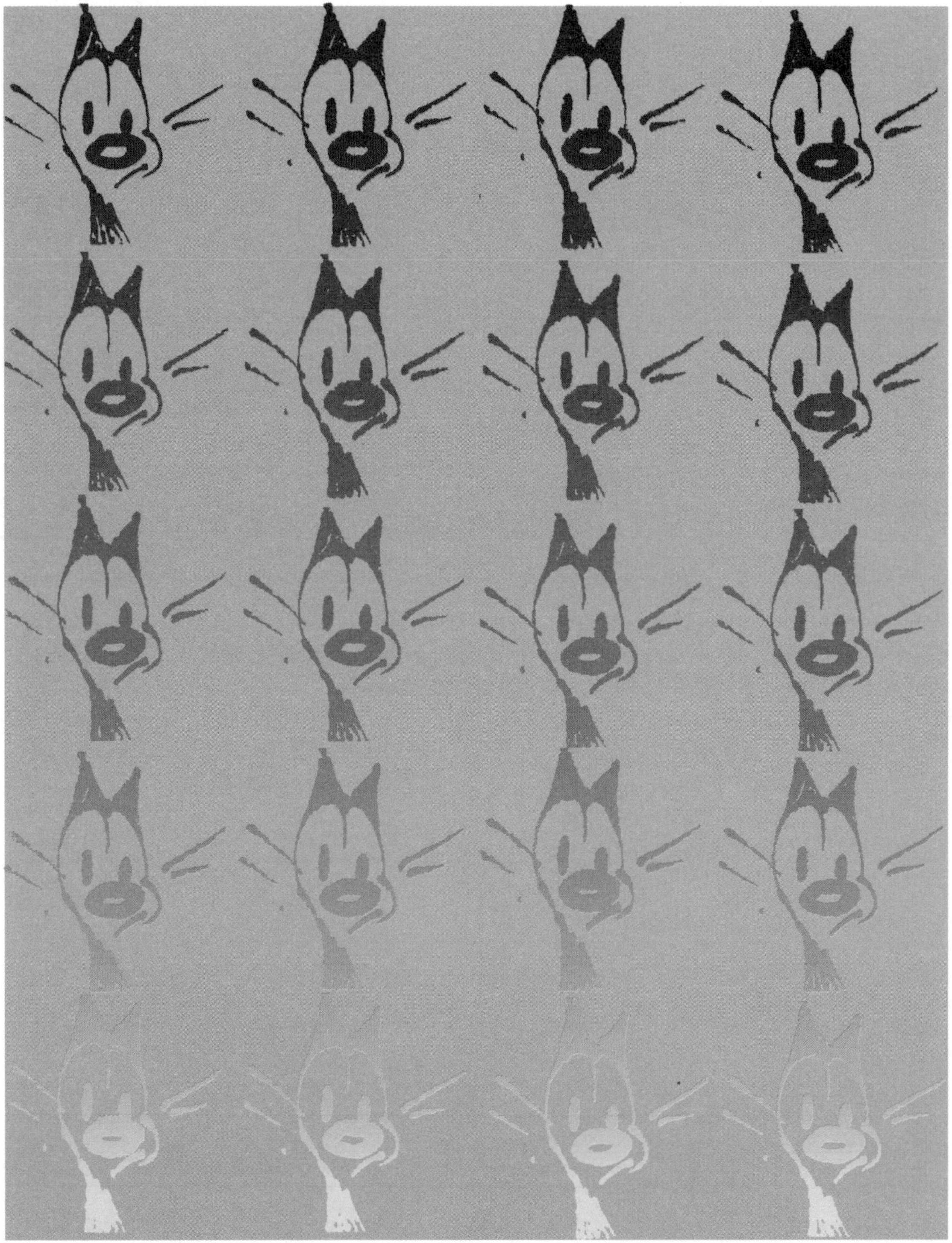

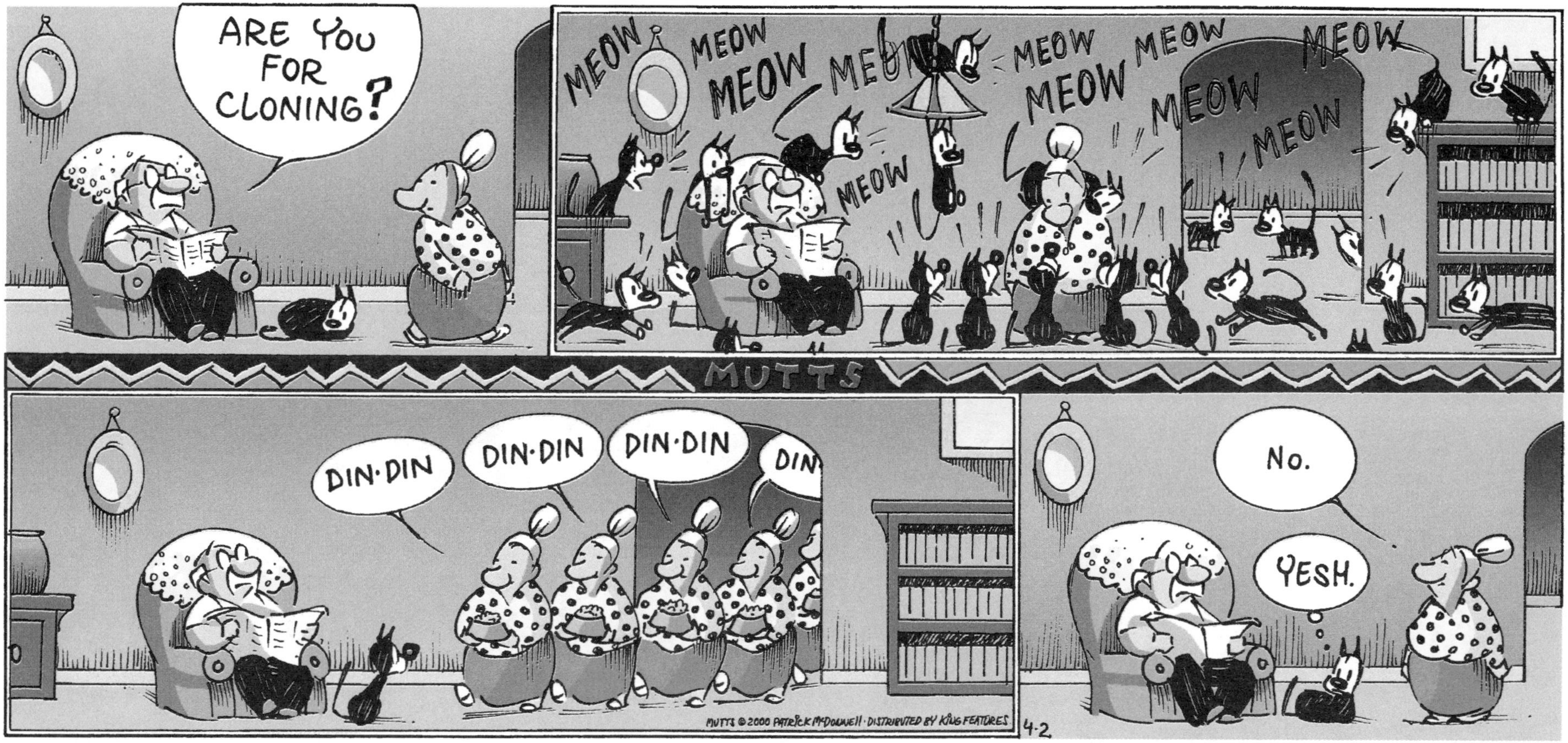
ARE YOU FOR CLONING?
MEOW
MEOW
MEOW
MEOW
MEOW
MEOW
MEOW
MEOW
MEOW
MEOW
MEOW
MUTTS
DIN·DIN
DIN·DIN
DIN·DIN
MUTTS © 2000 PATRICK McDONNELL · DISTRIBUTED BY KING FEATURES
4·2
No.
YESH.

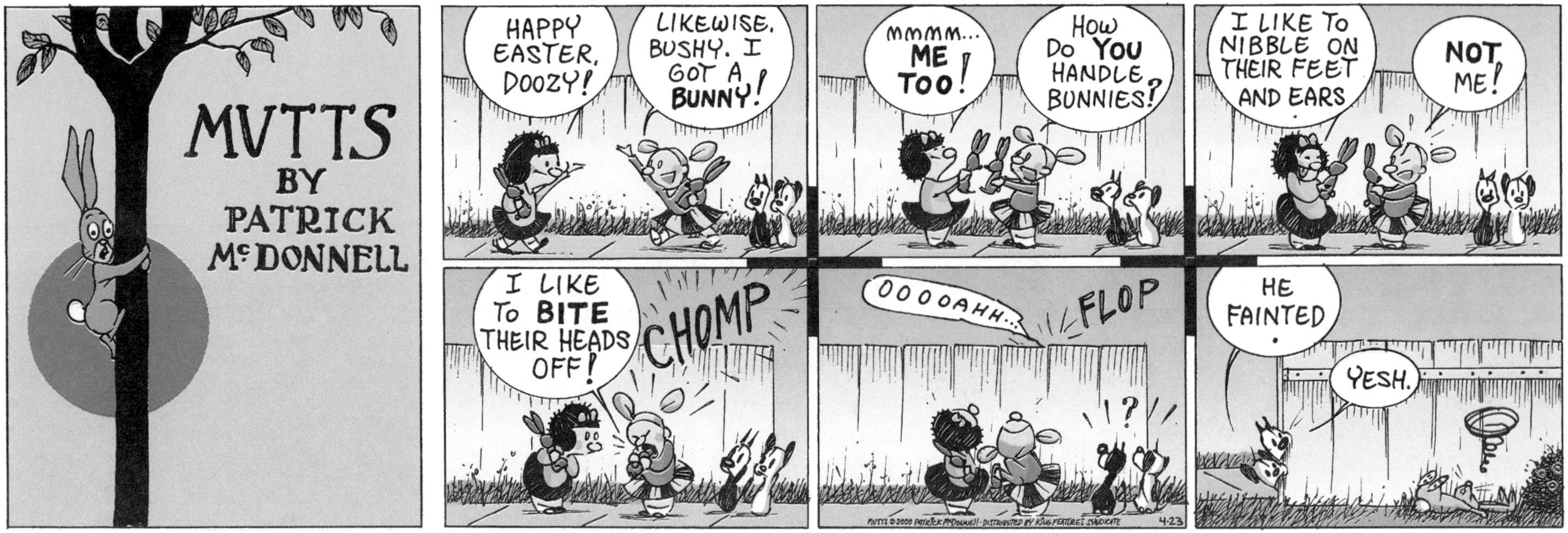
MUTTS
BY
PATRICK
McDONNELL
HAPPY EASTER, DOOZY!
LIKEWISE, BUSHY. I GOT A BUNNY!
MMMM... ME TOO!
HOW DO YOU HANDLE BUNNIES?
I LIKE TO NIBBLE ON THEIR FEET AND EARS.
NOT ME!
I LIKE TO BITE THEIR HEADS OFF!
CHOMP
OOOOAHH...
FLOP
?
HE FAINTED.
YESH.
MUTTS © 2000 PATRICK McDONNELL · DISTRIBUTED BY KING FEATURES SYNDICATE
4·23

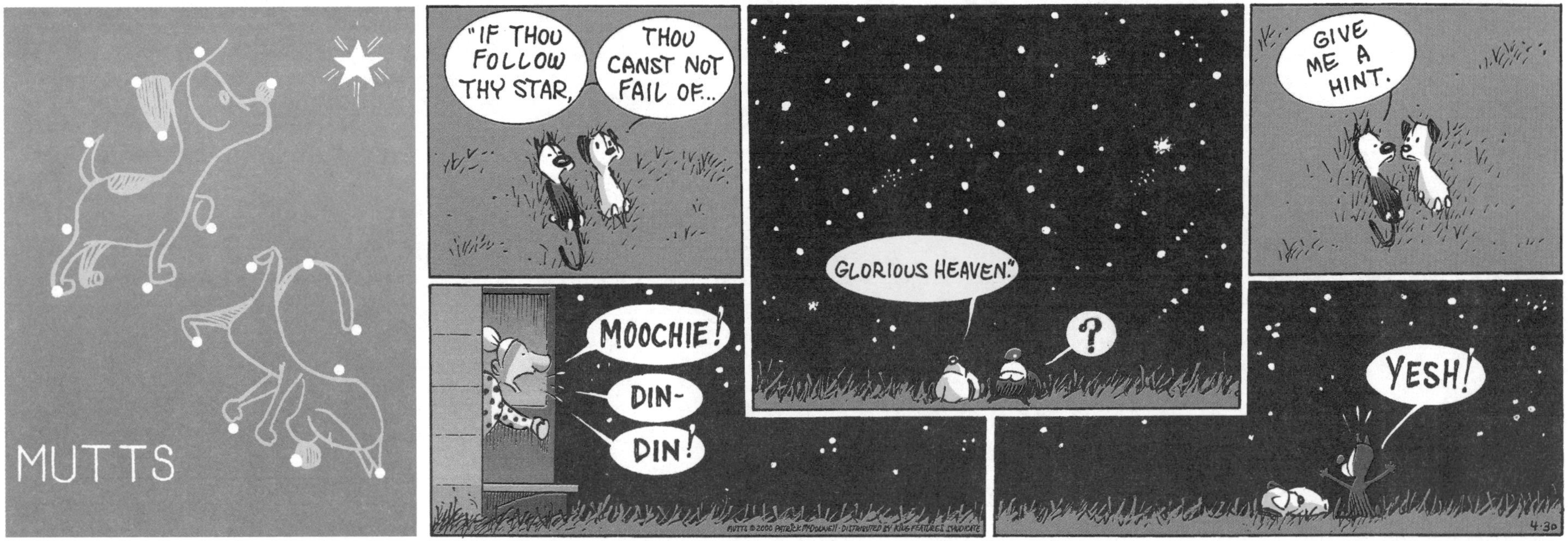
MUTTS
"IF THOU FOLLOW THY STAR,
THOU CANST NOT FAIL OF...
GLORIOUS HEAVEN."
?
GIVE ME A HINT.
MOOCHIE!
DIN-
DIN!
YESH!
MUTTS © 2000 PATRICK McDONNELL · DISTRIBUTED BY KING FEATURES SYNDICATE
4·30

Since 1994
Mutts
YESH!
COMICS
by McDONNELL

BREAKFAST TIME!
WHAT'S TODAY'S SHPECIAL?
MMMM... NICE VIEW.
CAN YOU SEND UP A TREAT TO THE GUEST ROOM!
LITTER CLEANED DAILY...
FLUFF IT UP THE WAY I LIKE IT.
I FEEL LIKE I RUN THE "MEOW" HOTEL.
MUTTS © 2000 PATRICK McDONNELL · DISTRIBUTED BY KING FEATURES SYNDICATE 6·25

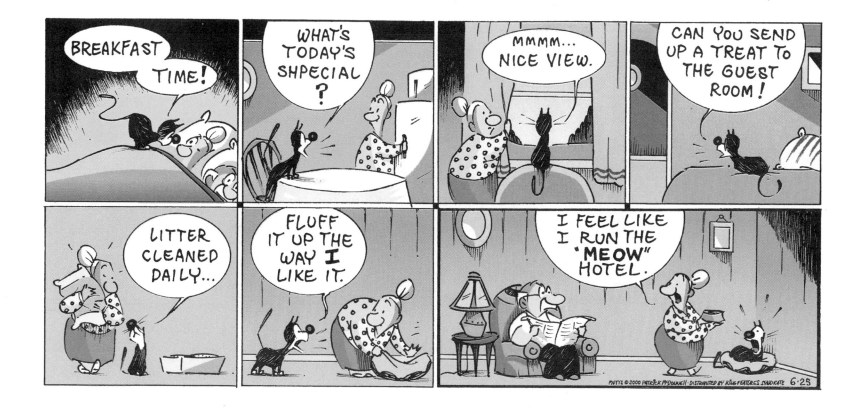

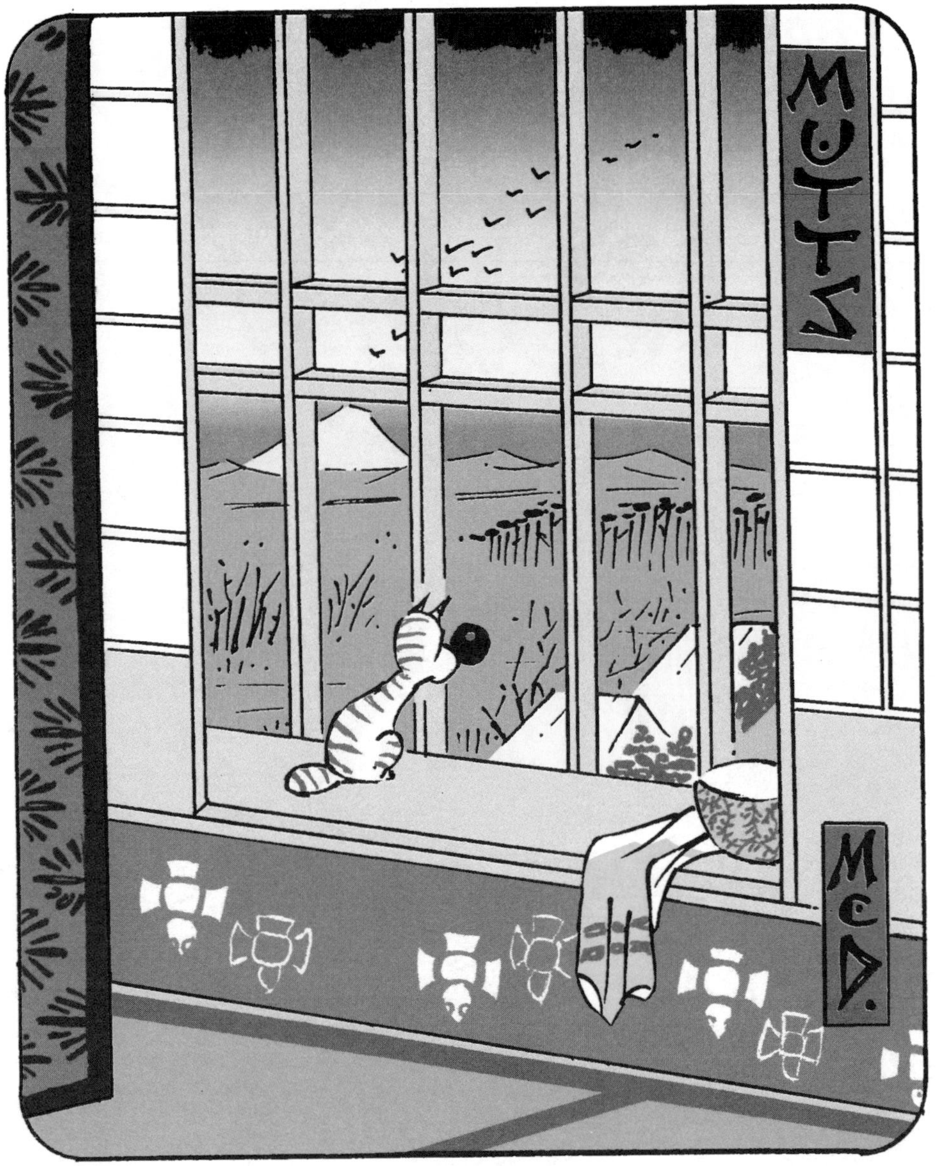
MUTTS
MCD.

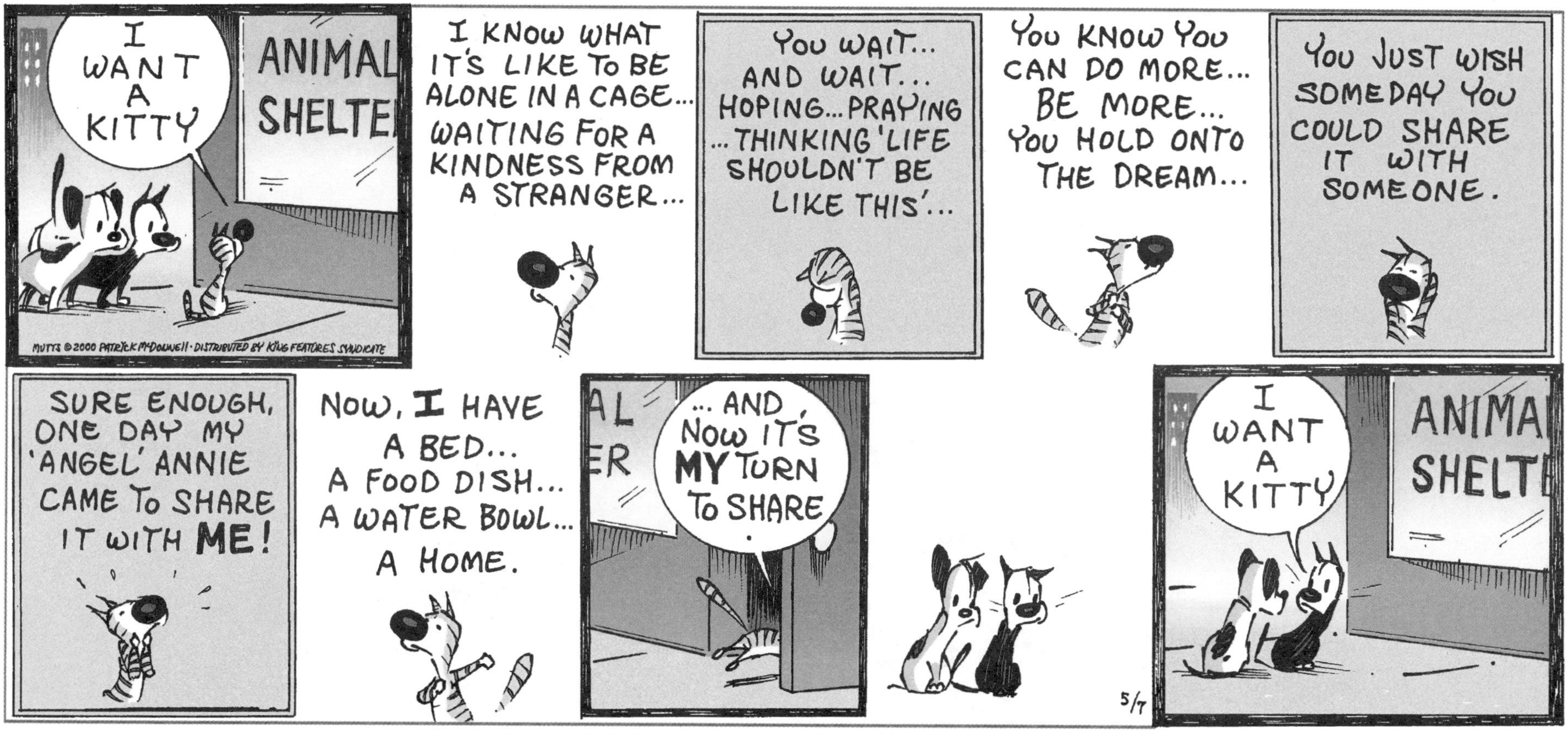
I WANT A KITTY
ANIMAL SHELTE
MUTTS © 2000 PATRICK McDONNELL · DISTRIBUTED BY KING FEATURES SYNDICATE
I KNOW WHAT IT'S LIKE TO BE ALONE IN A CAGE... WAITING FOR A KINDNESS FROM A STRANGER...
YOU WAIT... AND WAIT... HOPING... PRAYING ...THINKING 'LIFE SHOULDN'T BE LIKE THIS'...
YOU KNOW YOU CAN DO MORE... BE MORE... YOU HOLD ONTO THE DREAM...
YOU JUST WISH SOMEDAY YOU COULD SHARE IT WITH SOMEONE.
SURE ENOUGH, ONE DAY MY 'ANGEL' ANNIE CAME TO SHARE IT WITH ME!
NOW, I HAVE A BED... A FOOD DISH... A WATER BOWL... A HOME.
...AND NOW IT'S MY TURN TO SHARE.
5/7
I WANT A KITTY
ANIMA SHELTE

MUTTS
COMICUS STRIPUS

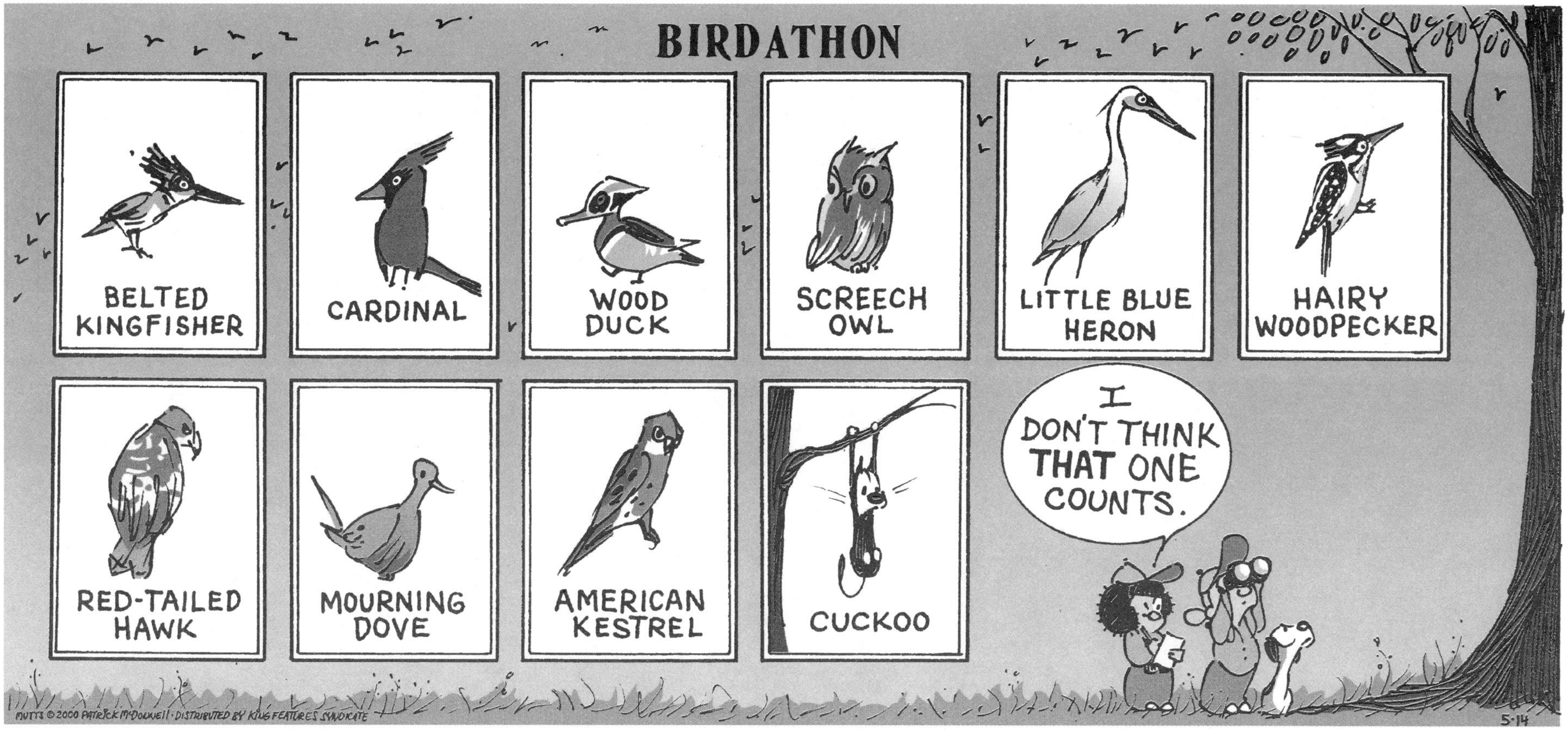
BIRDATHON
BELTED KINGFISHER
CARDINAL
WOOD DUCK
SCREECH OWL
LITTLE BLUE HERON
HAIRY WOODPECKER
RED-TAILED HAWK
MOURNING DOVE
AMERICAN KESTREL
CUCKOO
I DON'T THINK THAT ONE COUNTS.
MUTTS © 2000 PATRICK McDONNELL · DISTRIBUTED BY KING FEATURES SYNDICATE
5·14

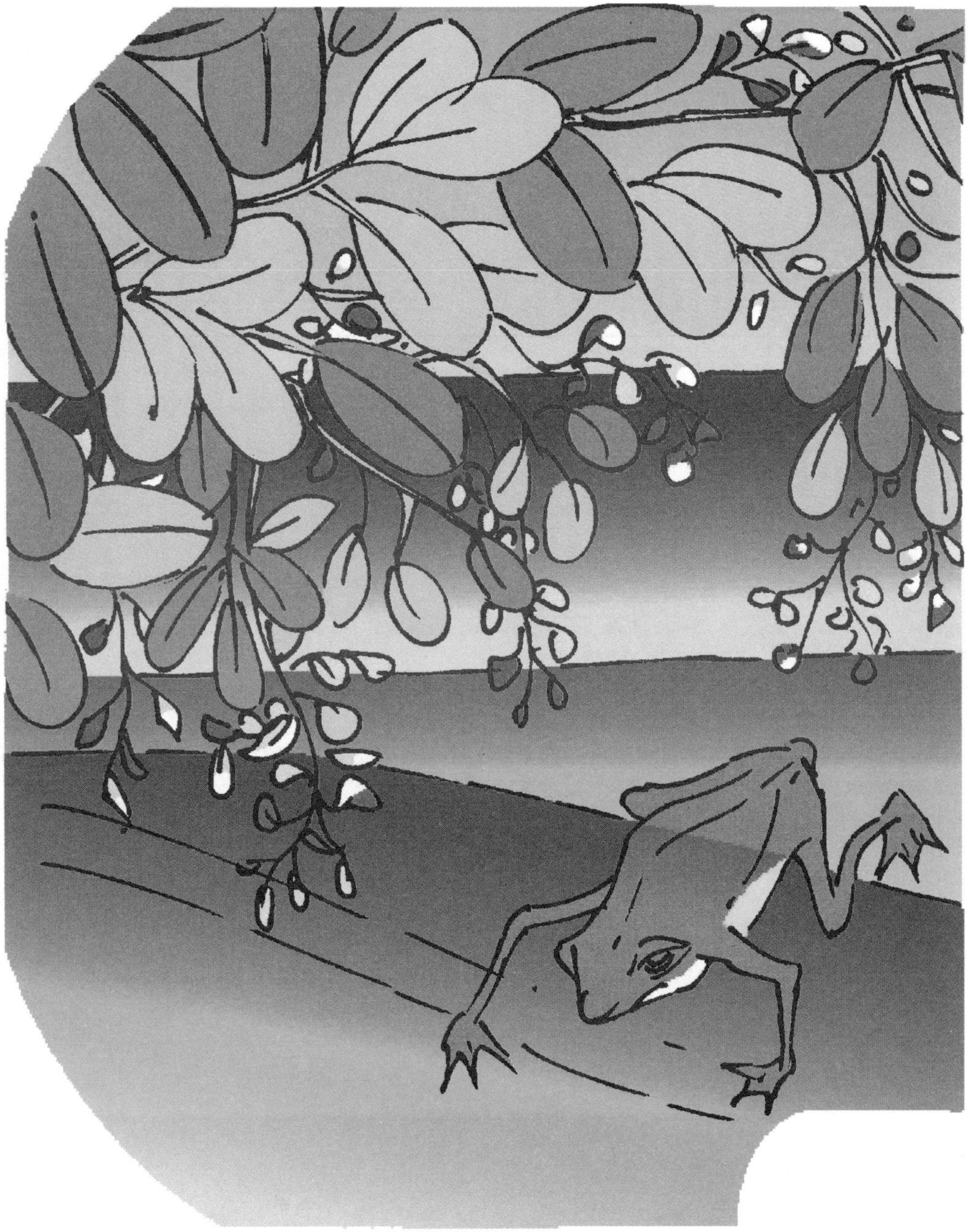

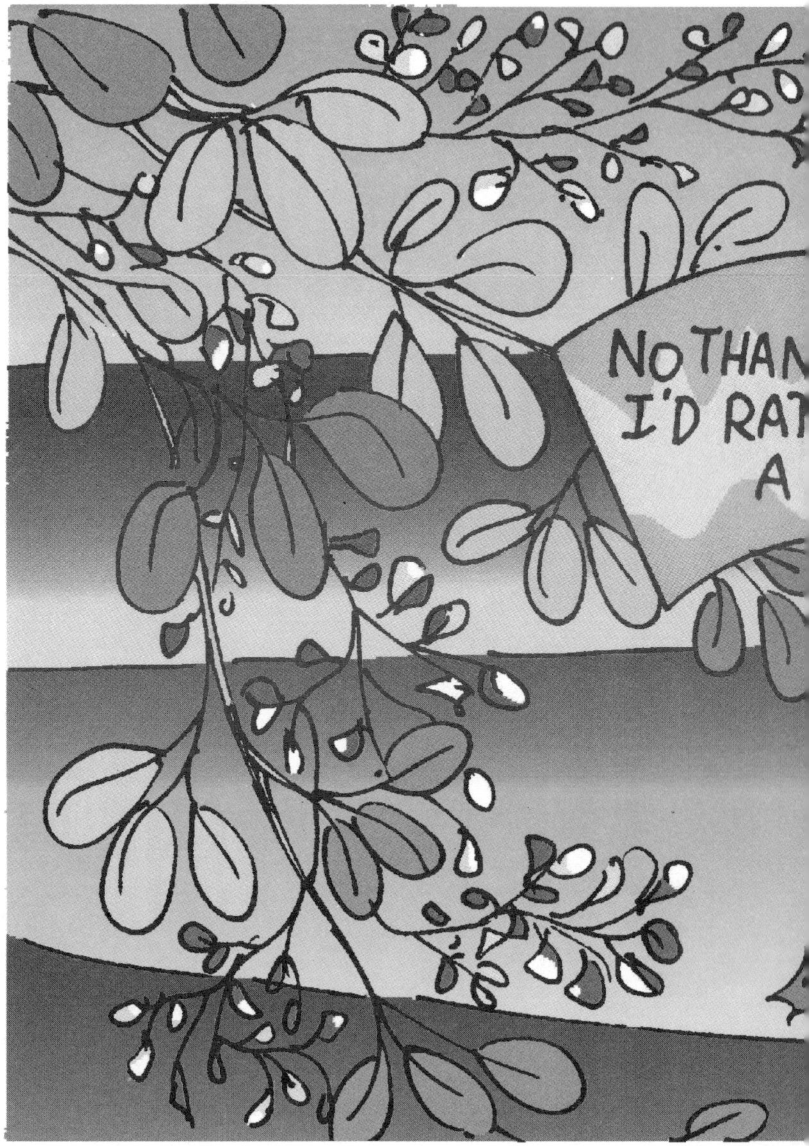
NO THAN
I'D RAT
A

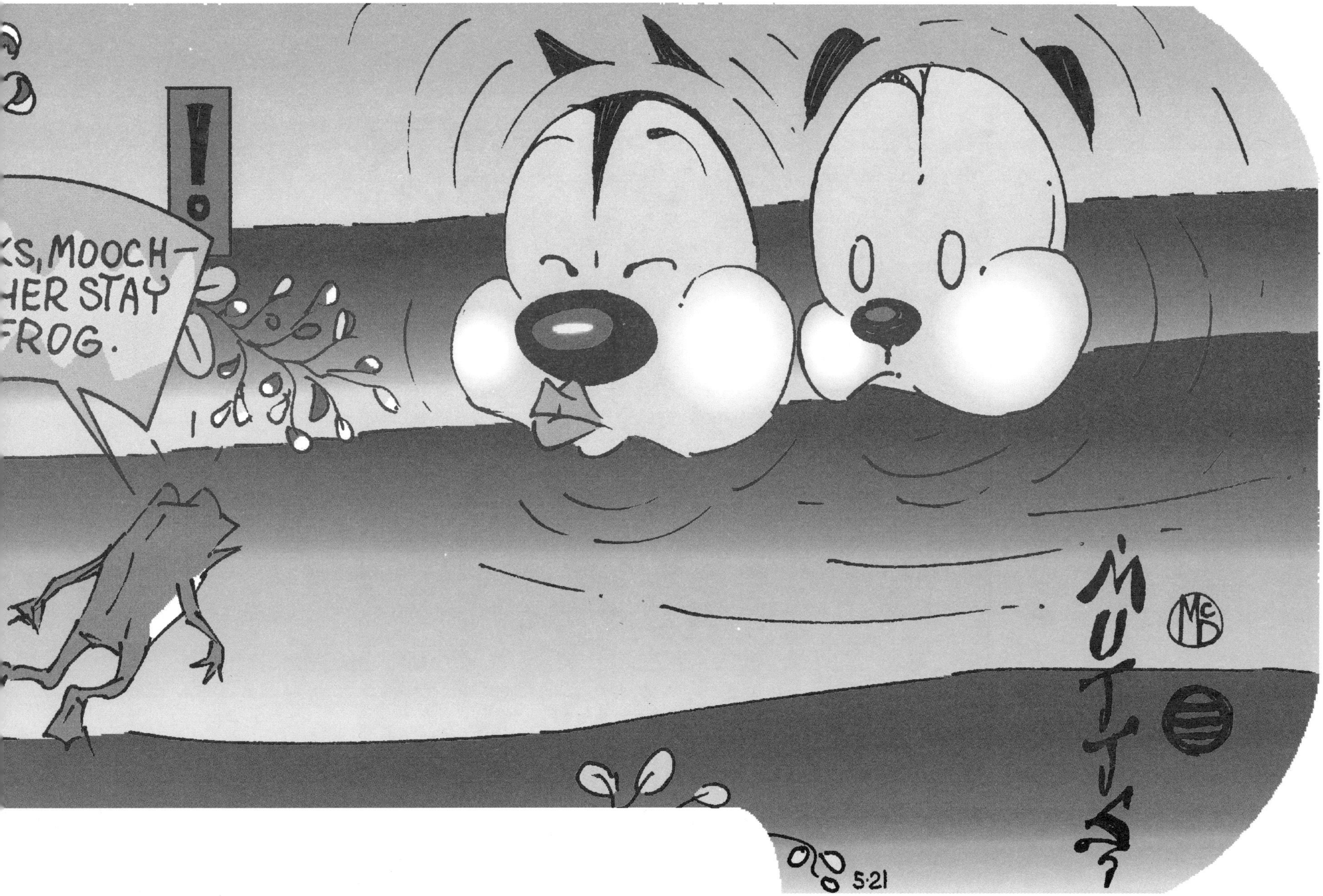

!
KS, MOOCH—
HER STAY
FROG.
MUTTS
5·21

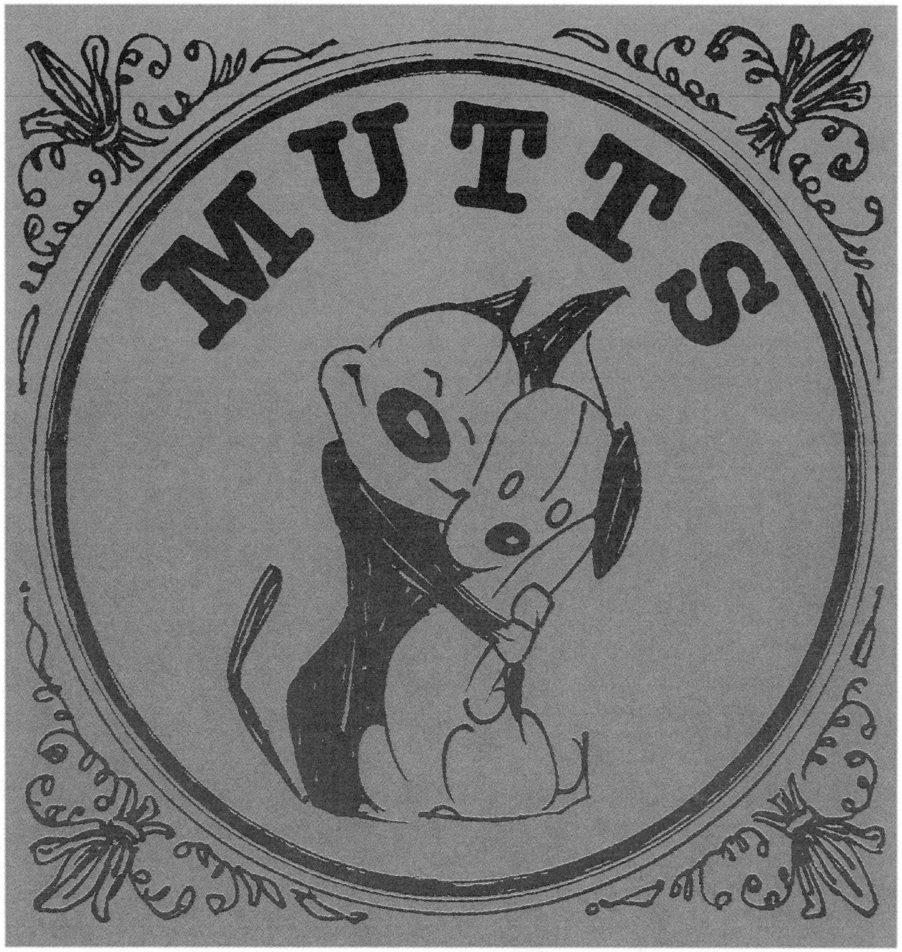
MUTTS

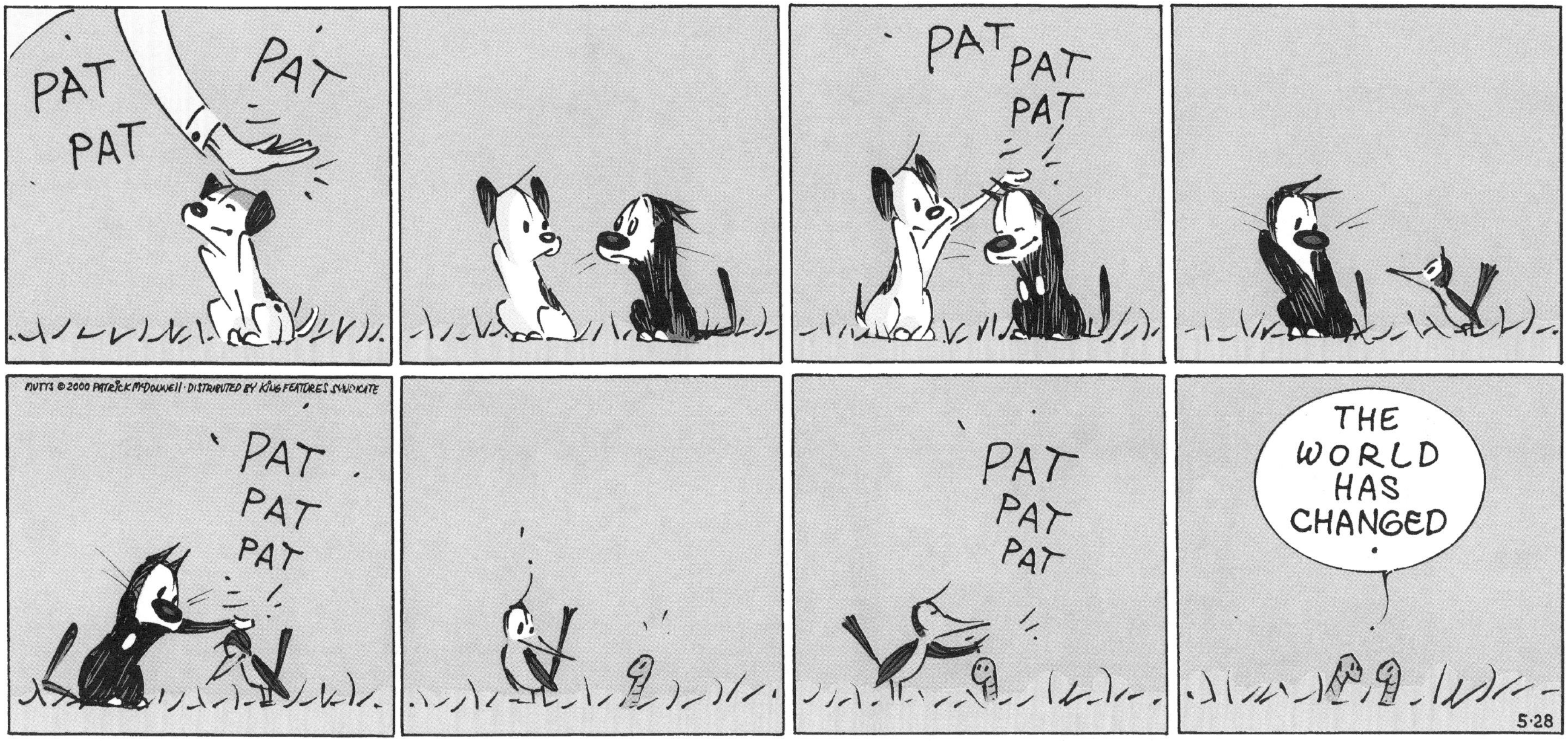
PAT
PAT
PAT
PAT
PAT
PAT
MUTTS © 2000 PATRICK McDONNELL · DISTRIBUTED BY KING FEATURES SYNDICATE
PAT
PAT
PAT
PAT
PAT
PAT
THE WORLD HAS CHANGED.
5·28

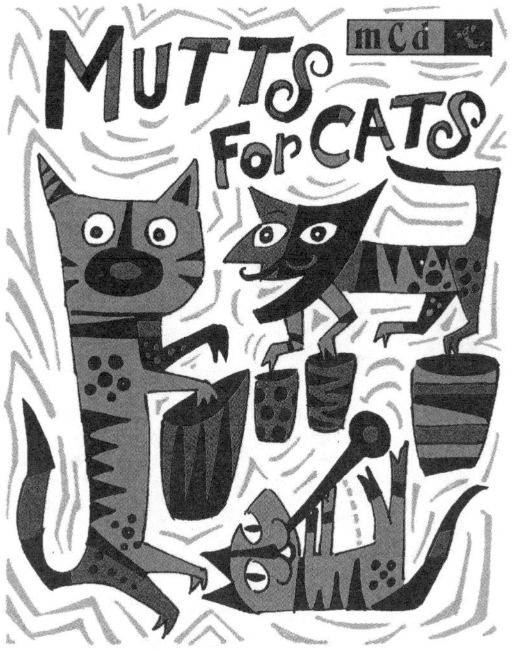
mCd
MUTTS
For CATS

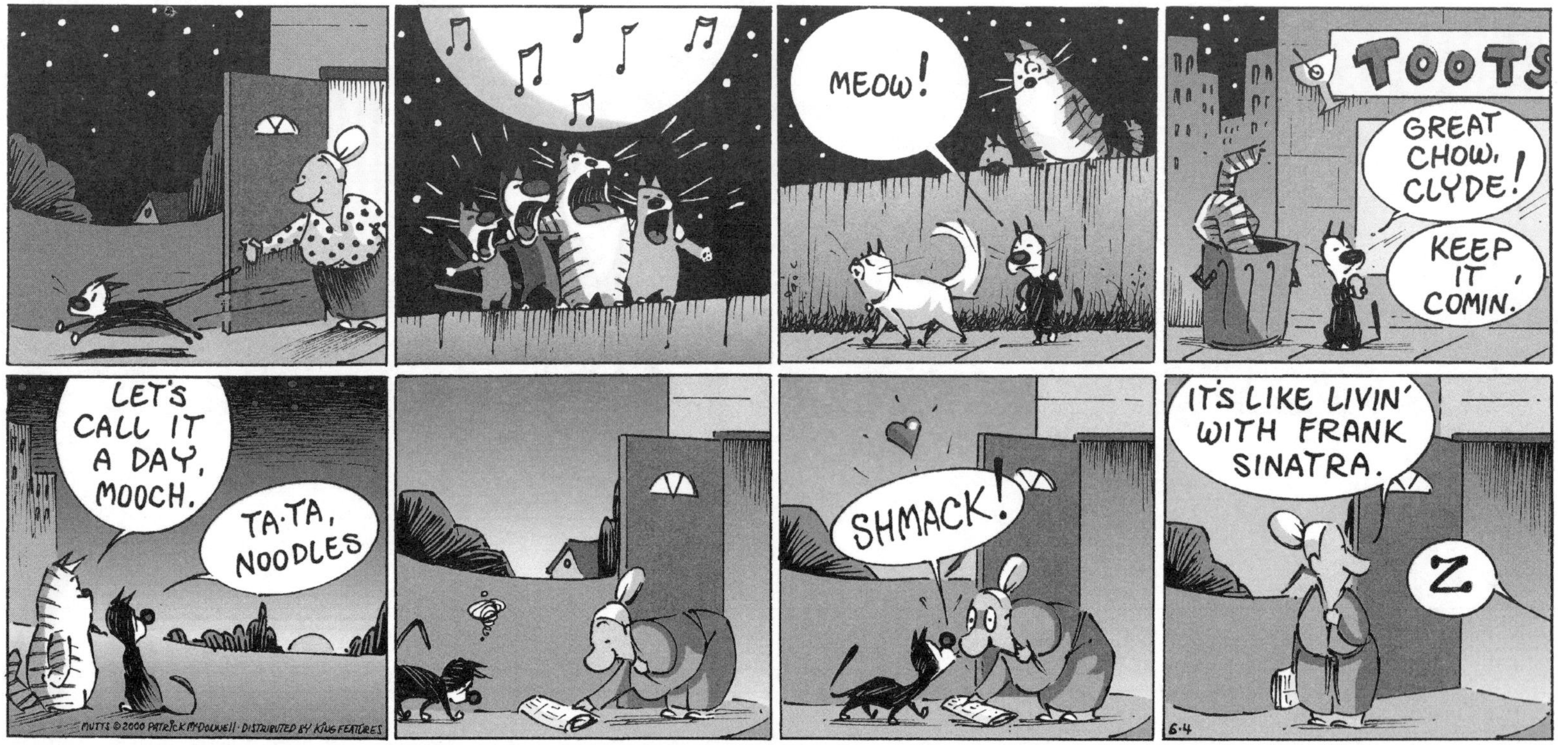
MEOW!
TOOTS
GREAT CHOW, CLYDE!
KEEP IT COMIN'.
LET'S CALL IT A DAY, MOOCH.
TA-TA, NOODLES
SHMACK!
IT'S LIKE LIVIN' WITH FRANK SINATRA.
Z
MUTTS © 2000 PATRICK McDONNELL · DISTRIBUTED BY KING FEATURES
6-4

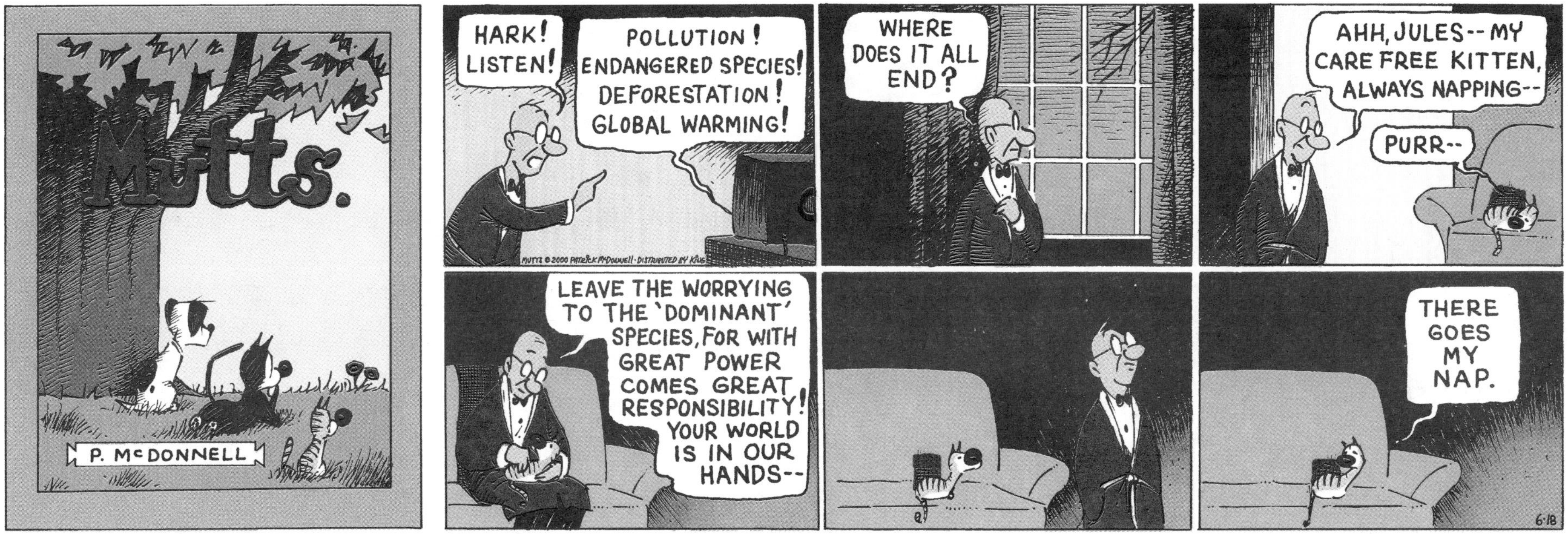
Mutts.
P. McDONNELL
HARK! LISTEN!
POLLUTION! ENDANGERED SPECIES! DEFORESTATION! GLOBAL WARMING!
WHERE DOES IT ALL END?
AHH, JULES-- MY CARE FREE KITTEN, ALWAYS NAPPING--
PURR--
LEAVE THE WORRYING TO THE 'DOMINANT' SPECIES, FOR WITH GREAT POWER COMES GREAT RESPONSIBILITY! YOUR WORLD IS IN OUR HANDS--
THERE GOES MY NAP.
6·18

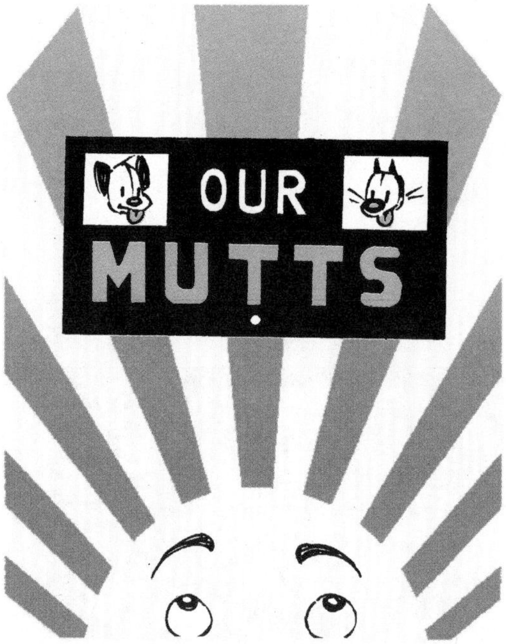
OUR
MUTTS

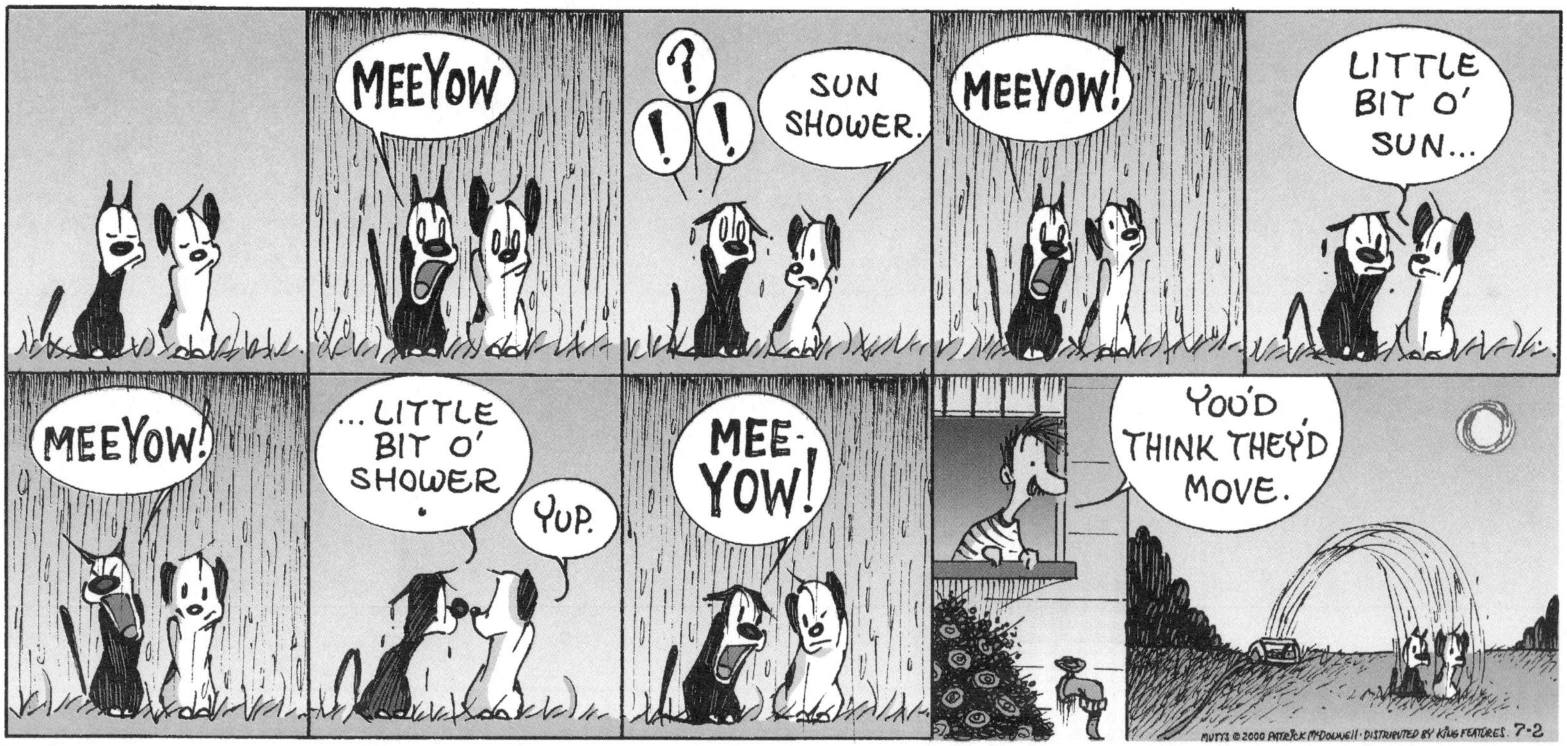
MEEYOW
?
!
!
SUN SHOWER.
MEEYOW!
LITTLE BIT O' SUN...
MEEYOW!
...LITTLE BIT O' SHOWER.
YUP.
MEE-YOW!
YOU'D THINK THEY'D MOVE.
MUTTS © 2000 PATRICK McDONNELL · DISTRIBUTED BY KING FEATURES. 7-2

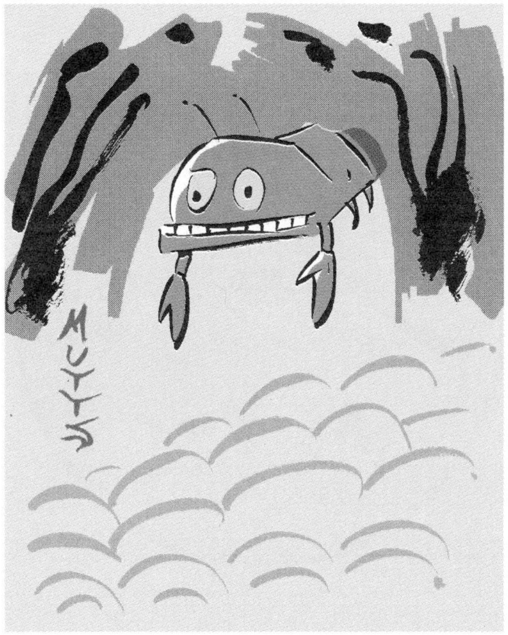
MUTTS

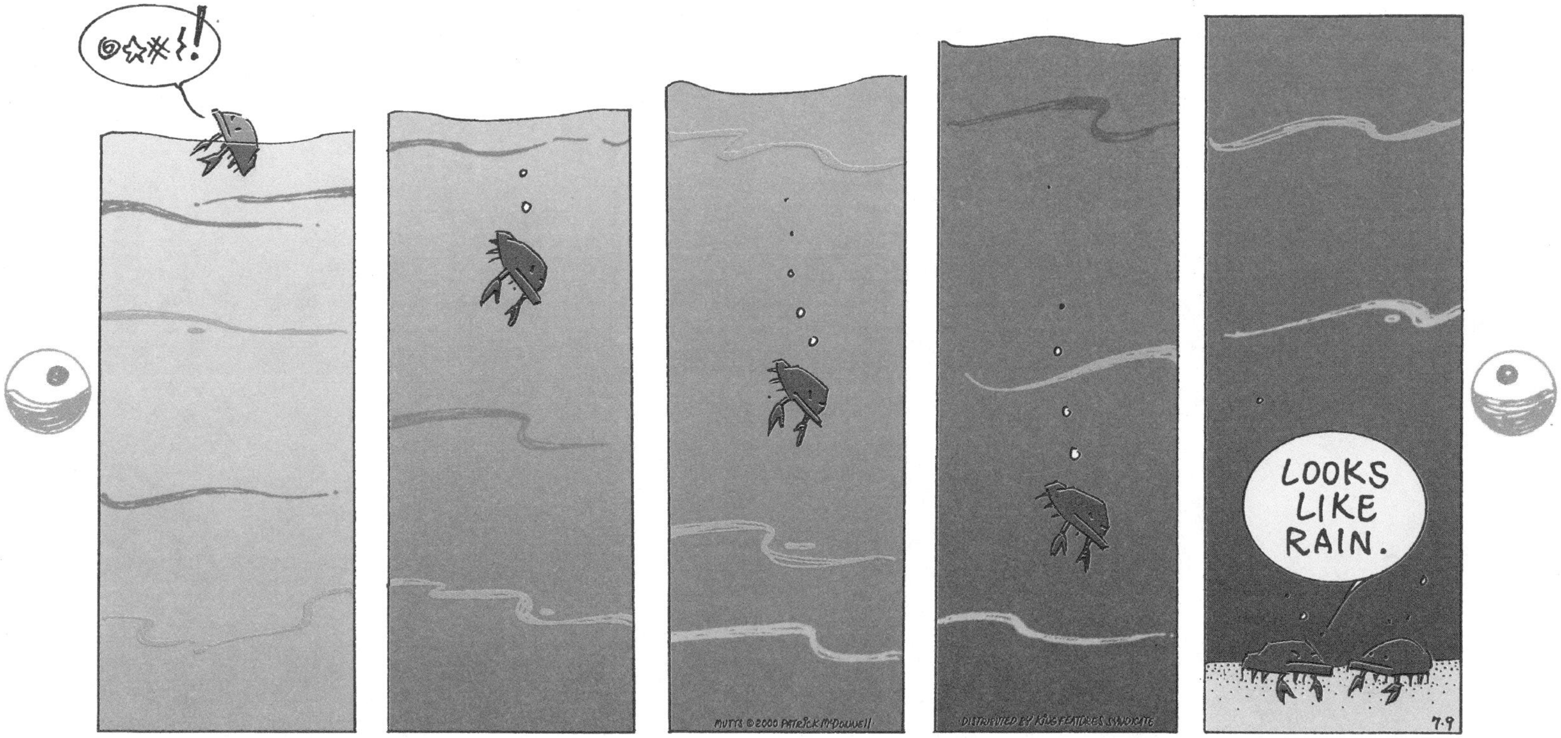
LOOKS LIKE RAIN.
MUTTS © 2000 PATRICK McDONNELL
DISTRIBUTED BY KING FEATURES SYNDICATE
7-9

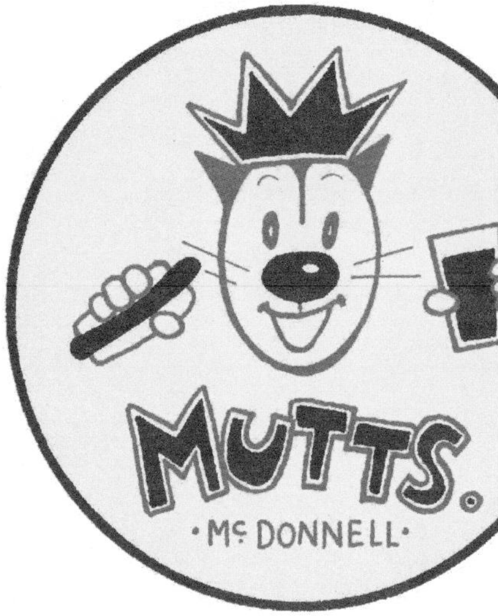
MUTTS.
·McDONNELL·

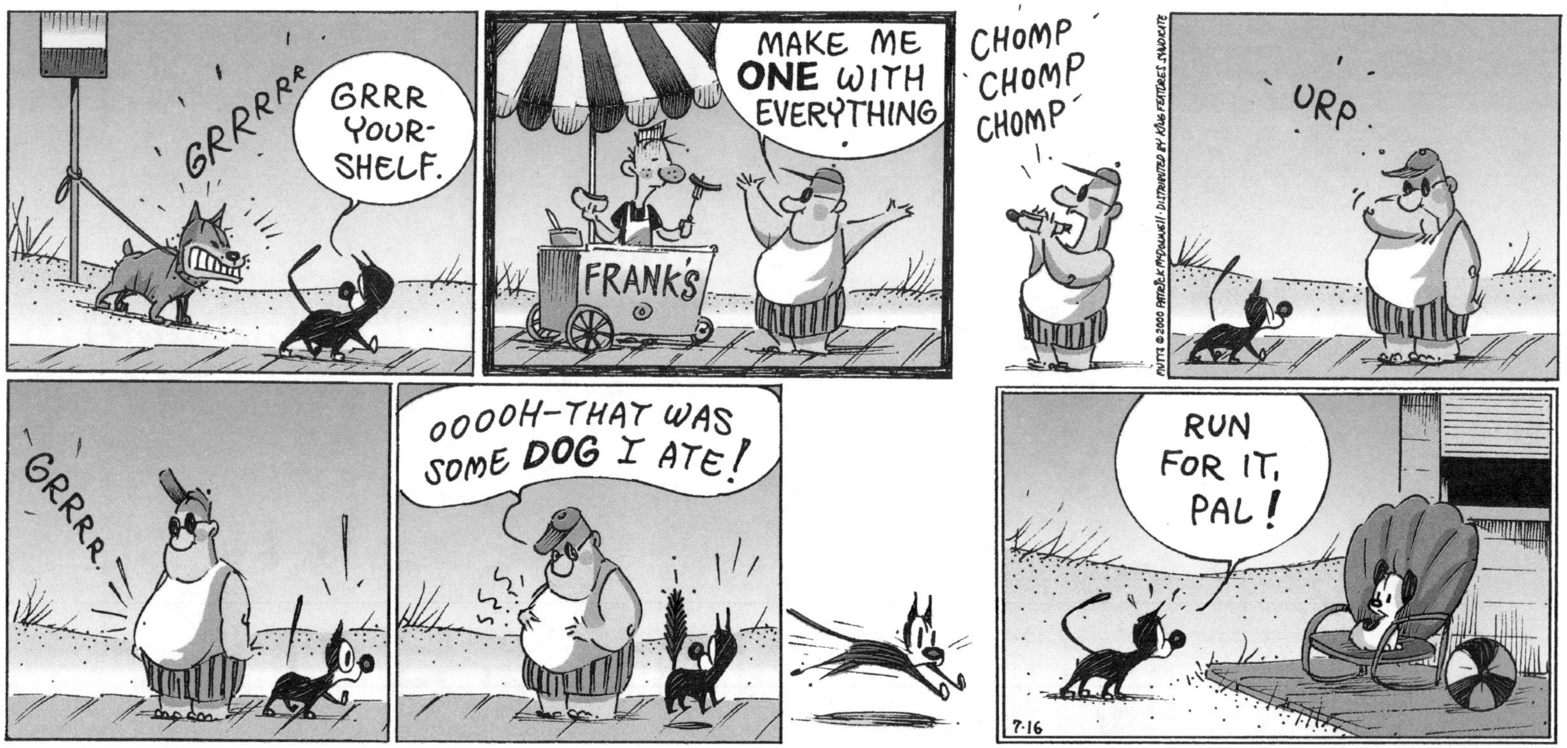
GRRRRR
GRRR YOUR-SHELF.
FRANK'S
MAKE ME ONE WITH EVERYTHING.
CHOMP CHOMP CHOMP
MUTTS © 2000 PATRICK McDONNELL · DISTRIBUTED BY KING FEATURES SYNDICATE
URP
GRRRR
OOOOH–THAT WAS SOME DOG I ATE!
RUN FOR IT, PAL!
7·16

900
001
101
301
910
011
111
311
930
031
131
331
950
051
151
351
970
071
171
371
m
u
tt
s

I'M GOING TO CUDDLE WITH A CUTTLE-FISH.
7·23
THEY COMMUNICATE BY CHANGING **COLOR**!
SLAP
MUST'VE BEEN SHOMETHIN' I SAID.
MUTTS © 2000 PATRICK McDONNELL · DISTRIBUTED BY KING FEATURES SYNDICATE

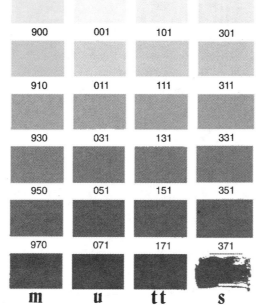

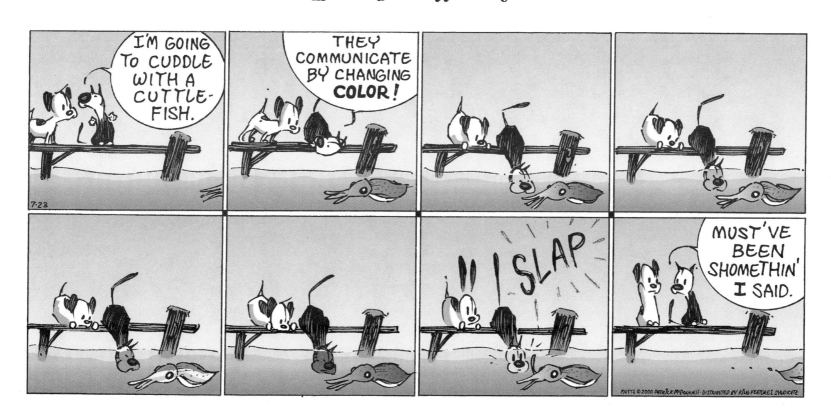

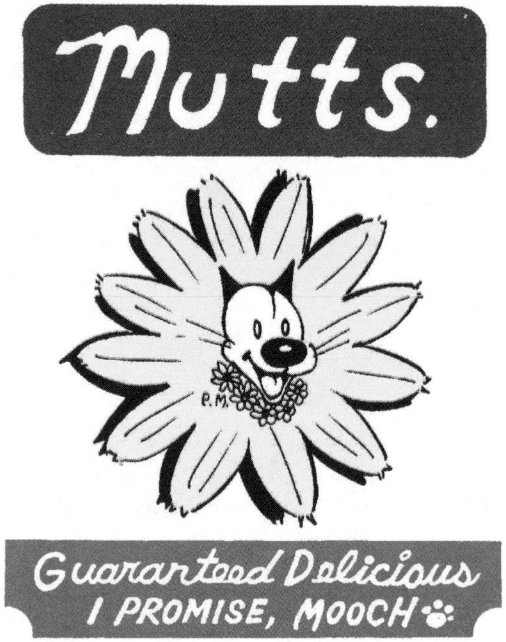
Mutts.
P.M.
Guaranteed Delicious
I PROMISE, MOOCH

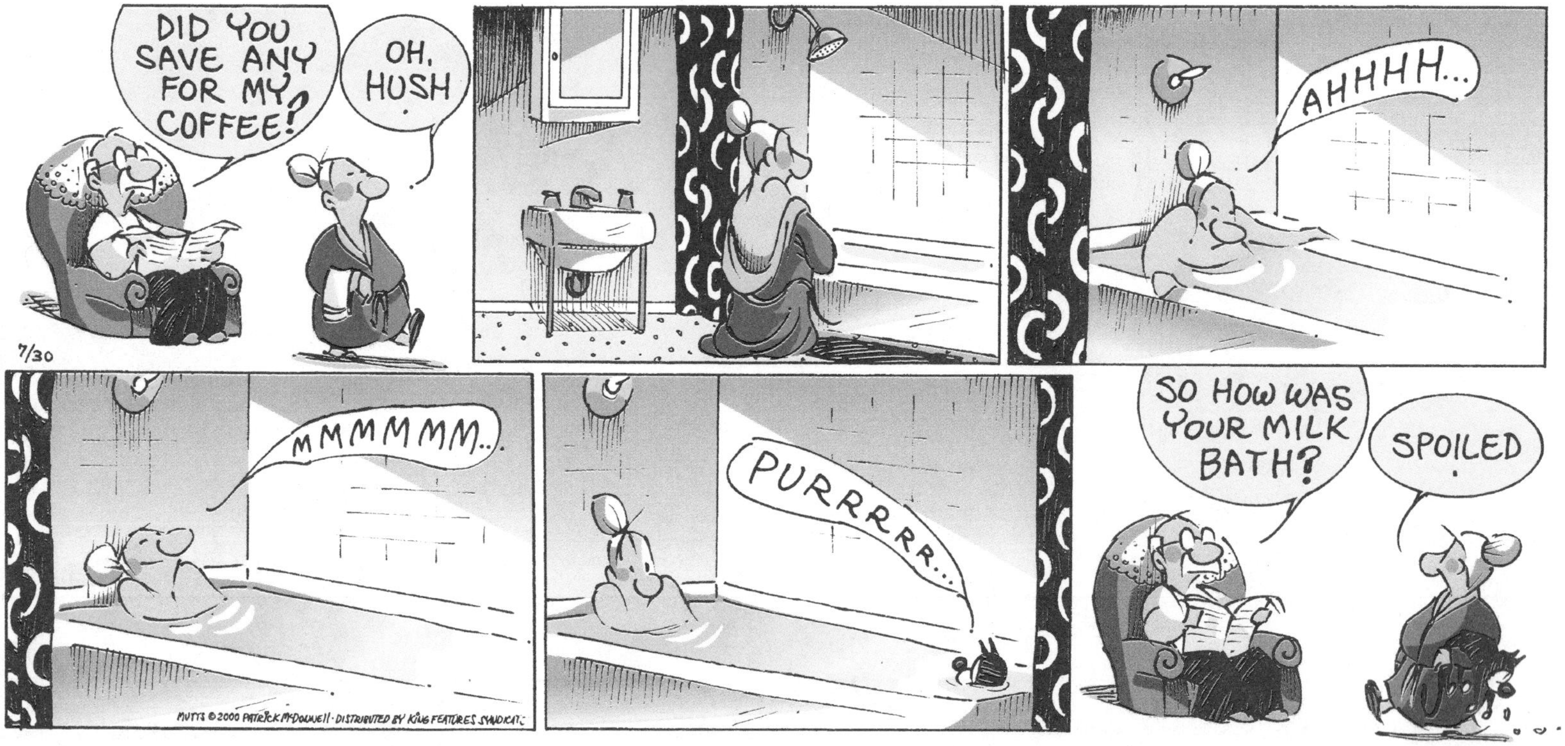
DID YOU SAVE ANY FOR MY COFFEE?
OH, HUSH.
7/30
AHHHH...
MMMMMM...
PURRRRRR...
MUTTS © 2000 PATRICK McDONNELL · DISTRIBUTED BY KING FEATURES SYNDICATE
SO HOW WAS YOUR MILK BATH?
SPOILED.

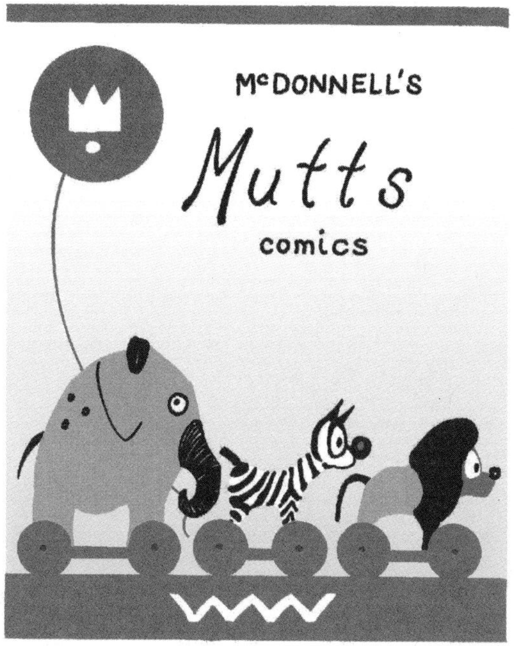
McDONNELL'S
Mutts
comics

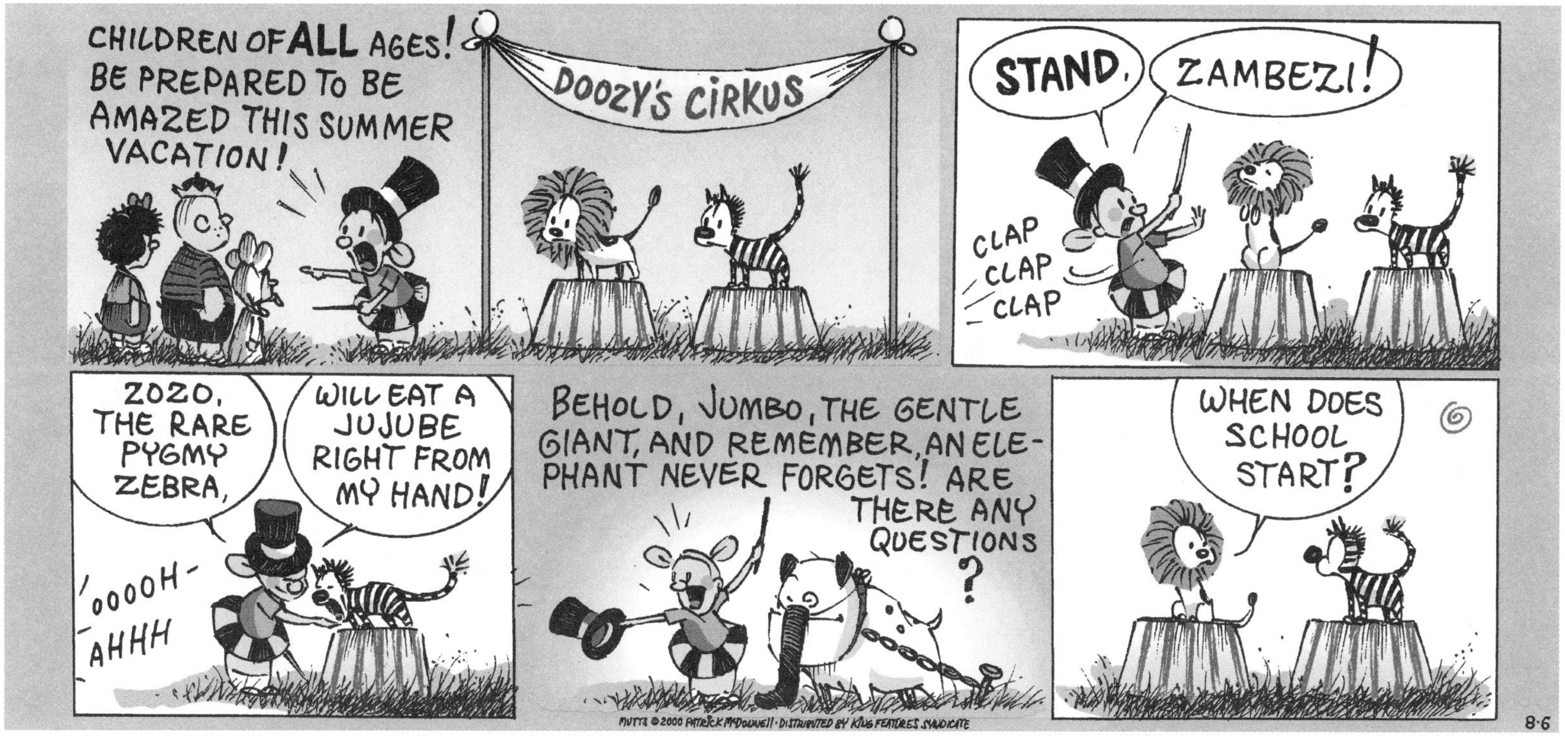
CHILDREN OF ALL AGES! BE PREPARED TO BE AMAZED THIS SUMMER VACATION!
DOOZY'S CIRKUS
STAND,
ZAMBEZI!
CLAP CLAP CLAP
ZOZO, THE RARE PYGMY ZEBRA,
WILL EAT A JUJUBE RIGHT FROM MY HAND!
OOOOH-AHHH
BEHOLD, JUMBO, THE GENTLE GIANT, AND REMEMBER, AN ELE-PHANT NEVER FORGETS! ARE THERE ANY QUESTIONS?
WHEN DOES SCHOOL START?
MUTTS © 2000 PATRICK McDONNELL · DISTRIBUTED BY KING FEATURES SYNDICATE
8·6

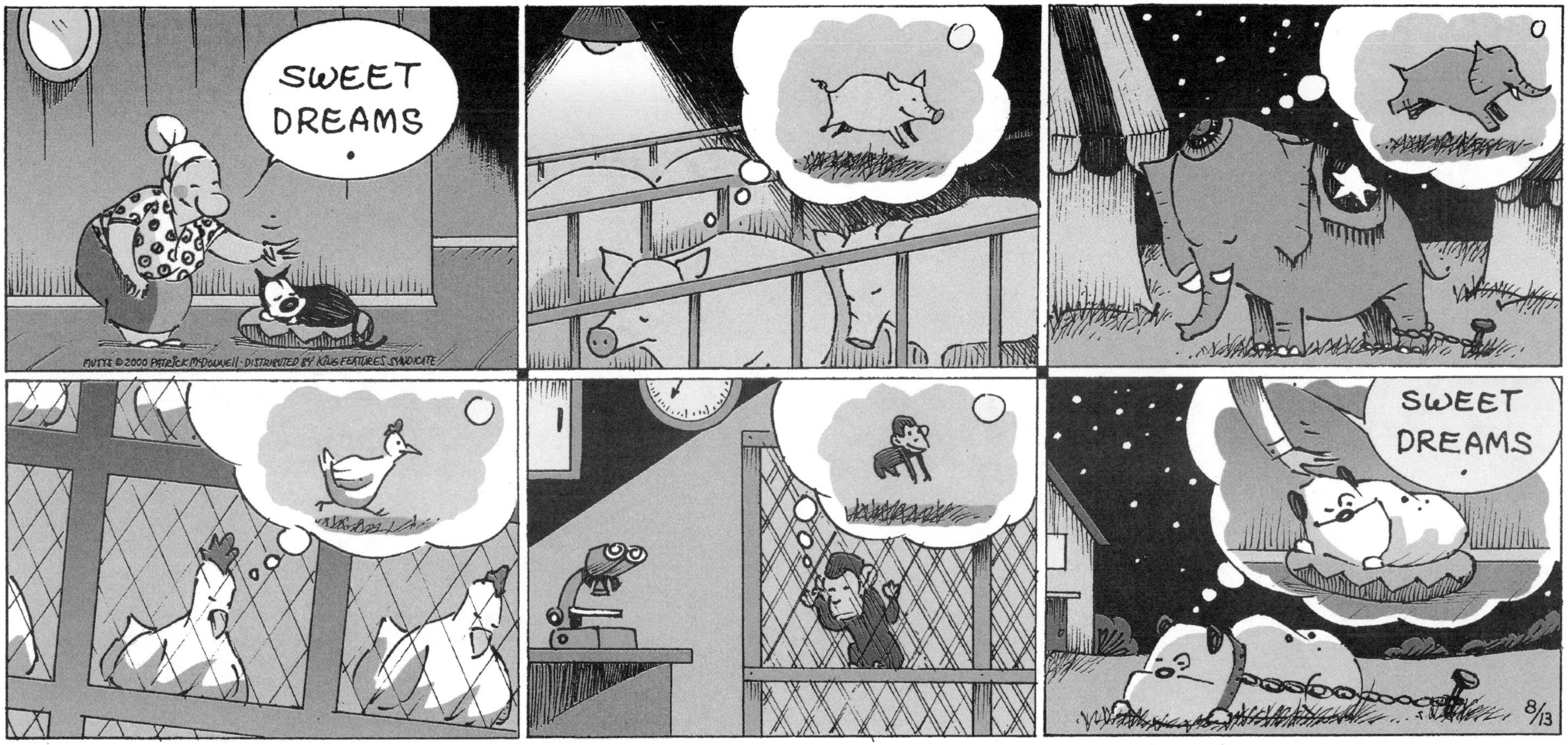
SWEET DREAMS.
MUTTS © 2000 PATRICK McDONNELL · DISTRIBUTED BY KING FEATURES SYNDICATE
SWEET DREAMS.
8/13

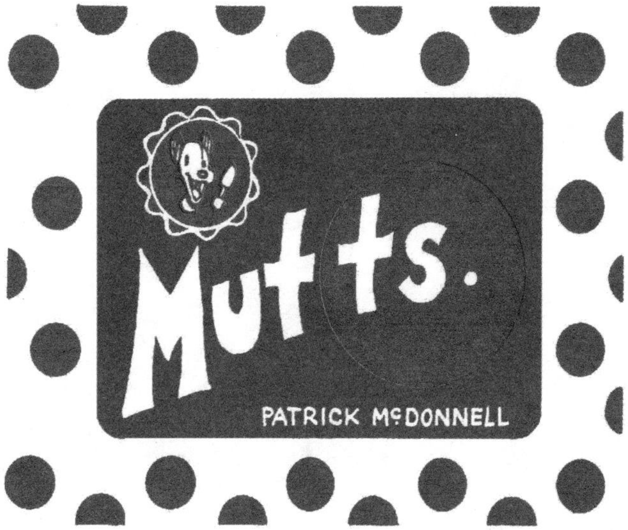
Mutts.
PATRICK McDONNELL

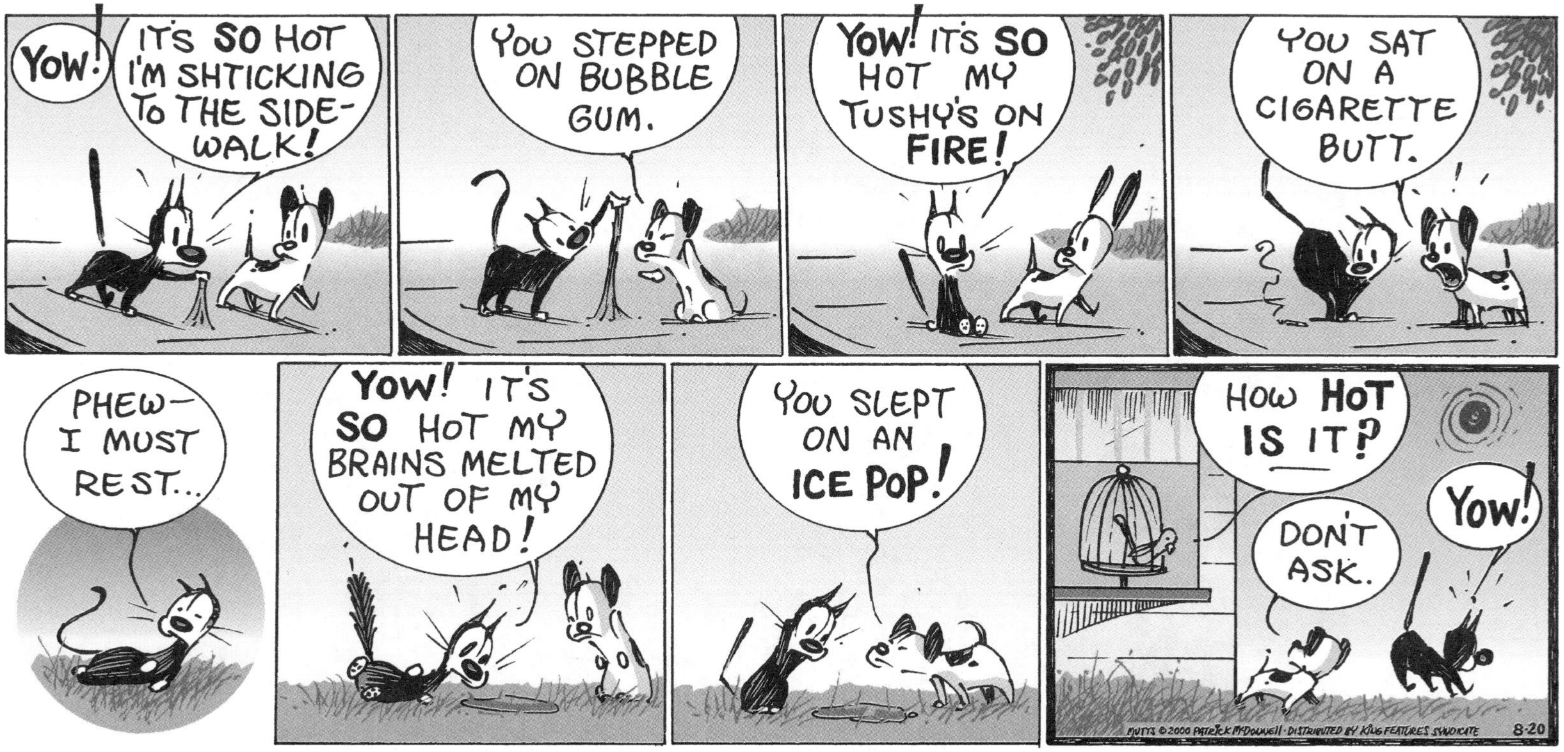
YOW!
IT'S SO HOT I'M SHTICKING TO THE SIDE-WALK!
YOU STEPPED ON BUBBLE GUM.
YOW! IT'S SO HOT MY TUSHY'S ON FIRE!
YOU SAT ON A CIGARETTE BUTT.
PHEW— I MUST REST...
YOW! IT'S SO HOT MY BRAINS MELTED OUT OF MY HEAD!
YOU SLEPT ON AN ICE POP!
HOW HOT IS IT?
DON'T ASK.
YOW!
MUTTS © 2000 PATRICK McDONNELL · DISTRIBUTED BY KING FEATURES SYNDICATE
8-20

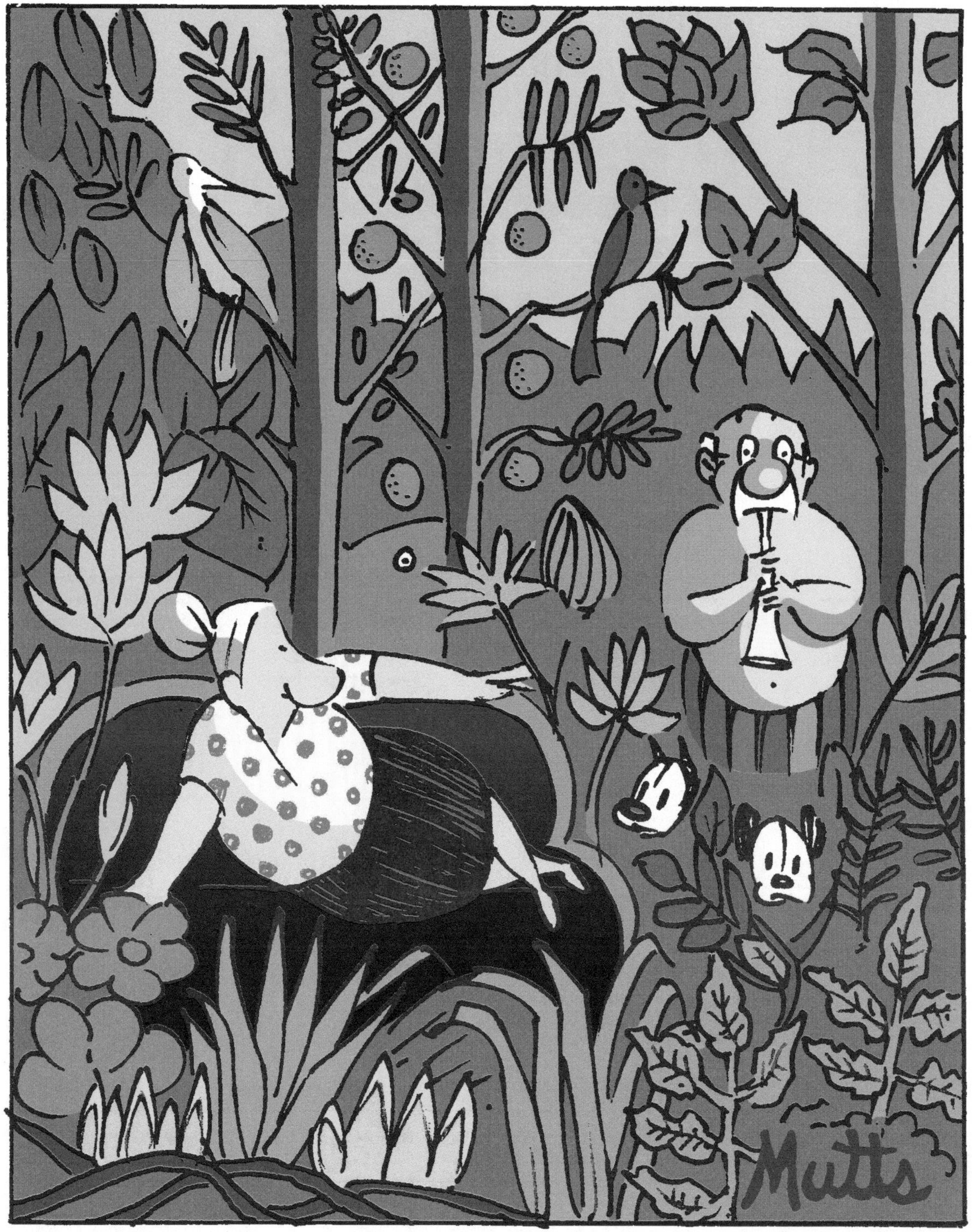
Mutts

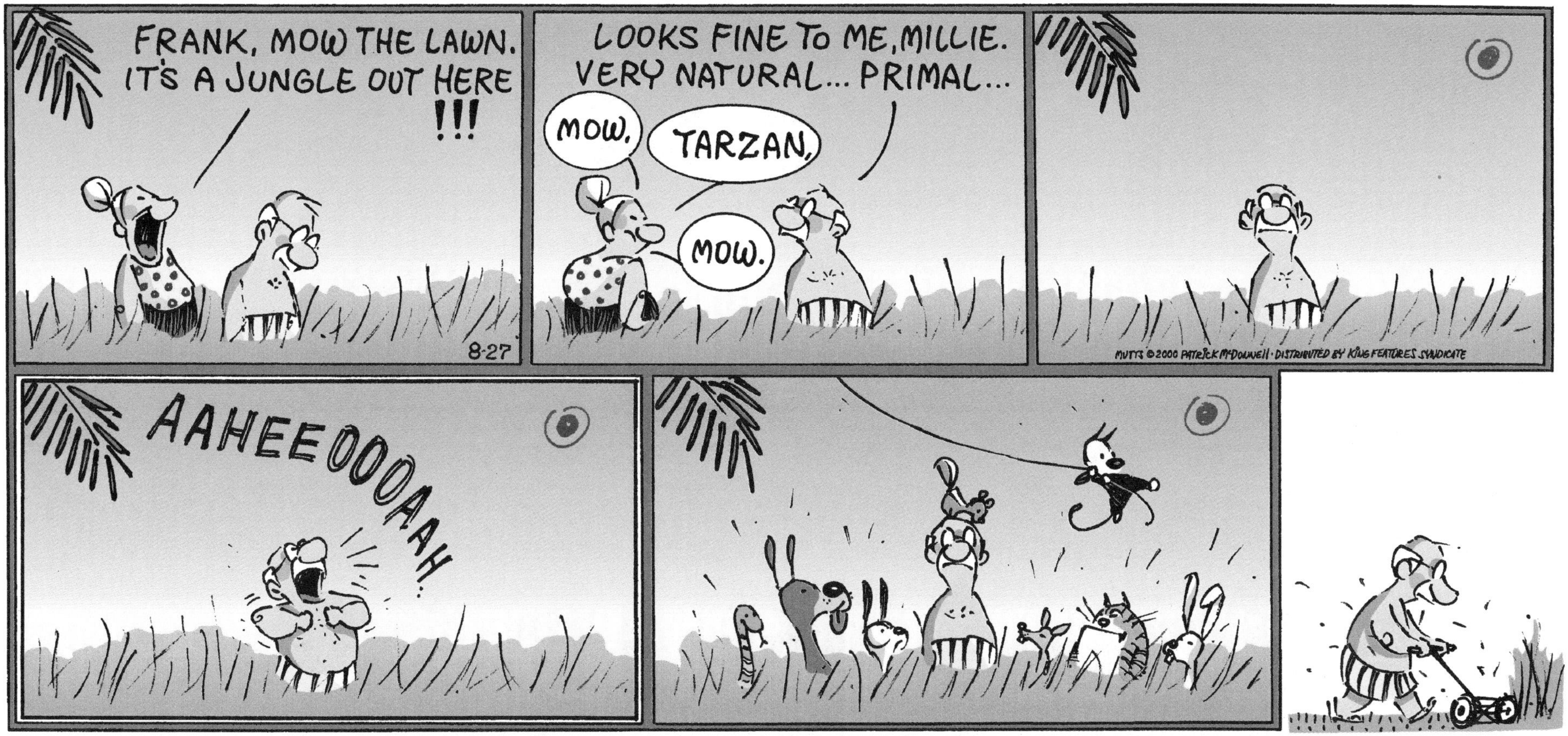
FRANK, MOW THE LAWN. IT'S A JUNGLE OUT HERE !!!
8·27
LOOKS FINE TO ME, MILLIE. VERY NATURAL... PRIMAL...
MOW,
TARZAN,
MOW.
MUTTS ©2000 PATRICK McDONNELL · DISTRIBUTED BY KING FEATURES SYNDICATE
AAHEEOOOAAH

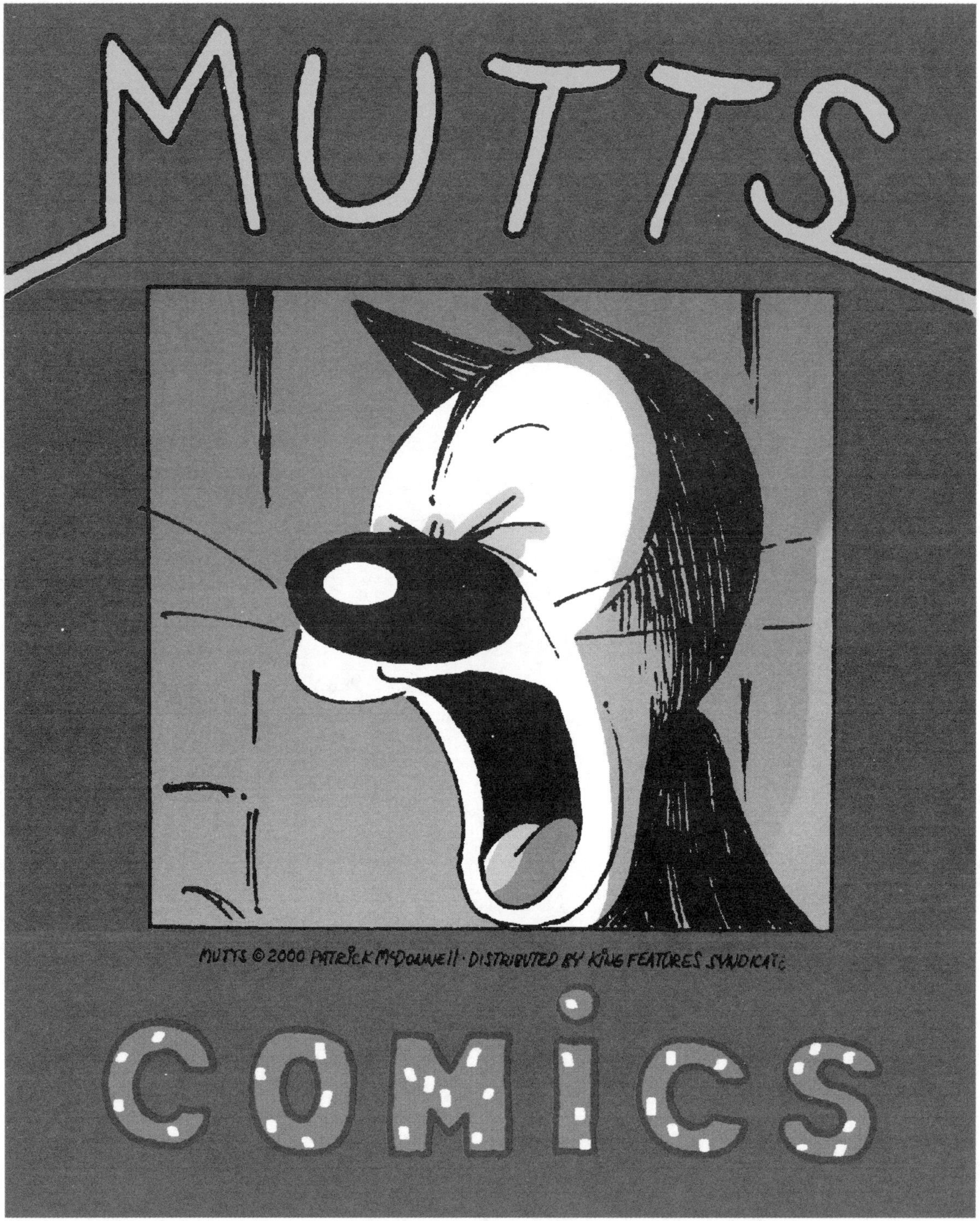
MUTTS
MUTTS © 2000 PATRICK McDONNELL · DISTRIBUTED BY KING FEATURES SYNDICATE
COMICS

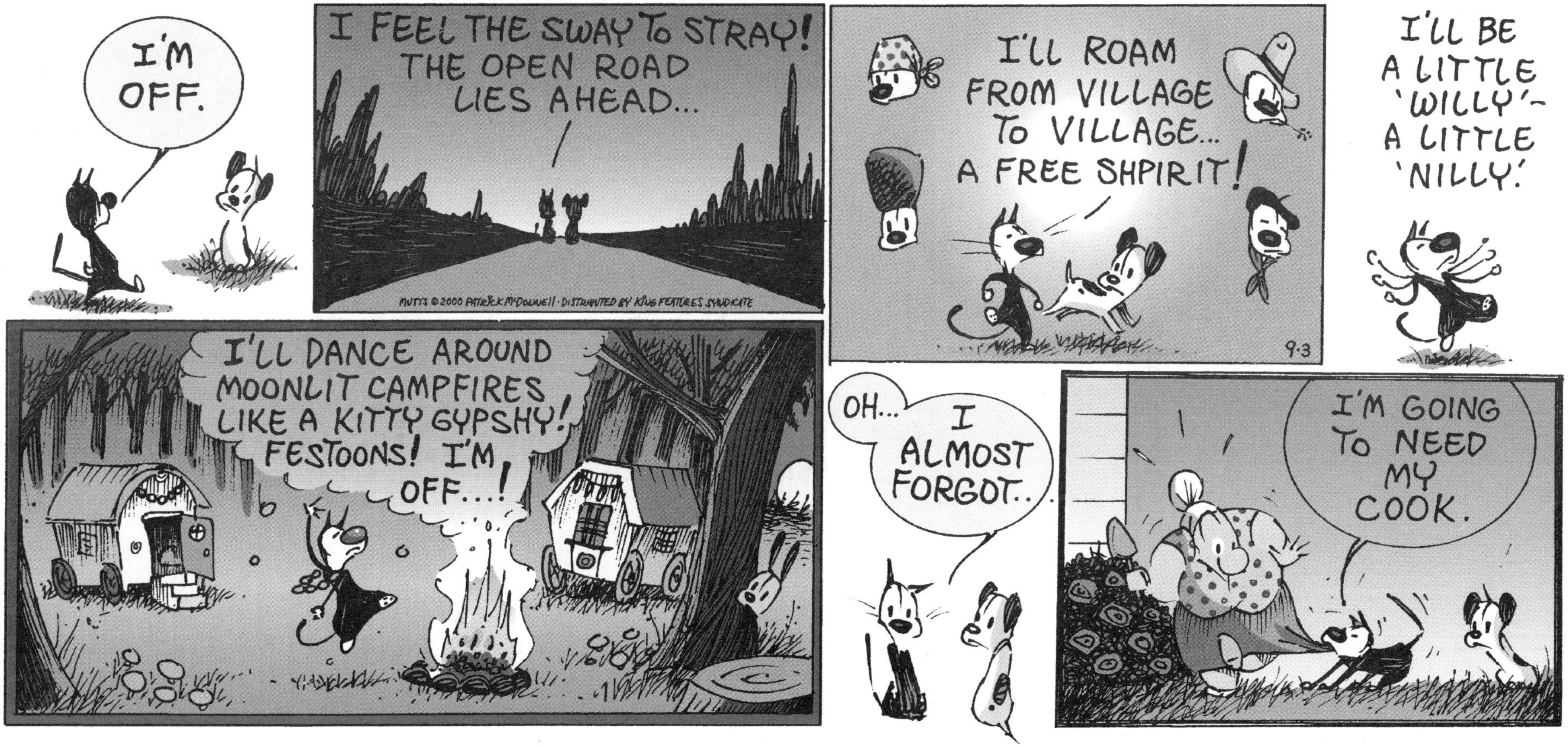
I'M OFF.
I FEEL THE SWAY TO STRAY! THE OPEN ROAD LIES AHEAD...
MUTTS © 2000 PATRICK McDONNELL · DISTRIBUTED BY KING FEATURES SYNDICATE
I'LL ROAM FROM VILLAGE TO VILLAGE... A FREE SHPIRIT!
9·3
I'LL BE A LITTLE 'WILLY'– A LITTLE 'NILLY.'
I'LL DANCE AROUND MOONLIT CAMPFIRES LIKE A KITTY GYPSHY! FESTOONS! I'M OFF....!
OH... I ALMOST FORGOT..
I'M GOING TO NEED MY COOK.

Mutts

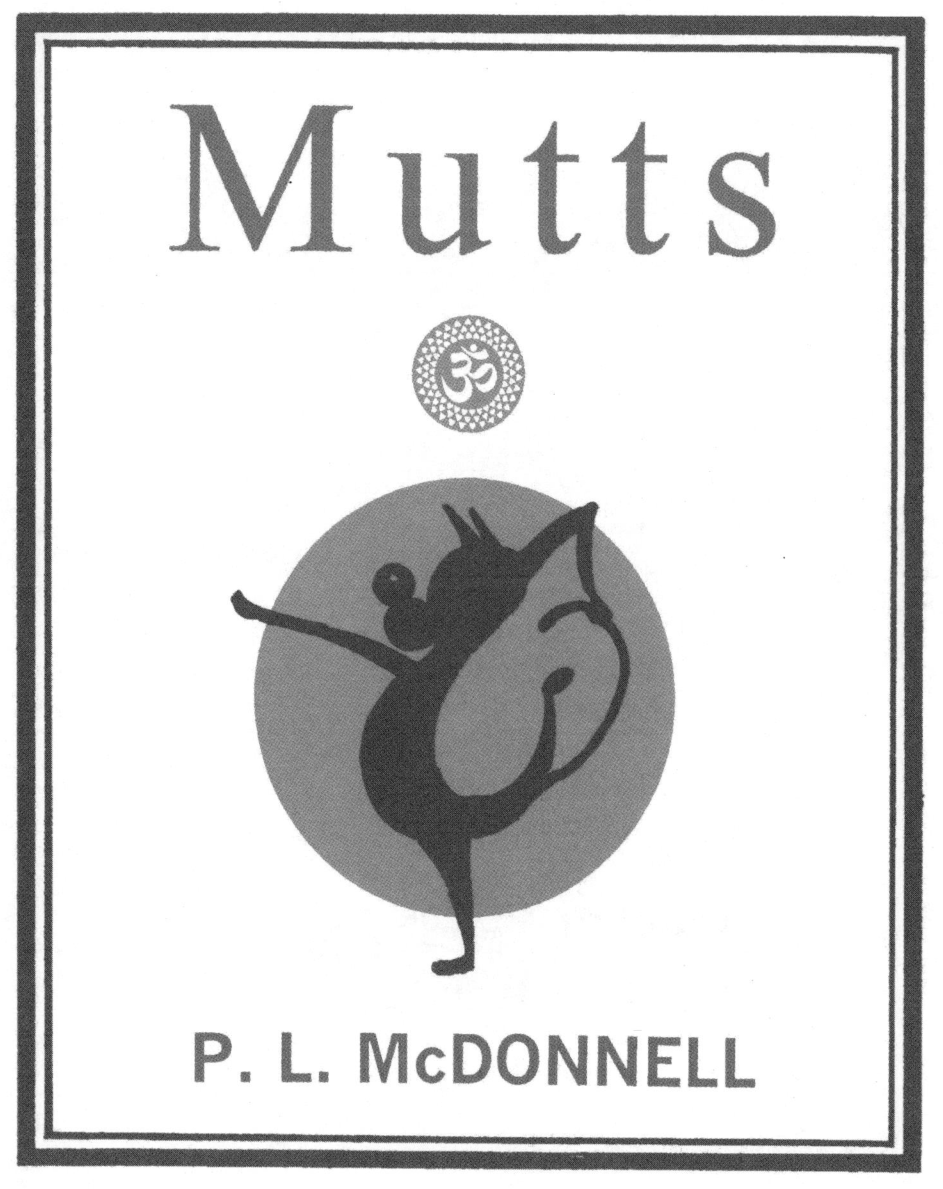

P. L. McDONNELL

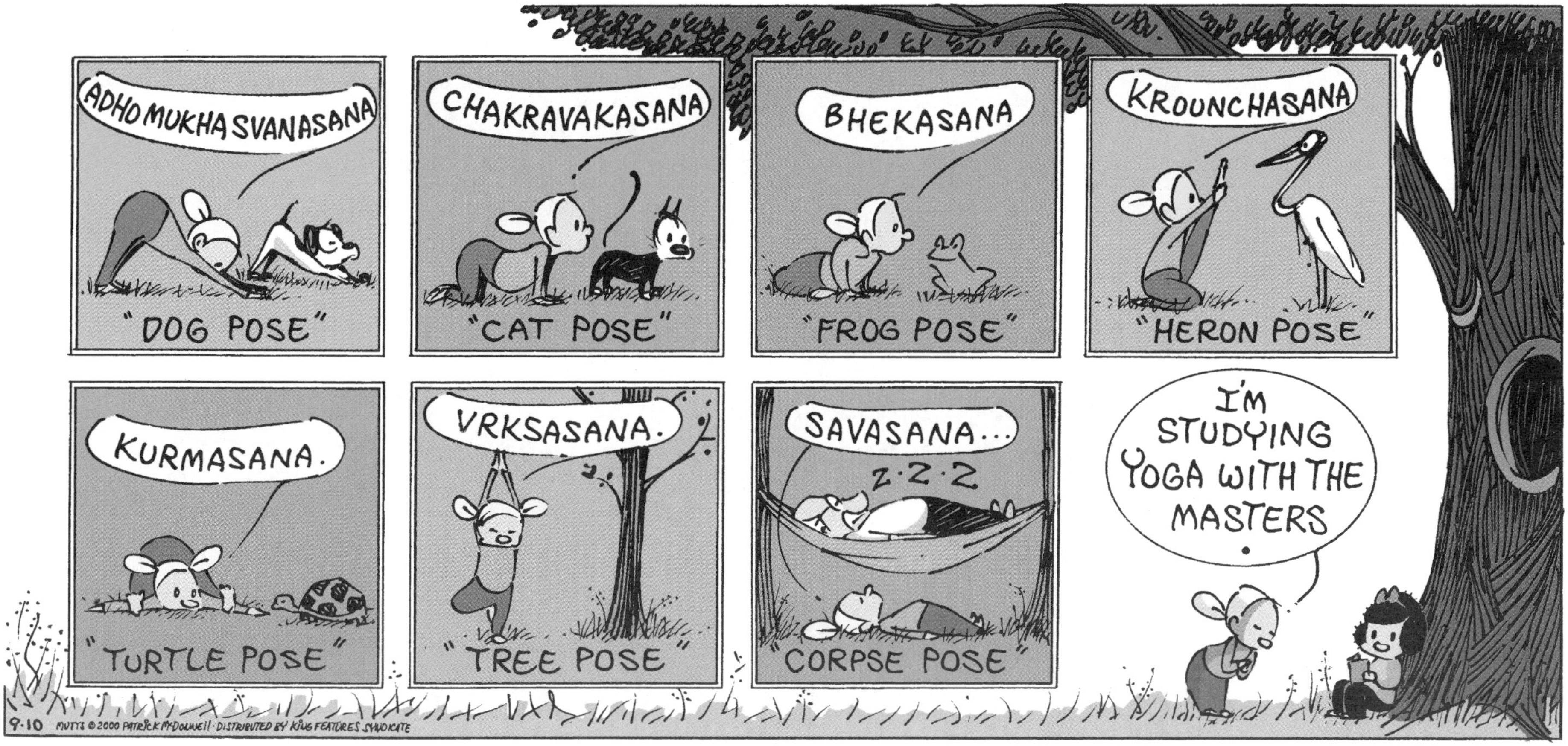
ADHO MUKHA SVANASANA
"DOG POSE"
CHAKRAVAKASANA
"CAT POSE"
BHEKASANA
"FROG POSE"
KROUNCHASANA
"HERON POSE"
KURMASANA.
"TURTLE POSE"
VRKSASANA.
"TREE POSE"
SAVASANA...
Z·Z·Z
"CORPSE POSE"
I'M STUDYING YOGA WITH THE MASTERS.
9·10 MUTTS © 2000 PATRICK McDONNELL · DISTRIBUTED BY KING FEATURES SYNDICATE

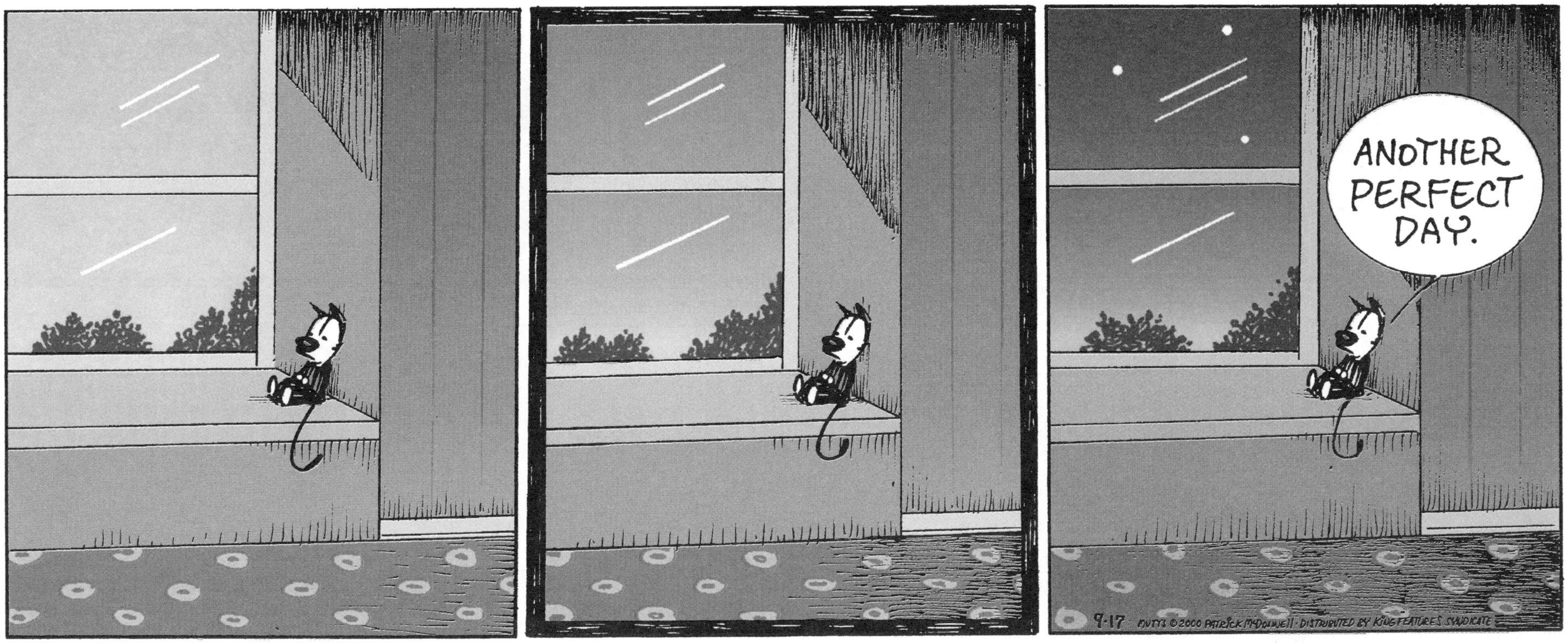
ANOTHER PERFECT DAY.
9·17 MUTTS © 2000 PATRICK McDONNELL · DISTRIBUTED BY KING FEATURES SYNDICATE

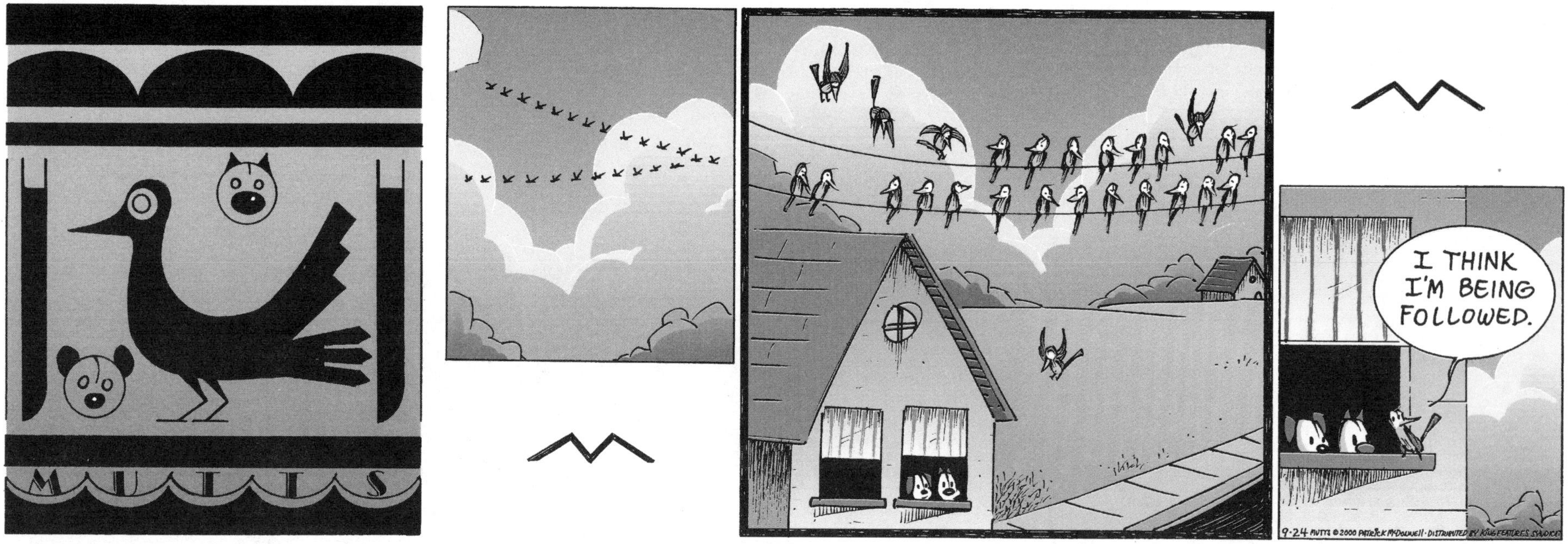
MUTTS
I THINK I'M BEING FOLLOWED.
9·24 MUTTS © 2000 PATRICK McDONNELL · DISTRIBUTED BY KING FEATURES SYNDICATE

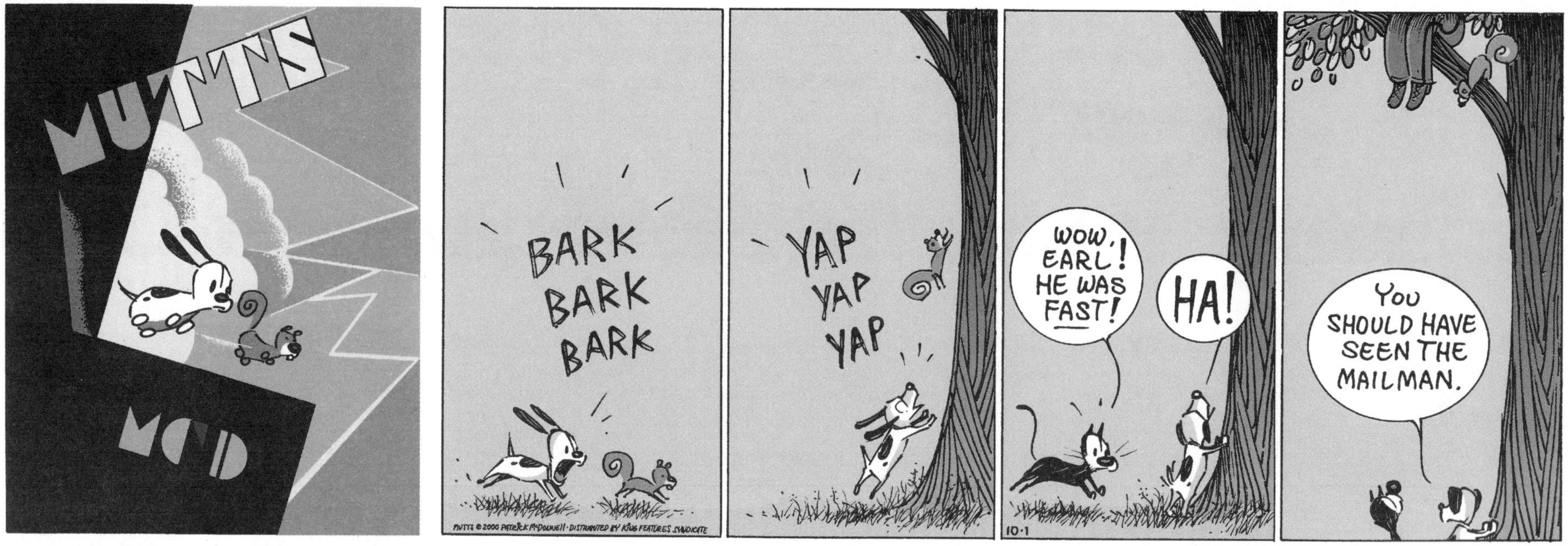
MUTTS
MCD
BARK BARK BARK
MUTTS © 2000 PATRICK McDONNELL · DISTRIBUTED BY KING FEATURES SYNDICATE
YAP YAP YAP
10·1
WOW, EARL! HE WAS FAST!
HA!
YOU SHOULD HAVE SEEN THE MAILMAN.

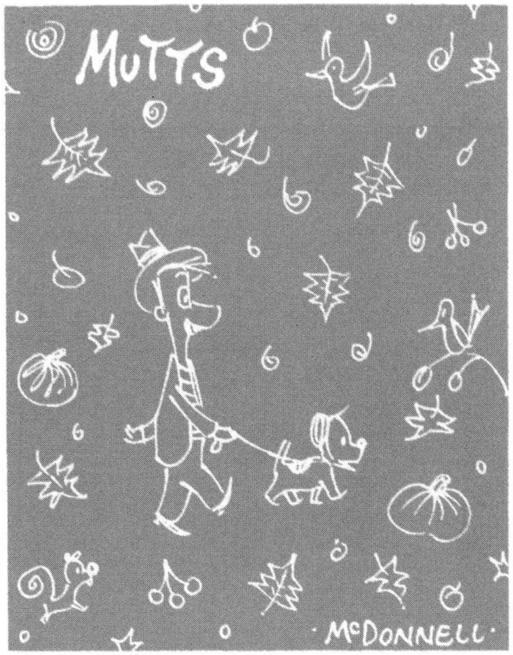
MUTTS
McDONNELL

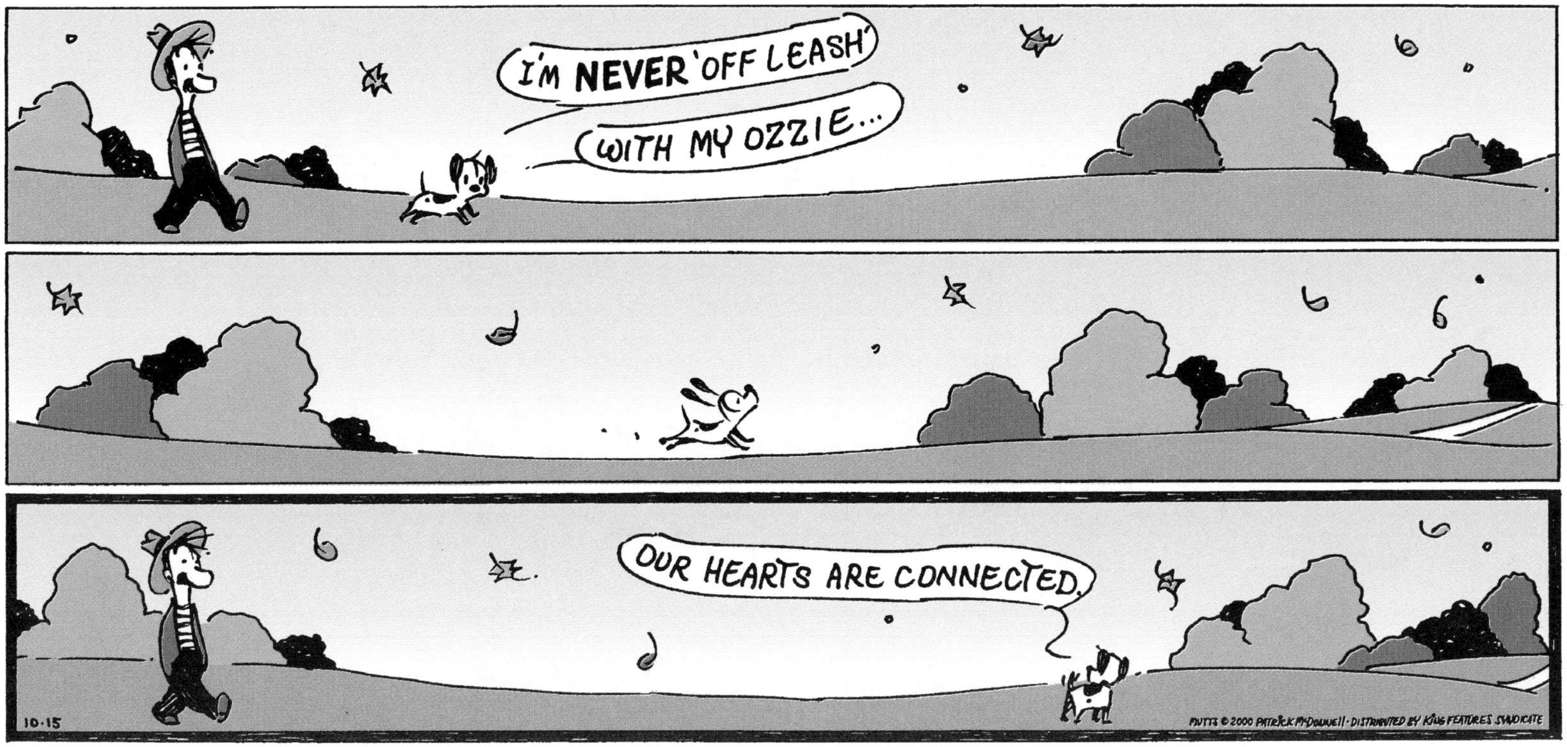
I'M NEVER 'OFF LEASH'
WITH MY OZZIE...
OUR HEARTS ARE CONNECTED.
10·15
MUTTS © 2000 PATRICK McDONNELL · DISTRIBUTED BY KING FEATURES SYNDICATE

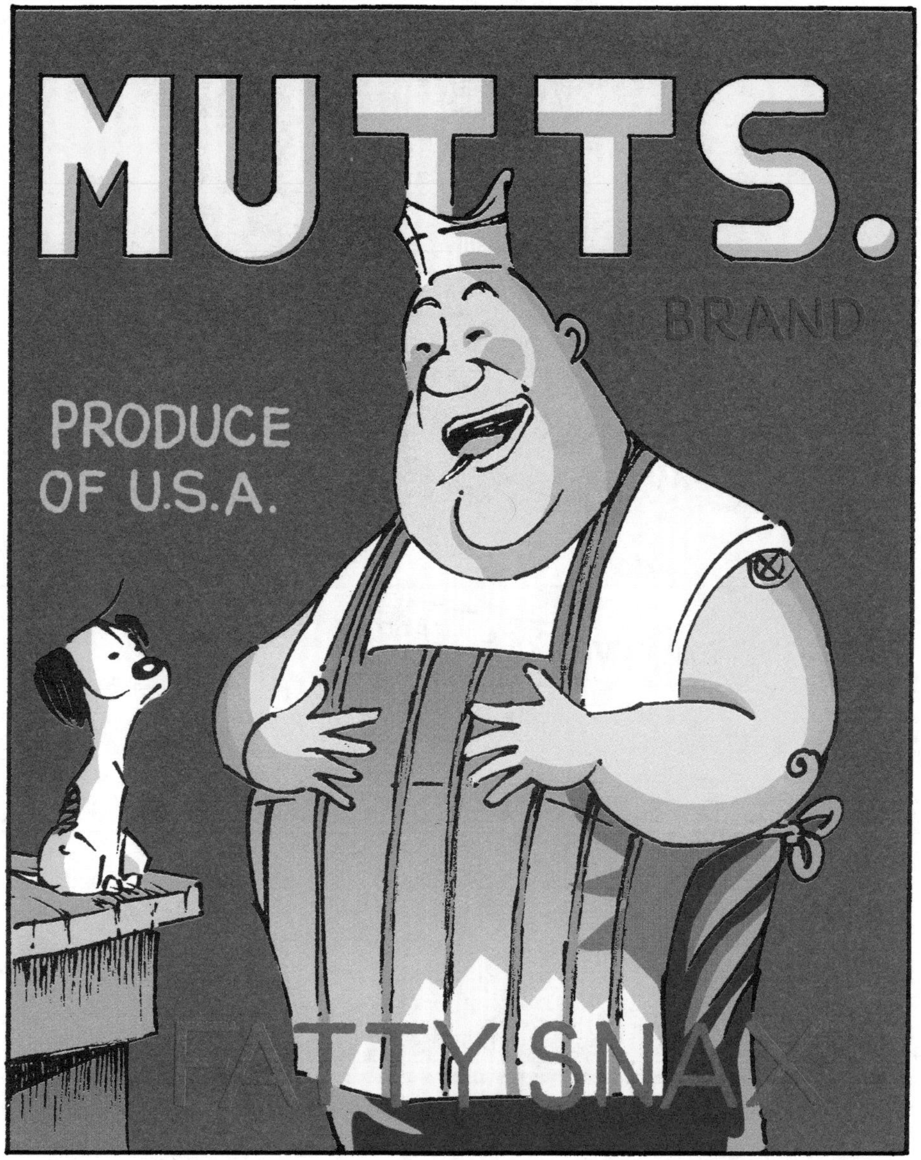
MUTTS.
BRAND
PRODUCE
OF U.S.A.
FATTY SNAX

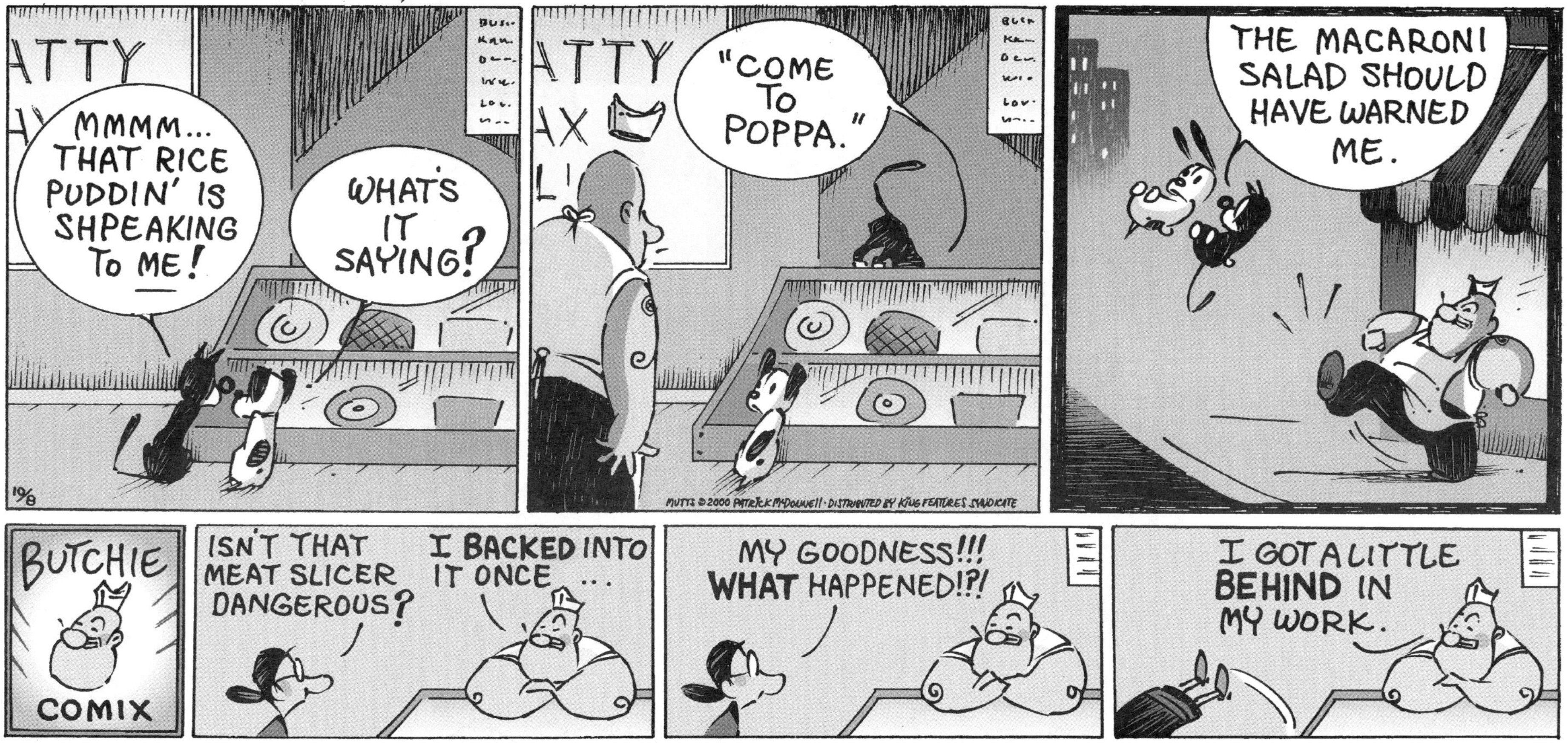
MMMM... THAT RICE PUDDIN' IS SHPEAKING TO ME!
WHAT'S IT SAYING?
10/8
"COME TO POPPA."
MUTTS © 2000 PATRICK McDONNELL · DISTRIBUTED BY KING FEATURES SYNDICATE
THE MACARONI SALAD SHOULD HAVE WARNED ME.
BUTCHIE COMIX
ISN'T THAT MEAT SLICER DANGEROUS?
I BACKED INTO IT ONCE ...
MY GOODNESS!!! WHAT HAPPENED!?!
I GOT A LITTLE BEHIND IN MY WORK.

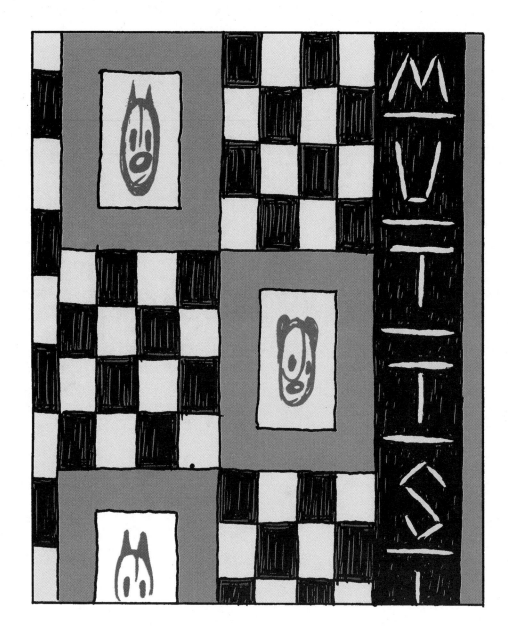

126

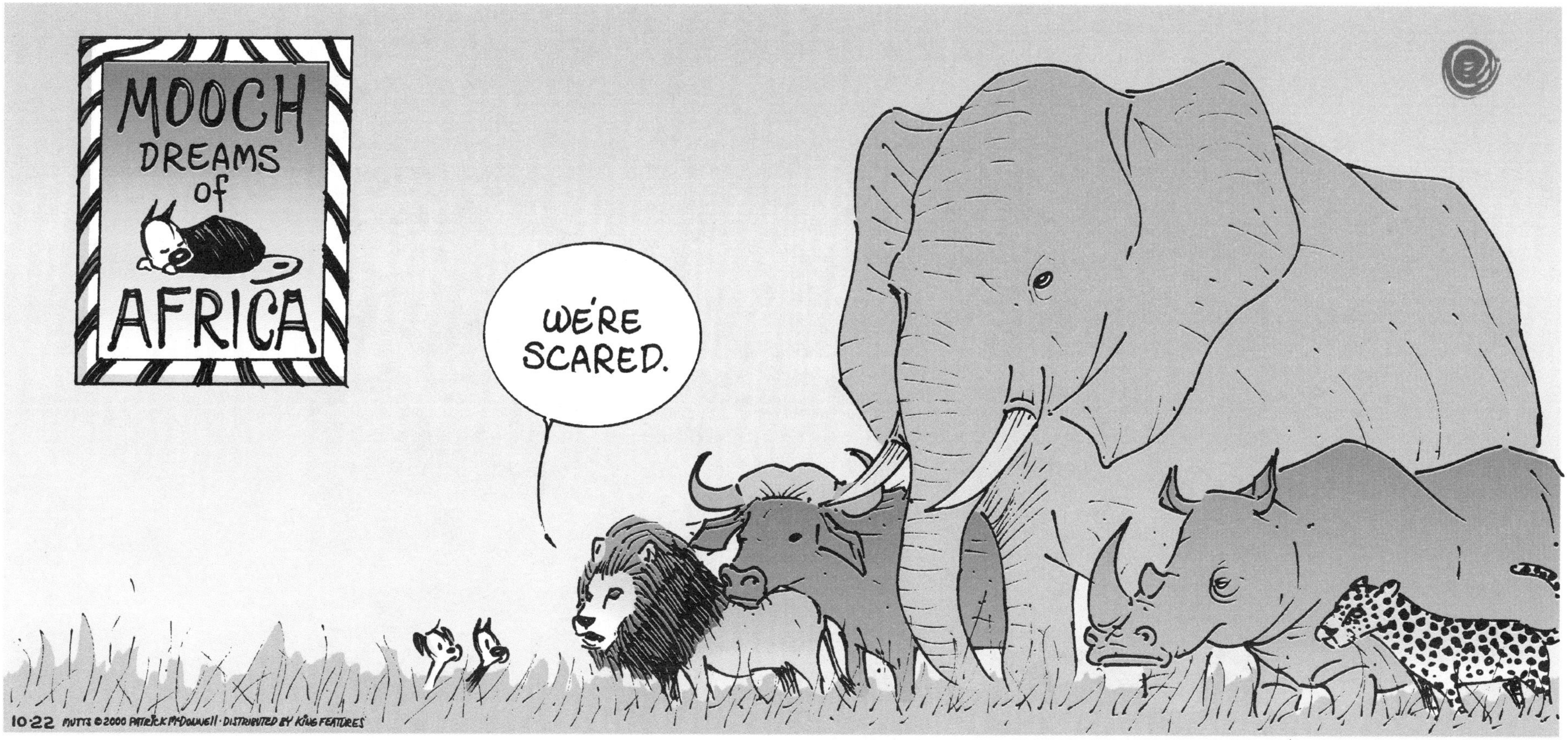
MOOCH DREAMS of AFRICA
WE'RE SCARED.
10·22 MUTTS © 2000 PATRICK McDONNELL · DISTRIBUTED BY KING FEATURES

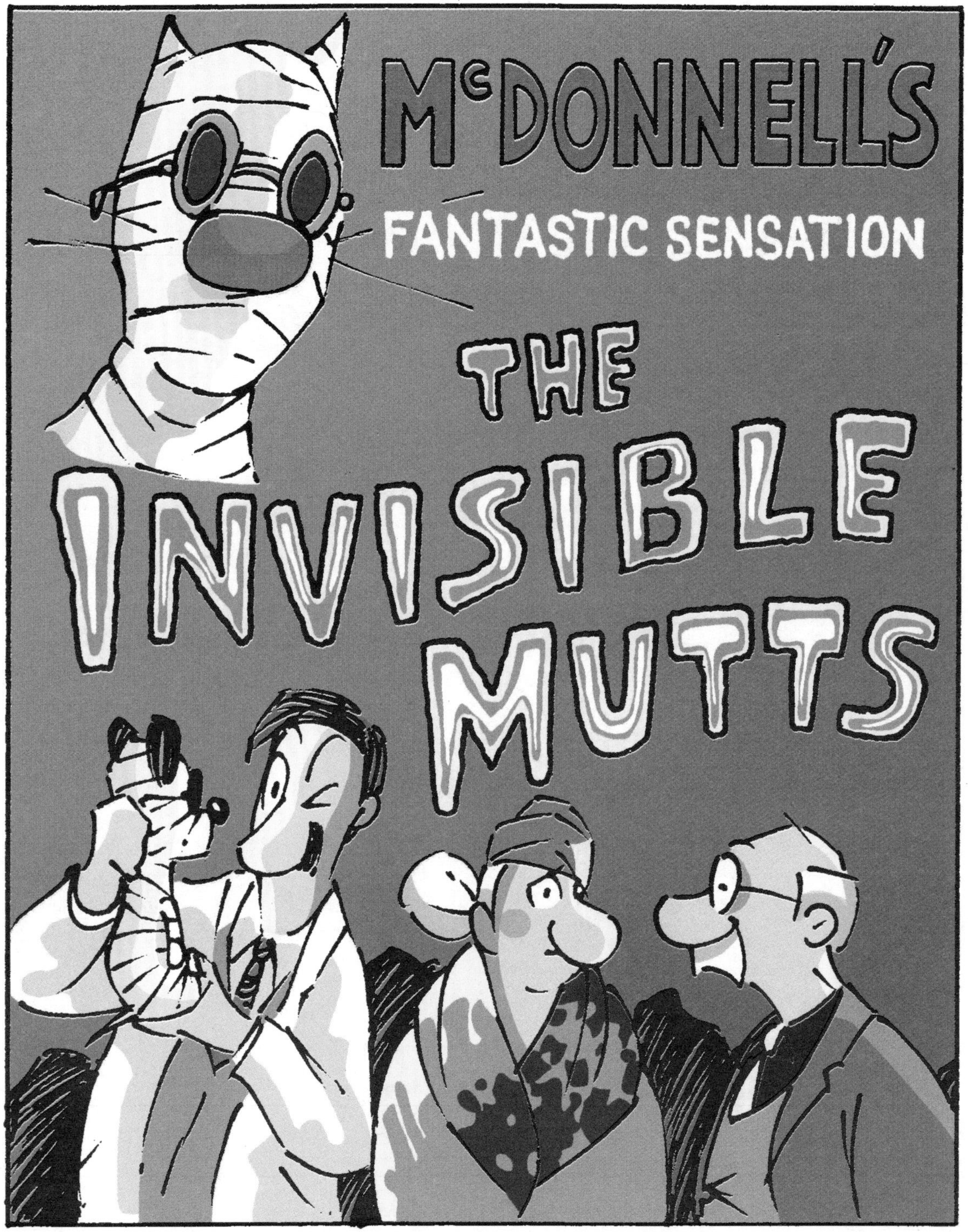
McDONNELL'S
FANTASTIC SENSATION
THE
INVISIBLE
MUTTS

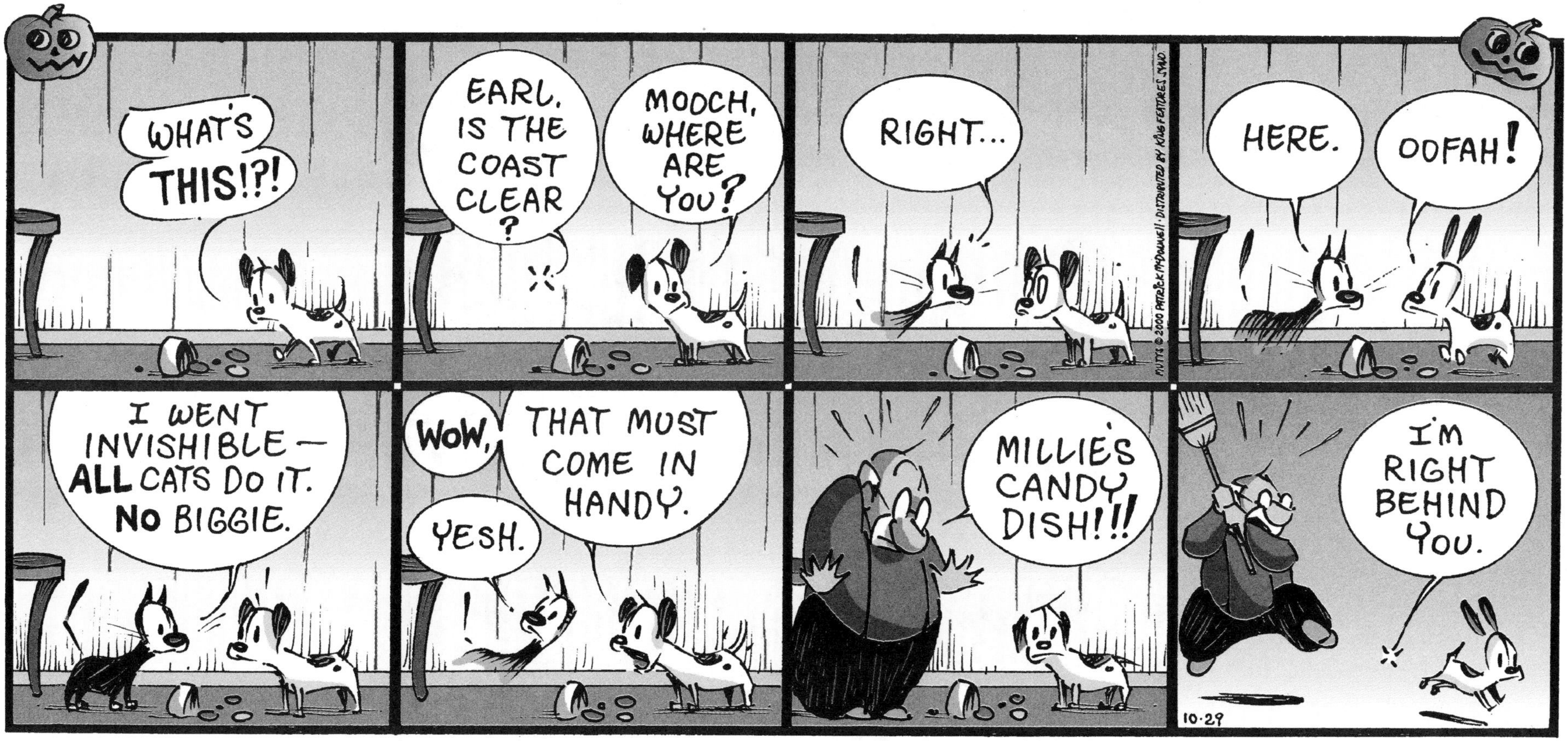
WHAT'S THIS!?!
EARL, IS THE COAST CLEAR?
MOOCH, WHERE ARE YOU?
RIGHT...
MUTTS © 2000 PATRICK McDONNELL · DISTRIBUTED BY KING FEATURES SYND.
HERE.
OOFAH!
I WENT INVISHIBLE — ALL CATS DO IT. NO BIGGIE.
WOW,
THAT MUST COME IN HANDY.
YESH.
MILLIE'S CANDY DISH!!!
I'M RIGHT BEHIND YOU.
10·29

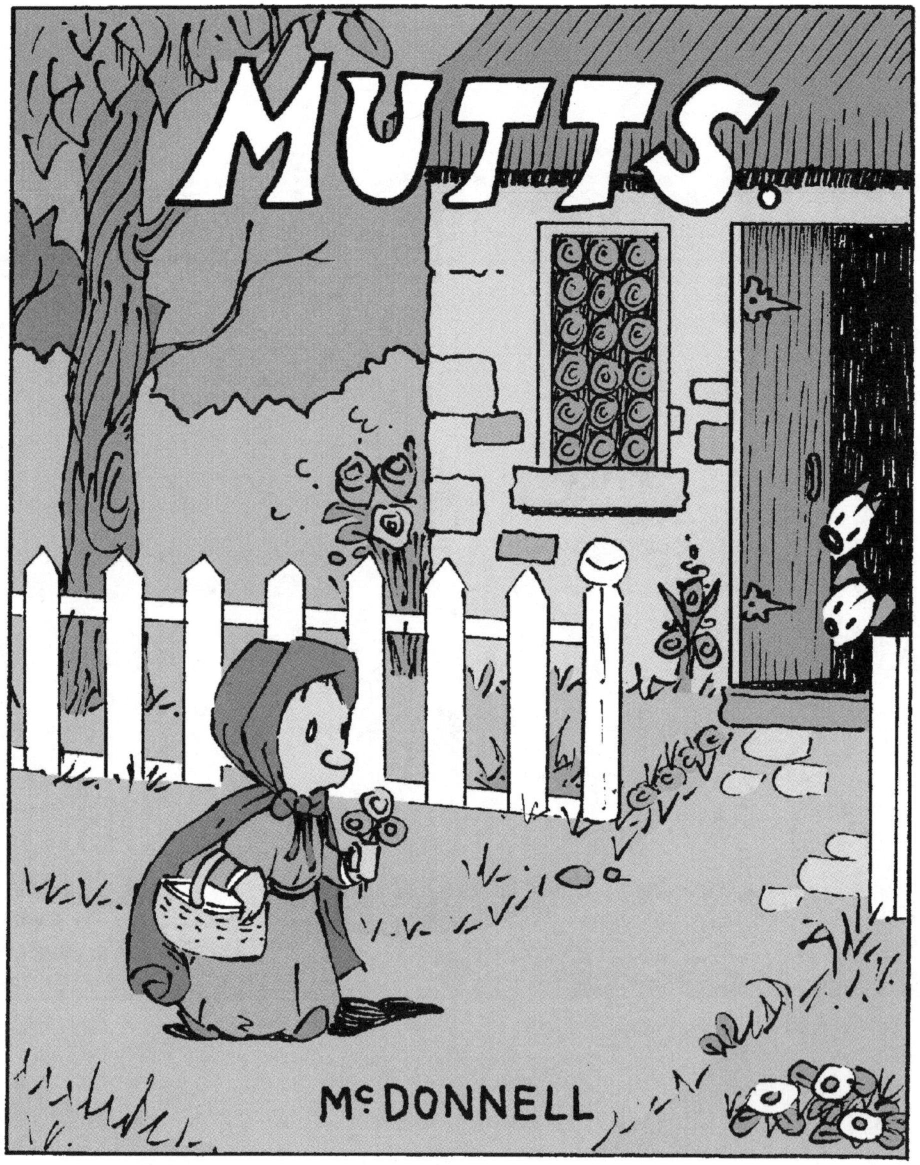
MUTTS.
McDONNELL

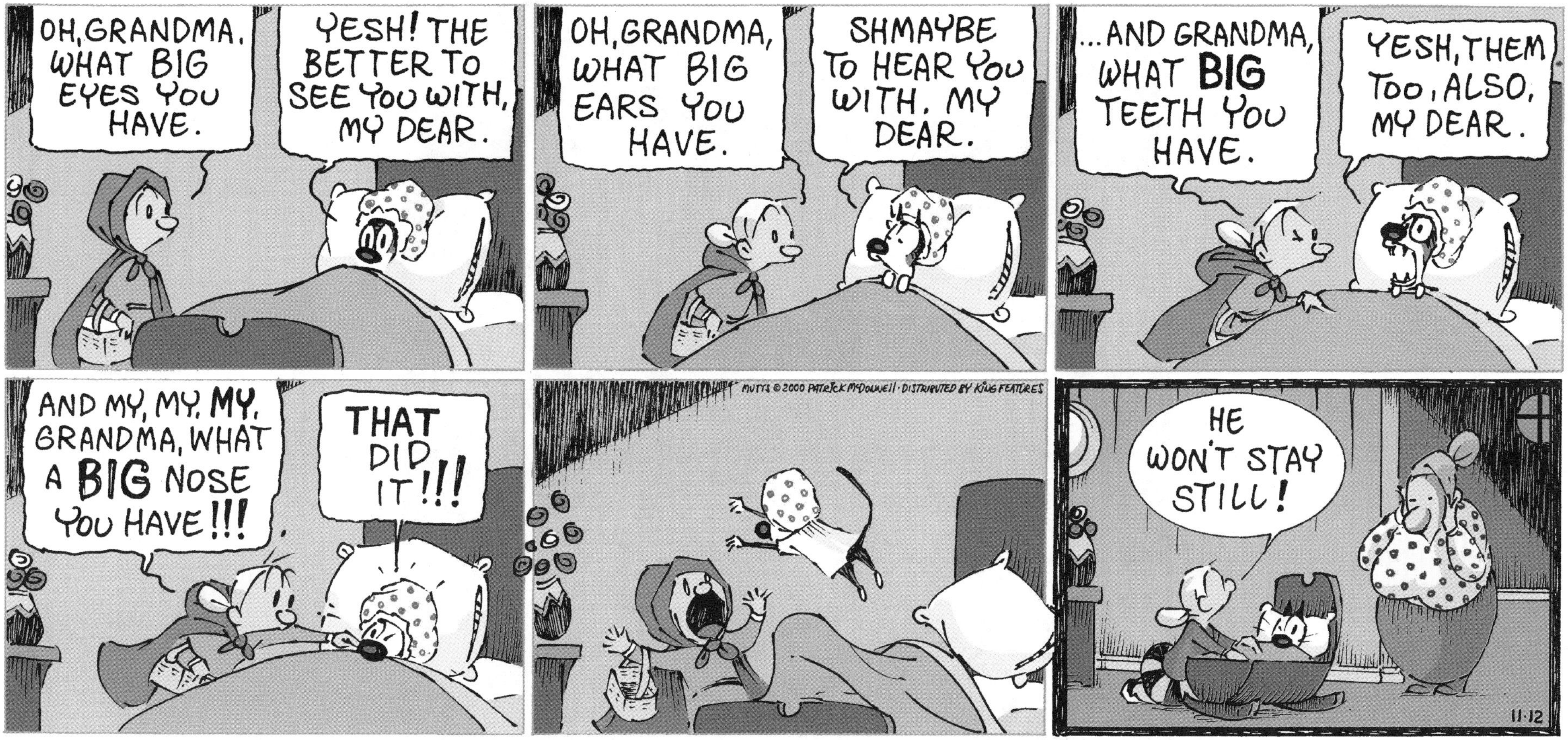
OH, GRANDMA, WHAT BIG EYES YOU HAVE.
YESH! THE BETTER TO SEE YOU WITH, MY DEAR.
OH, GRANDMA, WHAT BIG EARS YOU HAVE.
SHMAYBE TO HEAR YOU WITH, MY DEAR.
...AND GRANDMA, WHAT BIG TEETH YOU HAVE.
YESH, THEM TOO, ALSO, MY DEAR.
AND MY, MY, MY, GRANDMA, WHAT A BIG NOSE YOU HAVE!!!
THAT DID IT!!!
MUTTS © 2000 PATRICK McDONNELL · DISTRIBUTED BY KING FEATURES
HE WON'T STAY STILL!
11-12

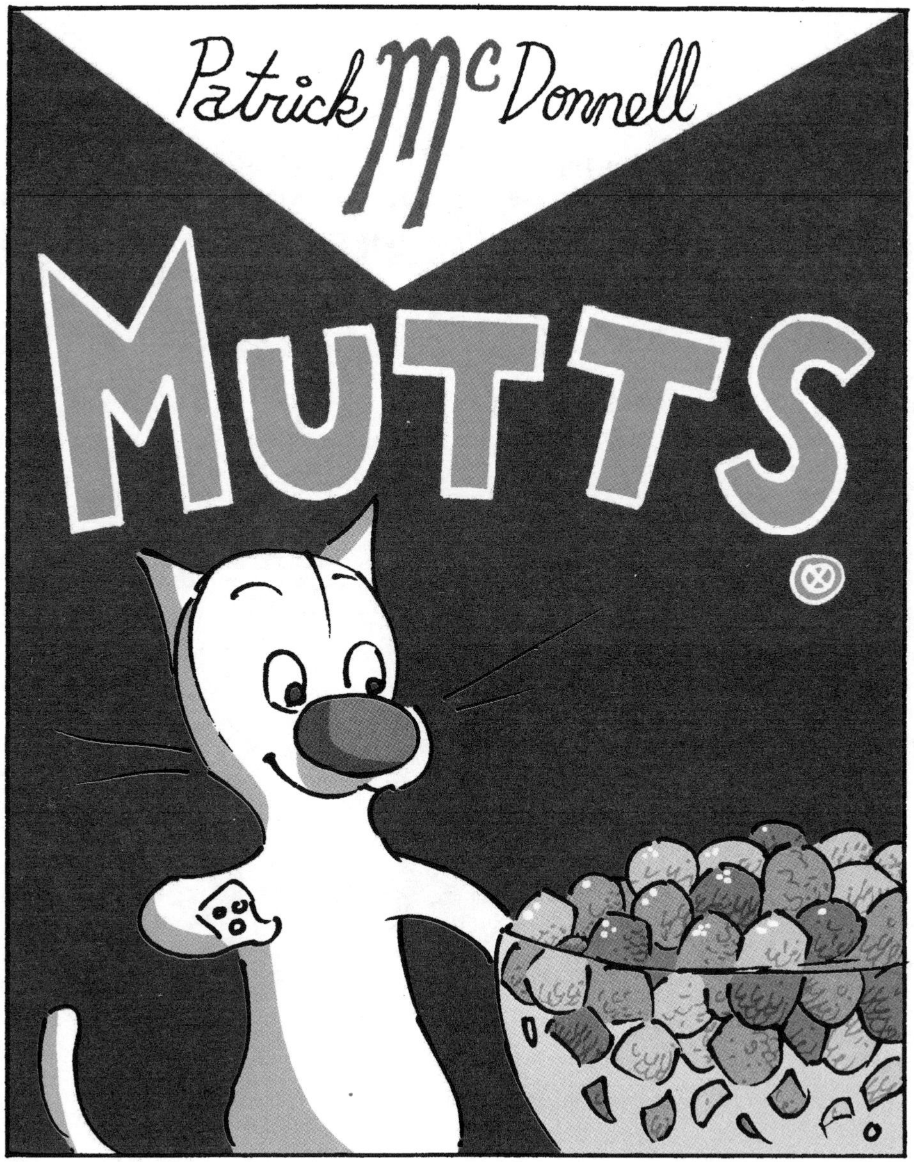
Patrick McDonnell
MUTTS

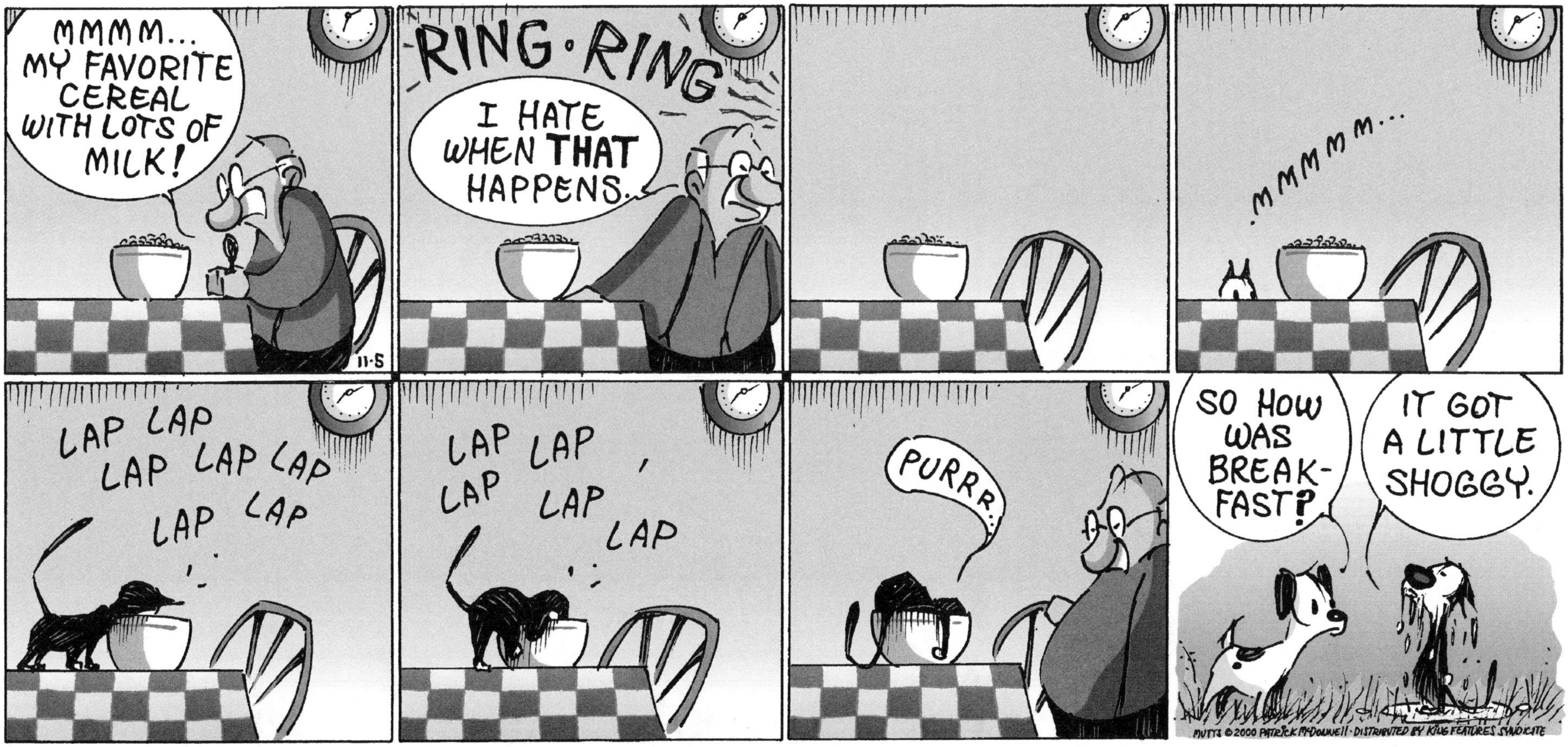
MMMM... MY FAVORITE CEREAL WITH LOTS OF MILK!
11-5
RING · RING
I HATE WHEN THAT HAPPENS.
MMMMM...
LAP LAP LAP LAP LAP LAP LAP
LAP LAP LAP LAP LAP
PURRR.
SO HOW WAS BREAK-FAST?
IT GOT A LITTLE SHOGGY.
MUTTS © 2000 PATRICK McDONNELL · DISTRIBUTED BY KING FEATURES SYNDICATE

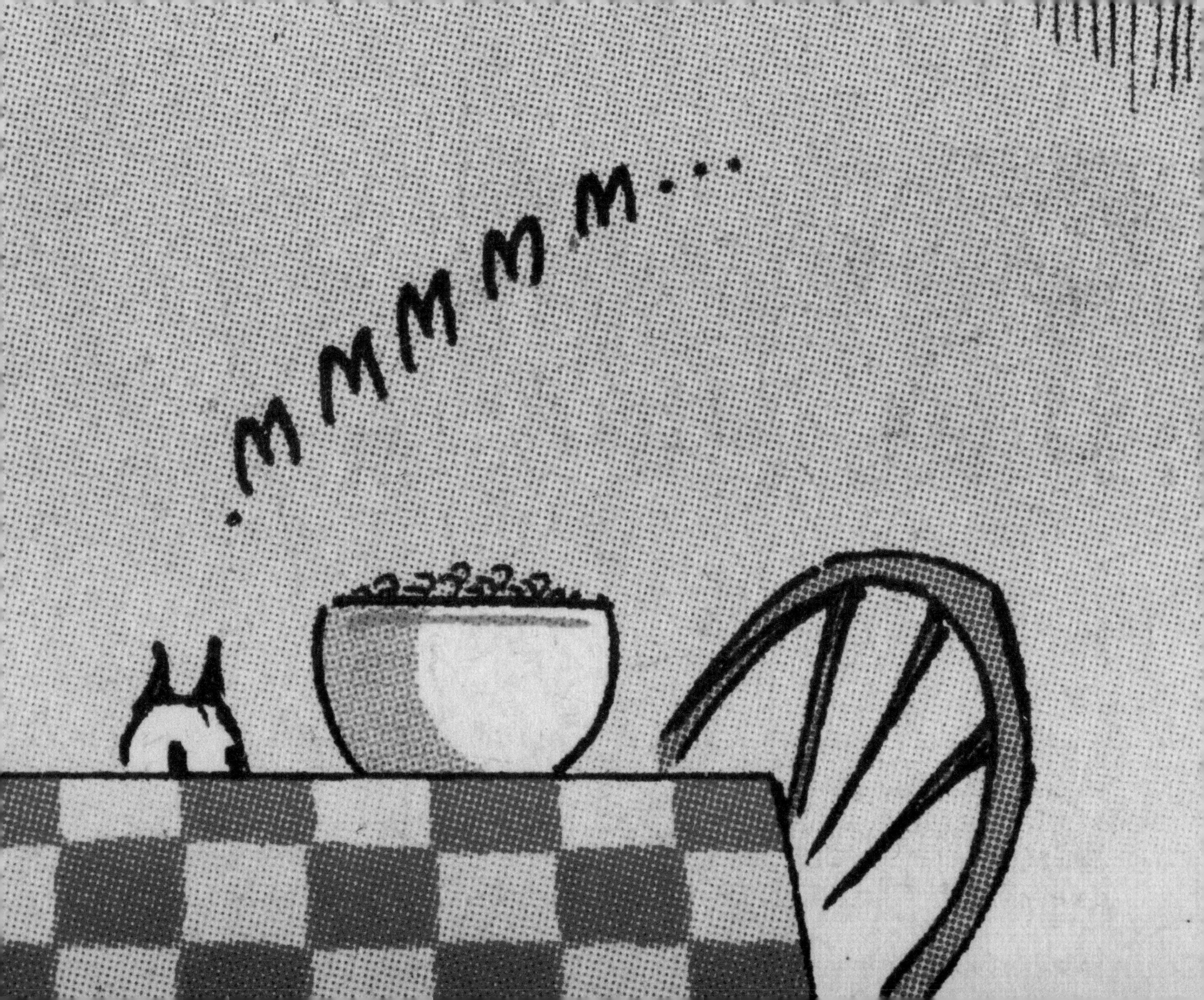

.MMMMMM...

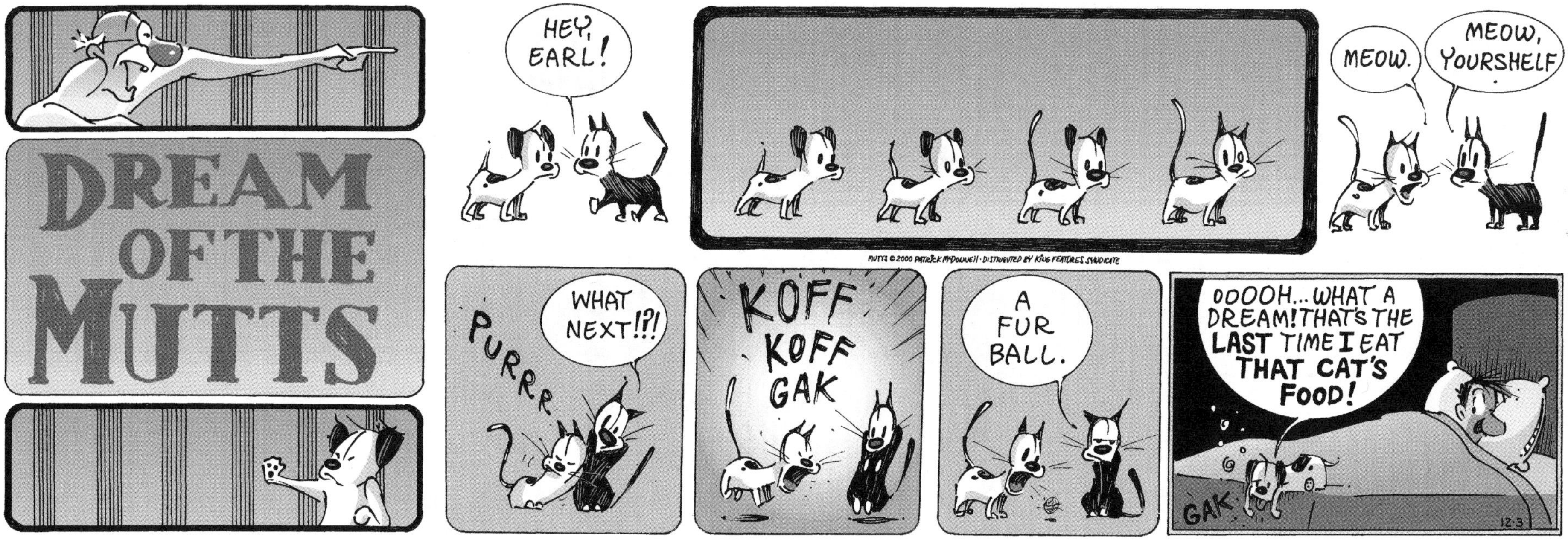
DREAM OF THE MUTTS
HEY, EARL!
MEOW.
MEOW, YOURSHELF.
MUTTS © 2000 PATRICK McDONNELL · DISTRIBUTED BY KING FEATURES SYNDICATE
PURRRR
WHAT NEXT!?!
KOFF KOFF GAK
A FUR BALL.
OOOOH...WHAT A DREAM! THAT'S THE LAST TIME I EAT THAT CAT'S FOOD!
GAK
12·3

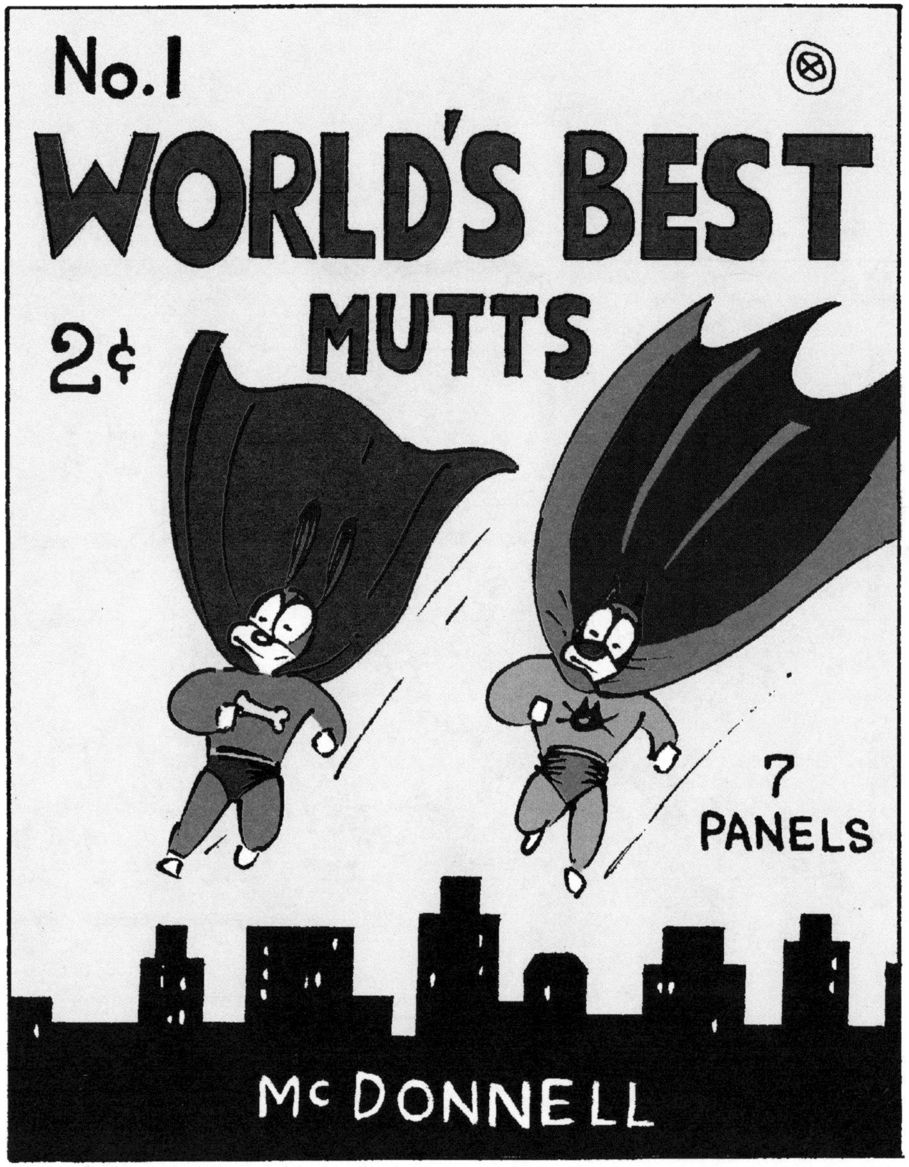
No. 1
WORLD'S BEST
MUTTS
2¢
7
PANELS
McDONNELL

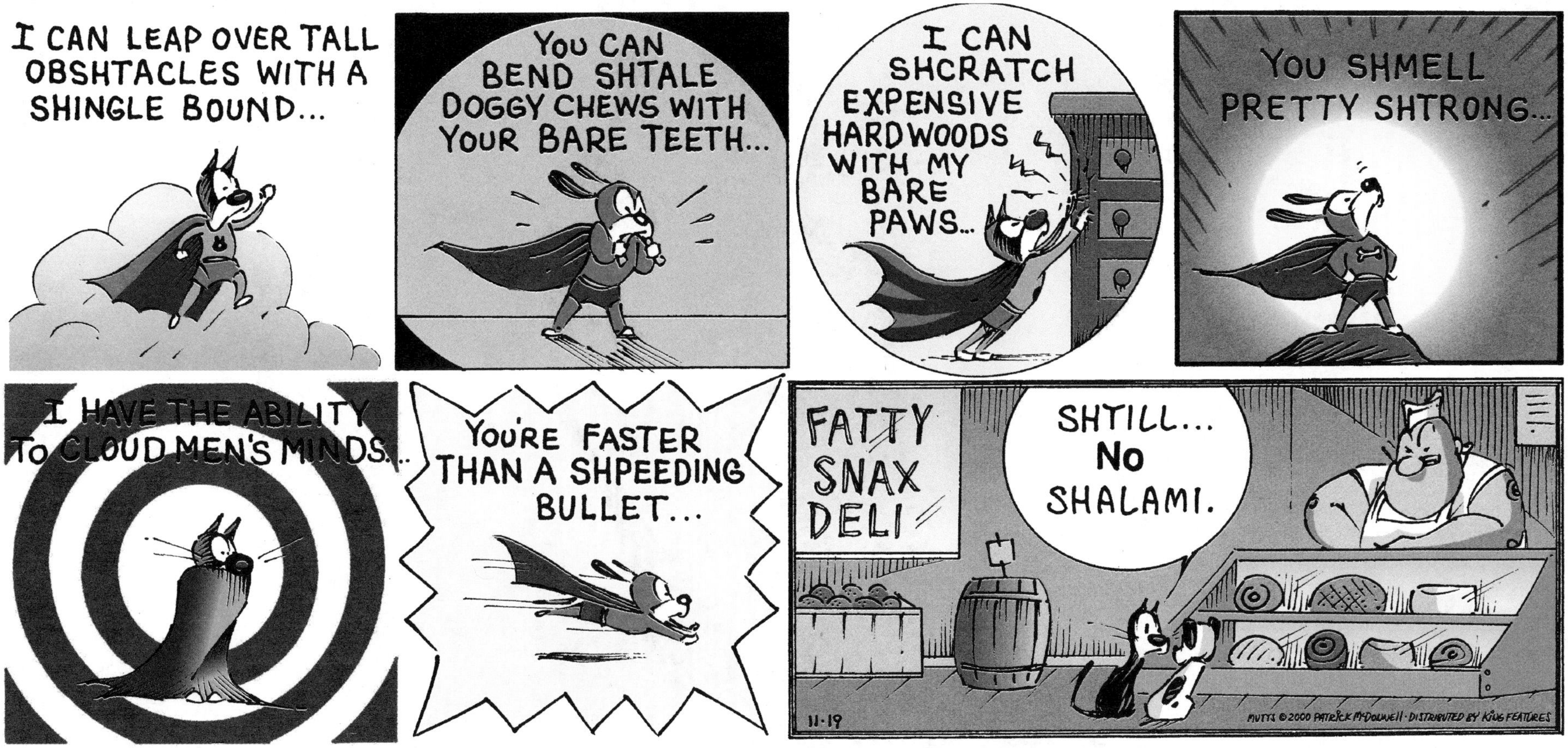
I CAN LEAP OVER TALL OBSHTACLES WITH A SHINGLE BOUND...
YOU CAN BEND SHTALE DOGGY CHEWS WITH YOUR BARE TEETH...
I CAN SHCRATCH EXPENSIVE HARDWOODS WITH MY BARE PAWS...
YOU SHMELL PRETTY SHTRONG...
I HAVE THE ABILITY TO CLOUD MEN'S MINDS...
YOU'RE FASTER THAN A SHPEEDING BULLET...
FATTY SNAX DELI
SHTILL... No SHALAMI.
11·19
MUTTS © 2000 PATRICK McDONNELL · DISTRIBUTED BY KING FEATURES

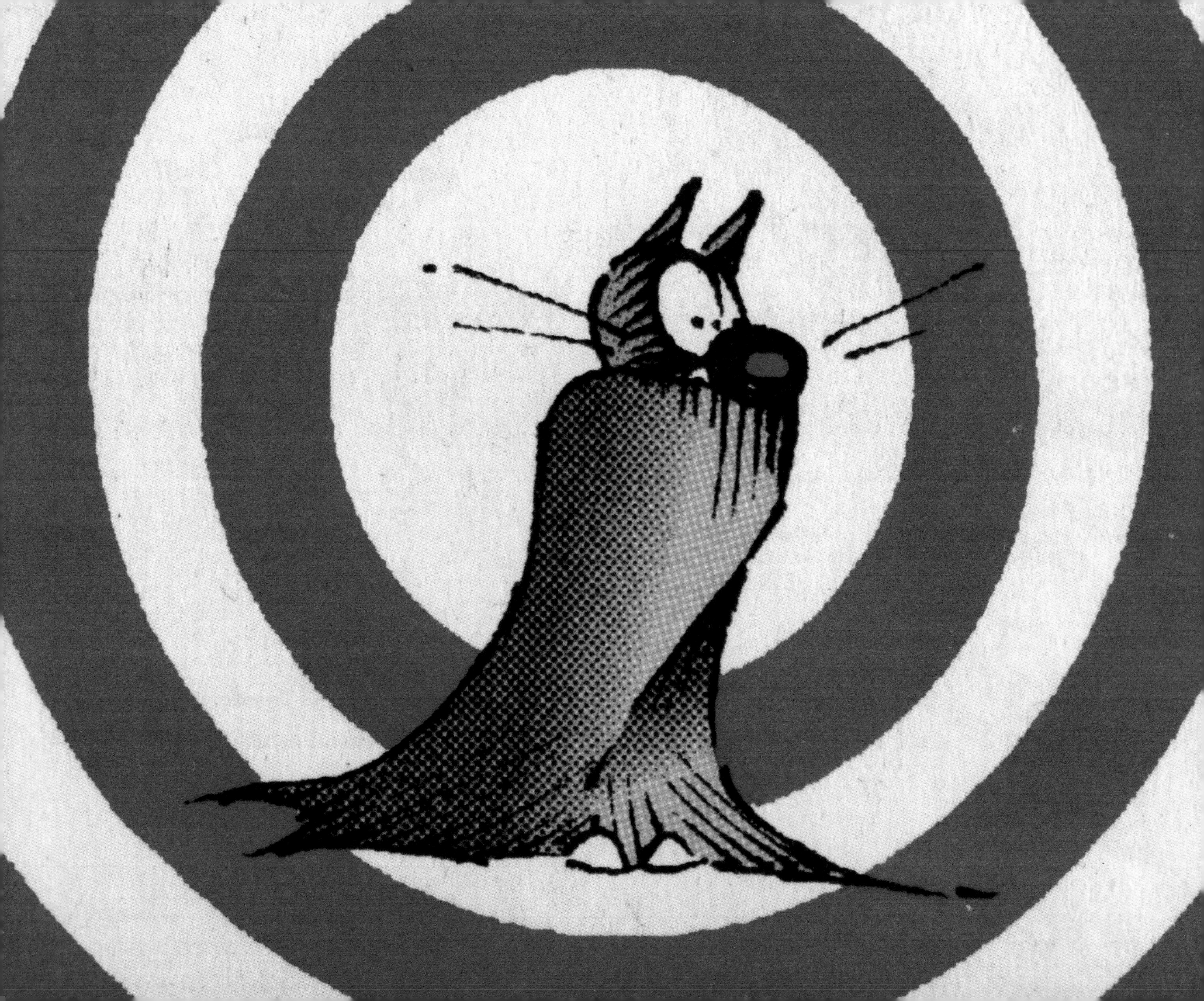

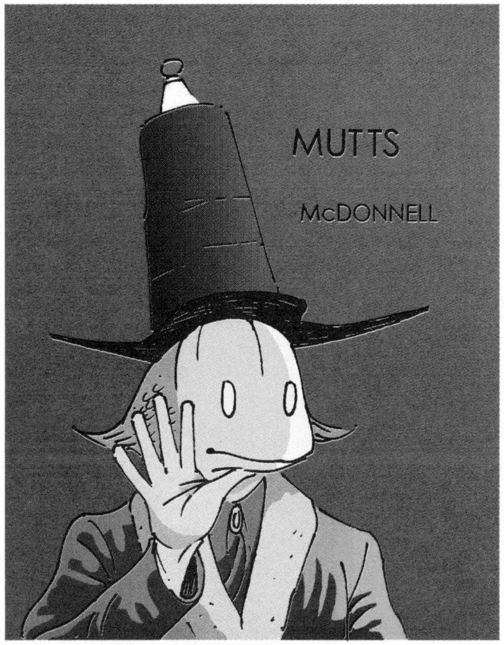
MUTTS
McDONNELL

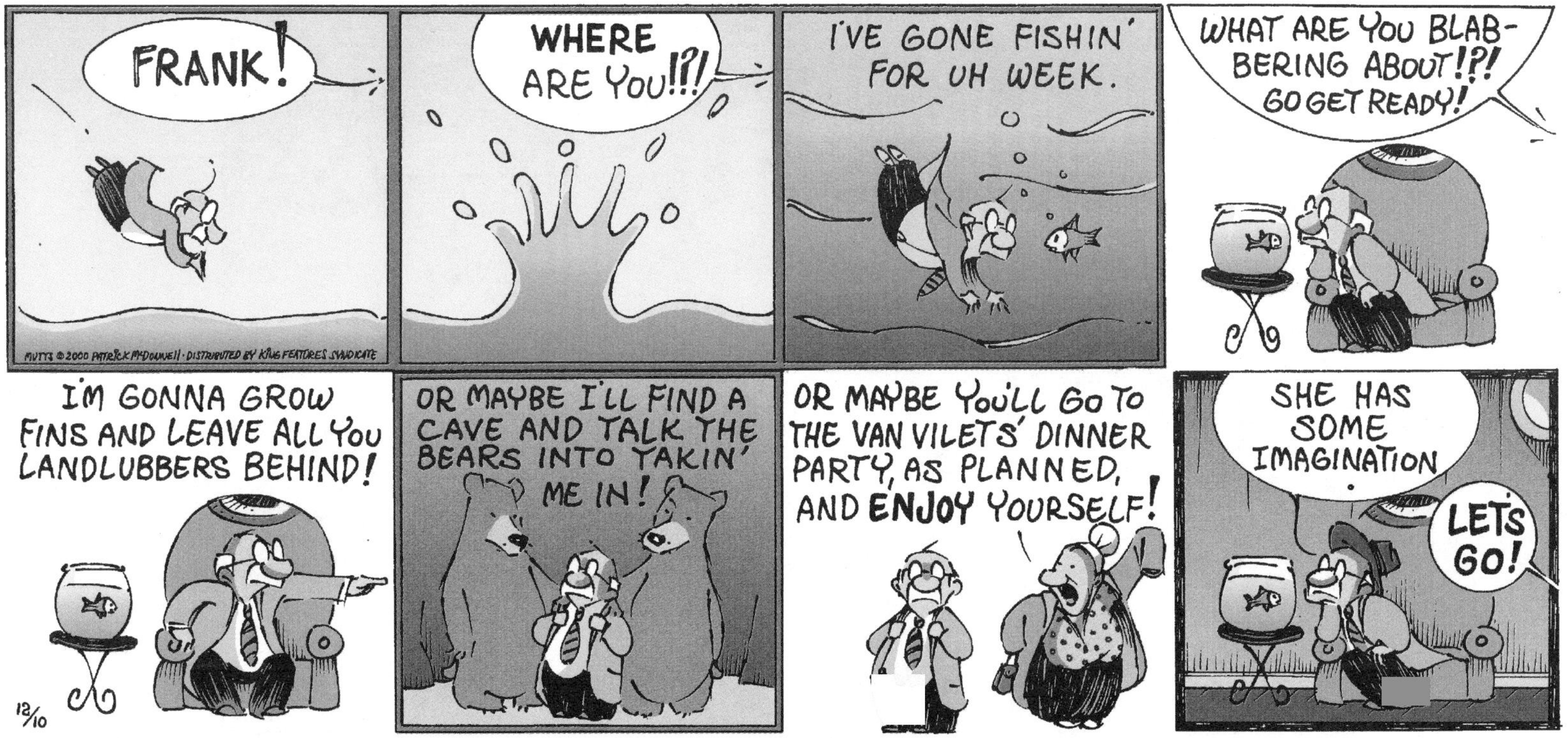
FRANK!
WHERE ARE YOU!?!
I'VE GONE FISHIN' FOR UH WEEK.
WHAT ARE YOU BLABBERING ABOUT!?! GO GET READY!
I'M GONNA GROW FINS AND LEAVE ALL YOU LANDLUBBERS BEHIND!
OR MAYBE I'LL FIND A CAVE AND TALK THE BEARS INTO TAKIN' ME IN!
OR MAYBE YOU'LL GO TO THE VAN VILETS' DINNER PARTY, AS PLANNED, AND ENJOY YOURSELF!
SHE HAS SOME IMAGINATION.
LET'S GO!
MUTTS © 2000 PATRICK McDONNELL · DISTRIBUTED BY KING FEATURES SYNDICATE
12/10

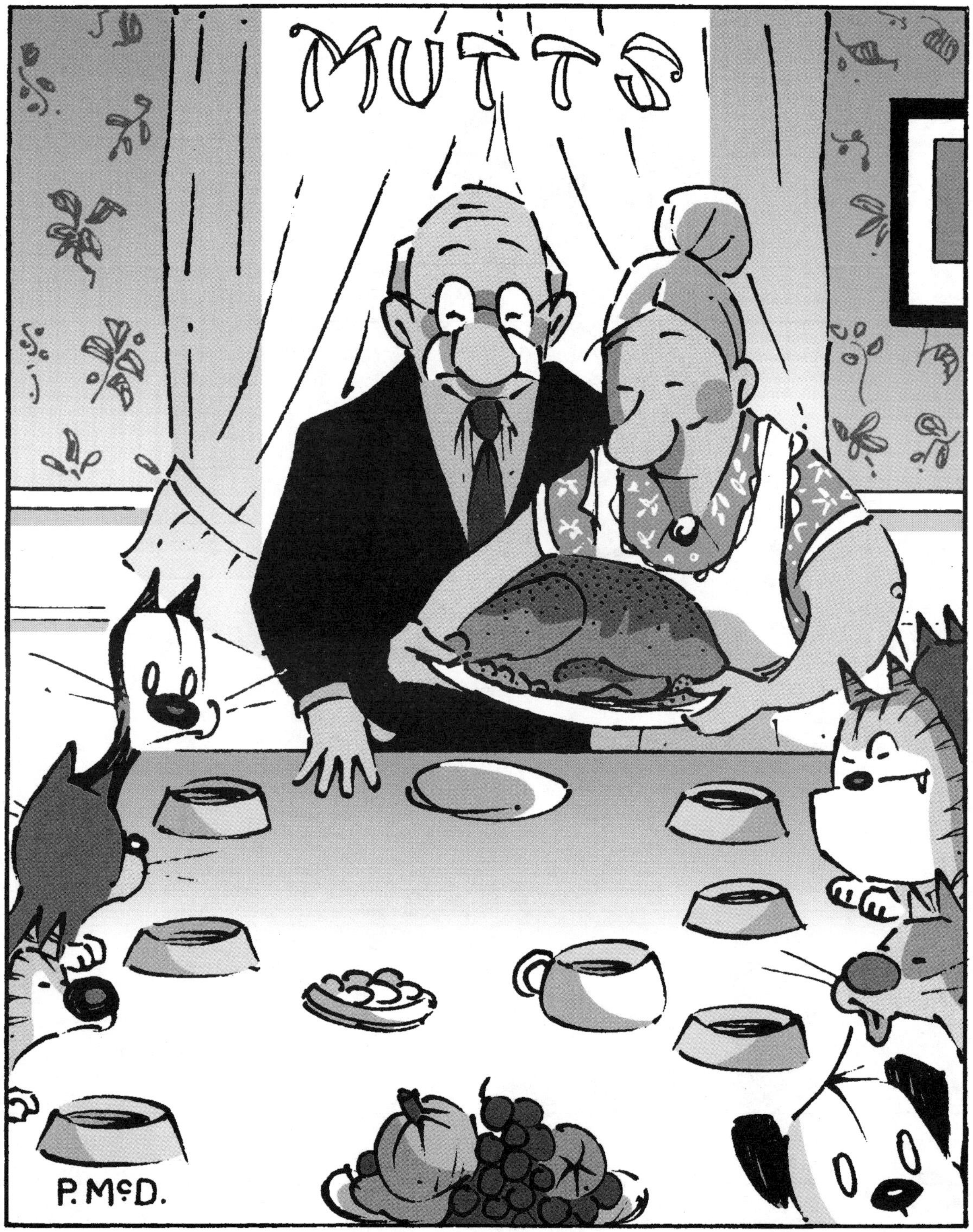
MUTTS
P. McD.

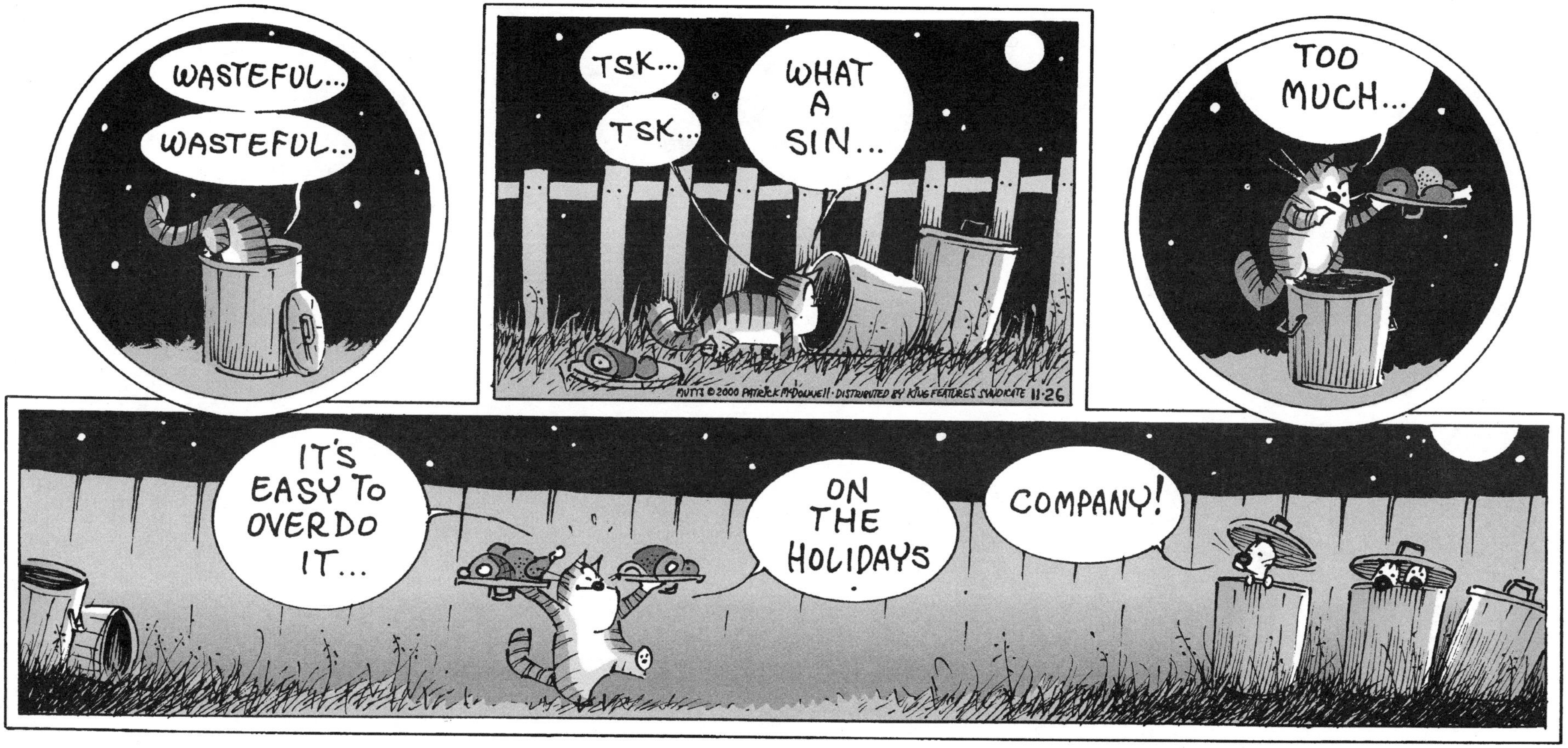
WASTEFUL...
WASTEFUL...
TSK...
TSK...
WHAT A SIN...
MUTTS © 2000 PATRICK McDONNELL · DISTRIBUTED BY KING FEATURES SYNDICATE 11·26
TOO MUCH...
IT'S EASY TO OVERDO IT...
ON THE HOLIDAYS.
COMPANY!

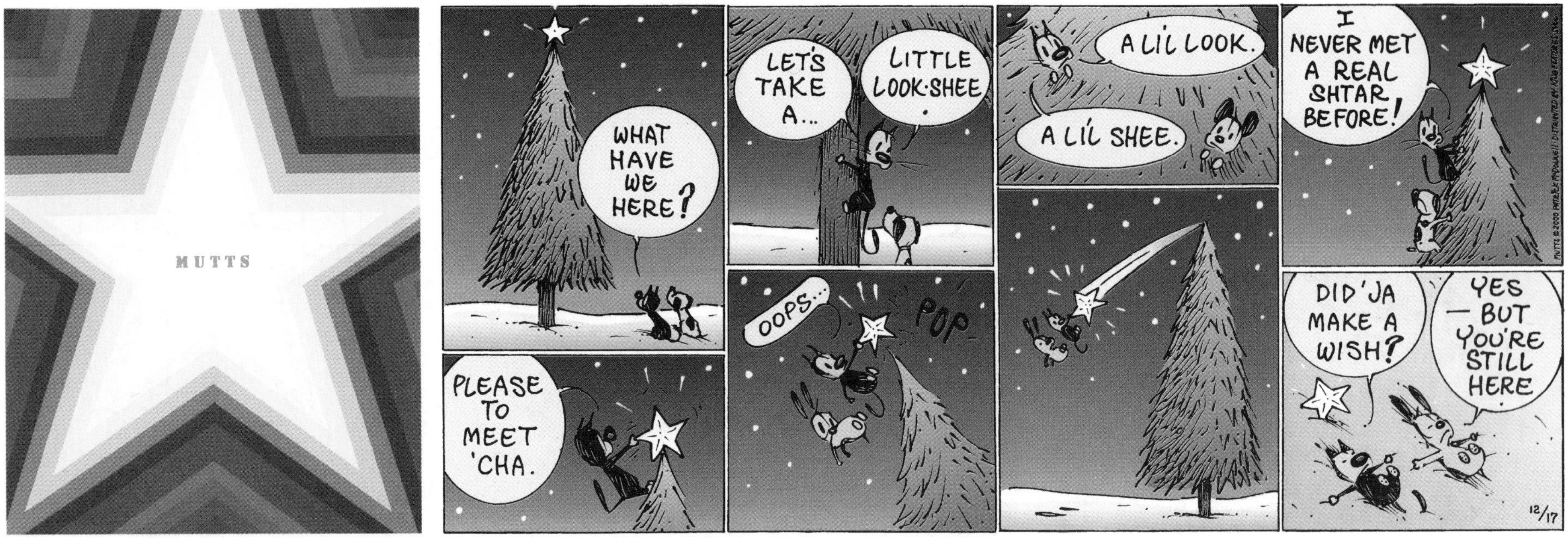
MUTTS
WHAT HAVE WE HERE?
PLEASE TO MEET 'CHA.
LET'S TAKE A...
LITTLE LOOK-SHEE.
OOPS...
POP
A LI'L LOOK.
A LI'L SHEE.
I NEVER MET A REAL SHTAR BEFORE!
DID'JA MAKE A WISH?
YES—BUT YOU'RE STILL HERE.
12/17

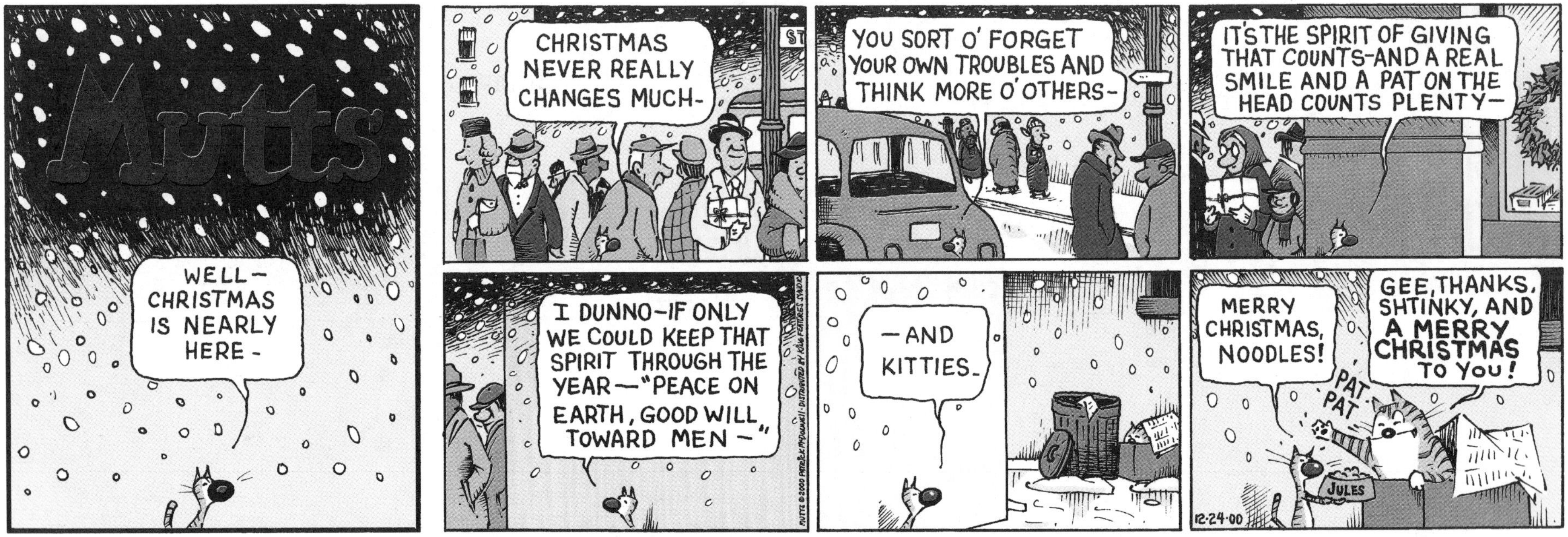
Mutts
WELL—CHRISTMAS IS NEARLY HERE-
CHRISTMAS NEVER REALLY CHANGES MUCH-
YOU SORT O' FORGET YOUR OWN TROUBLES AND THINK MORE O' OTHERS-
IT'S THE SPIRIT OF GIVING THAT COUNTS—AND A REAL SMILE AND A PAT ON THE HEAD COUNTS PLENTY—
I DUNNO—IF ONLY WE COULD KEEP THAT SPIRIT THROUGH THE YEAR—"PEACE ON EARTH, GOOD WILL TOWARD MEN—"
—AND KITTIES.
MERRY CHRISTMAS, NOODLES!
GEE, THANKS, SHTINKY, AND A MERRY CHRISTMAS TO YOU!
PAT PAT
JULES
12-24-00

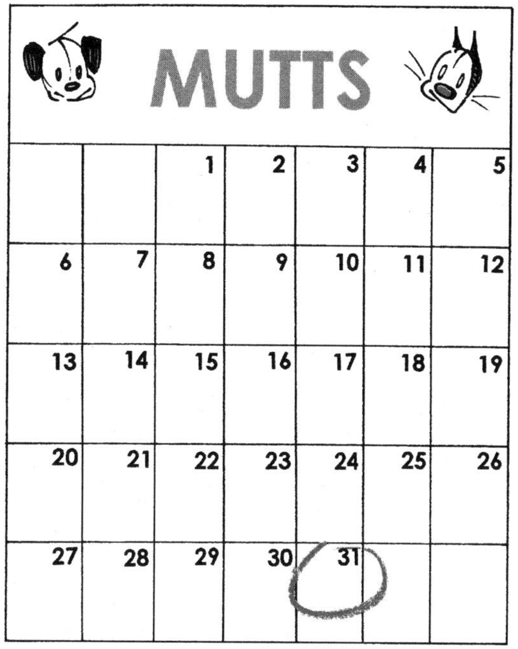
MUTTS
1 2 3 4 5
6 7 8 9 10 11 12
13 14 15 16 17 18 19
20 21 22 23 24 25 26
27 28 29 30 31

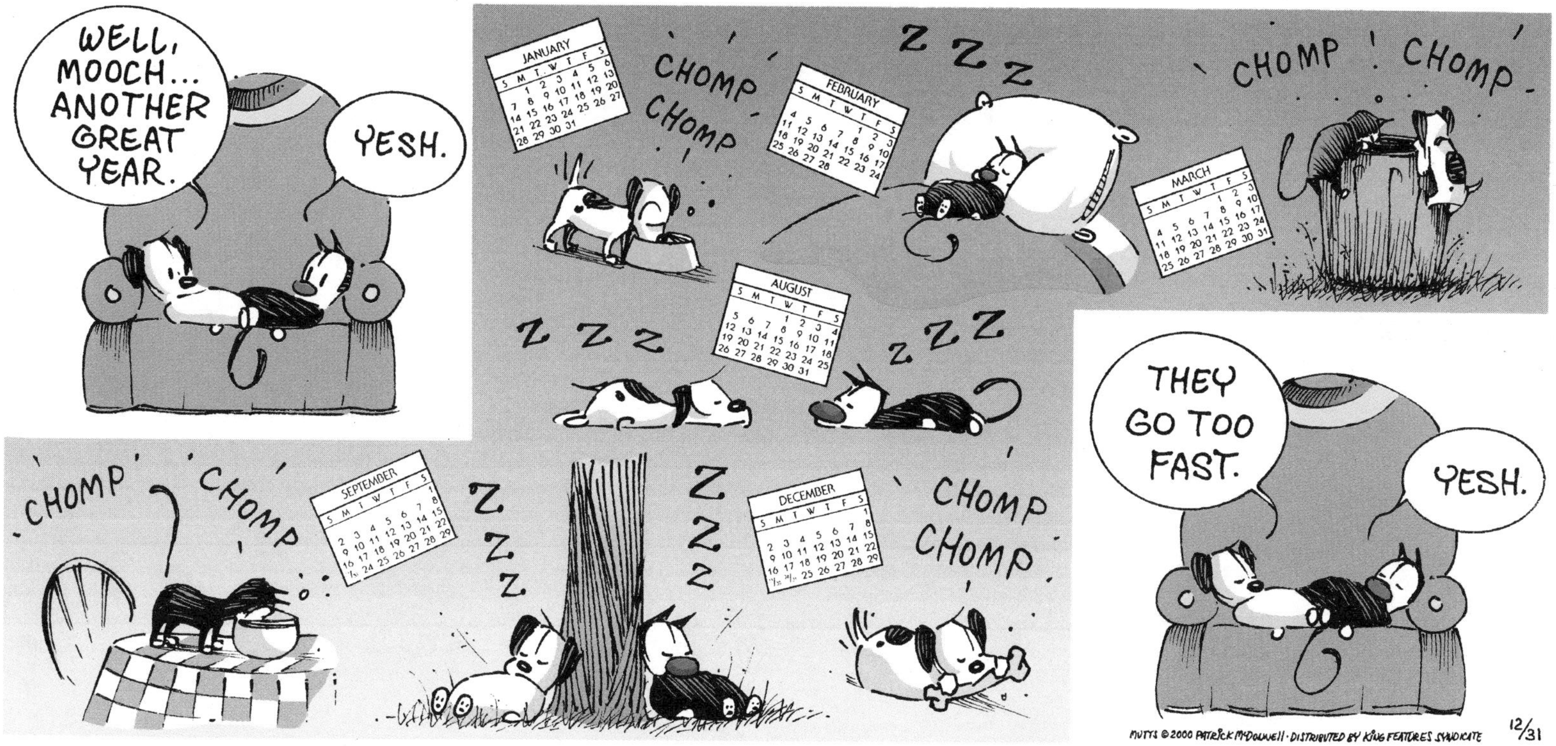
WELL, MOOCH... ANOTHER GREAT YEAR.
YESH.
JANUARY
CHOMP CHOMP
FEBRUARY
Z Z Z
MARCH
CHOMP CHOMP
AUGUST
Z Z Z
Z Z Z
SEPTEMBER
CHOMP CHOMP
Z Z Z
Z Z Z
DECEMBER
CHOMP CHOMP
THEY GO TOO FAST.
YESH.

 12/31